Rebecca Pendragon

Magic Is All Around Us

Gary Green

ISBN: 978-93-95131-09-4

First Edition: 2023
Rs. 200/-

ROCHAK PUBLISHING
HIG 45 Kaushambi Kunj, Kalindipuram
Allahabad - 211011 (U.P.) India
http://www.rochakpublishing.com
Tel: +(91) 9415091004
E-mail: info@rochakpublishing.com

Printed at VCORE CONNECT LLP.

Contents

1. Grandma's Little Secret

Rebecca watched the light November snow swirl around in her mother's grave as the casket was lowered to its final resting place. She focused on the snow. She couldn't think about the casket and what it meant. She was only twelve after all. She had never known her father. He was a soldier and died when she was a baby. Now her mother was gone—killed in a car crash.

Her grandmother, Naomi, stood by her side. Rebecca didn't know her well. She lived way across the country in Minnesota. While she had visited for a week every summer she could remember, she didn't know her well. Now Rebecca was going to have to live with her. Not only did she lose her mother, but she was moving away from her friends. She couldn't even cry. She had an emptiness in the pit of her stomach and just felt numb.

There had been a memorial service, of course. All her mom's friends and her own friends had been in attendance as well as her only living relative, Naomi. It was cold and most of the attendees did not linger at the grave. Soon only Rebecca and Naomi remained.

They spoke very little as they walked to Naomi's rental car. They had cleaned out the apartment and packed Rebecca's things already. Their next stop was the airport. While Naomi was technically retired, she had a busy life to get back to.

Naomi for her part, while grieving the loss of her only child, was worried about Rebecca. She knew that so much loss at such an early age would be difficult. So, she let Rebecca sit in silence as they rode to the airport and again as they flew back to her home in Minnesota. There would be plenty of time to guide her through the grieving process when they got home.

*   *   *

Naomi's home was a 160-acre farm in central Minnesota. The majority of the farm was gravel hills, left by the glaciers thousands of years ago, covered with ancient oaks. However, there were a few fertile valleys where she grew food for her animals and a 12-acre pond that was clean enough to swim in and deep enough to keep fish through the winter. Naomi loved the farm and her life there. She felt a deep bond with her animals and even with the ancient oaks. She had hoped that the beauty and serenity of the place would help Rebecca adjust to the loss of her mother and the other major changes to her life as it had helped her many times in the past.

However, as the long Minnesota winter turned to spring Rebecca was not doing well. She was not doing well in school and had not made any friends. To Naomi she seemed to be just going through the motions.

As Naomi walked from the barn to the house she noticed Max, her dog, waiting at the end of the long driveway for Rebecca to get off the school bus. Max, while technically a mutt, obviously had some Sheltie and Blue Heeler ancestors, as he had the shape of the Sheltie and the multi-colored eyes of the Blue Heeler, but the size and black color of a Lab. Naomi had adopted him from a shelter and taught him to herd. People said Naomi had a way with animals that bordered on the supernatural.

Rebecca got off the bus and ignored Max as she walked to the house. Rebecca shuffled slowly down the driveway, her dark mood in clear contrast to the beautiful early spring day. Naomi was tempted to watch the whole scene, but she had bread in the oven and as a special treat had made cinnamon rolls—extra gooey. She had formulated a plan.

Rebecca could smell the fresh bread and cinnamon rolls before she opened the door. While her mood was dark, as usual, she did like it when her grandma baked.

"Hi Rebecca, sit down at the table. I thought we'd have a treat." Naomi said cheerfully.

"OK" said Rebecca as she hung her book bag and jacket on the pegs by the door.

"Beautiful day, don't you think?' Naomi said.

"Yeah, it's OK I guess" Rebecca was noncommittal.

As they dug into their rolls Naomi said, "I'm worried about you."

Rebecca had felt something like this was coming. She knew her Grandma was worried. She could see it in her face and hear it in her voice, even though she had never actually said it. She knew it was coming and she had been dreading it. She just sat quietly and focused on her roll, hoping to endure until Grandma got tired of trying and left her alone.

"You have been moping around since you got here." That felt like an accusation. Rebecca stopped eating and slumped in her chair. "I know you feel bad, but as far as I know you haven't even cried once, have you?"

"No. . . . I'm just kind of . . . numb," Rebecca said quietly.

Naomi went on. "I'm not accusing you of anything, just stating a fact. I don't want you to feel bad just because I noticed I know it has been hard for you, losing your mom and moving way out here in the sticks with me. I know this, but I didn't see any other choice. Did you?'

"No"

"I've been thinking, trying to find a way to help you get through this. I have tried to make a comfortable home for you here. I have encouraged you to try some different things to maybe have some fun, to forget about your pain for a moment. Nothing seems to work." Naomi paused briefly before going on.

"So, I've decided to tell you a secret. I'm going to tell you a story, a true story, but you have to promise never to tell anyone."

Rebecca was a bit dubious but responded, “Ok, I promise.”

“As you know, I grew up on a farm. It was a lot like this one. I guess maybe that’s why I fell in love with this one the moment I saw it. Anyway, my dad had horses—not riding horses like Sadie and Bert. These were purebred Belgians. Their back was as high as my head and as wide as this table. I wanted to ride them, but Dad said it was too dangerous. Besides, he needed them for the farm work.”

“Didn’t he have tractors?”

“Nobody had tractors back then.” Naomi replied.

“How old are you anyway Grandma?”

Naomi chuckled and replied, “You’d be surprised.”

“Anyway,” she went on. “I begged and begged. So, one Christmas day when I was about your age he offered me a deal. He said if I could prove I was able to take care of a horse by taking care of those Belgians he would buy me a horse to ride for my birthday in April.”

“I was overjoyed. I worked every day after school cleaning out their stalls. I fed them every morning before school and again when I got home. It was hard work, but I did it. I worked through the winter and spring. On the morning of my birthday, I went to the barn as usual and there she was.

She was the most beautiful thing I had ever seen. I named her Jasmine. I rode her everywhere. We had a big patch of woods and I most especially loved to ride her on trails through the woods.

Way in the back of our farm was a big hill. There were no trees on this hill, and you could see for miles. There was a big rock on top of the hill I called ‘The Dragon Head’ because it looked like a dragon’s head. Before I got Jasmine I used to walk out there and sit on this rock where I could see the river two miles away. Sometimes I would read there and sometimes I would just sit and dream. It was my favorite place in all the world.

I still went there after I got Jasmine. I would sit and read, and she would graze on the grass around Dragon Head. I loved those times—almost as much as I loved galloping across the hay field on the way home. Jasmine loved to run, and I loved her to run. It was like flying.

I had hoped that you would love riding as much as I do. It would be something fun we could do together. Would you be willing to try?"

"Maybe" Rebecca replied, still a bit dubious about the whole conversation. Also, she was kind of scared of the horses and was beginning to worry that this conversation was leading to her being forced to take care of them.

"We'll see, I guess. Let's just put that to one side for a bit while I finish my story. Let's see, where was I? Oh yes, galloping across the hay field. One day we were going back to the barn at a full gallop and Jasmine stepped in a badger hole. I went flying and hit the ground with a thud. I was a bit bruised but mostly OK. But Jasmine had clearly broken her leg, the bone was sticking out of her skin. I ran to the house with tears in my eyes.

I told Dad what had happened, and he told me to stay in the house and ran out. He was back in a few minutes for his rifle. I knew what that meant. I threw my arms around him and begged him to stop.

He put his hand on my shoulder and looked me in the eyes. He said, 'It's the only thing to do. If we don't put her down that leg will get gangrene. That will kill her. It's a slow painful way to go. Now let me do this. It's for the best. You stay here.'

I went to my room and cried on my bed until I heard the shot. My heart broke. I cried until I fell asleep. I had only had Jasmine for a few months, but I loved her and she loved me. I was crushed. I still went to that hill almost every day and sat on the Dragon's Head. I usually brought a book, but often I just sat and cried.

I was sitting there one sunny autumn day. The trees were turning, and the view was breath-taking. I started thinking about how great it would be if I could be riding Jasmine, galloping across the hay field again and I started to cry again. Then I felt it. I could swear the ground moved. Then I heard a deep voice say, 'What are you going on about?'

I don't mind saying that scared me. I couldn't see anyone around. I slid off the rock and looked around and still couldn't see anyone.

'Who's there?' I said. Then I saw it. Right there on the side of that big rock was a great big eye. I was petrified. I just stood there, tears drying on my cheeks. Then the rock started to move. The Dragon's Head was really a *dragon's head*!"

"Oh, come on Grandma. I thought you said this was a true story."

Naomi smiled and chuckled a bit, then said, "I did say that. Tell you what. When I am finished with the story if you still don't think it is true, we'll just say I made it up. But I really want to finish this story. I think you'll like the end."

"Well, OK. But you should know I'm not buying any of this." Said Rebecca, reaching for another roll.

"'Alright, Dear. Now where was I? Oh yeah, the dragon' eye. So, there I was looking a real dragon in the eye and too scared to move or even scream.

Then he spoke again. 'Fear not. I will not harm you. Long years I have rested on this hill—hiding really. I have been alone for centuries. Then you came. I came to treasure those times when you sat on my head, reading or just enjoying the view. I hadn't realized how lonely I was. You see I am the last of my kind. Dragons live a very long time, but they can be killed. We were hunted and I am the last.'

We just stared at each other for a while. Finally, he said, 'What is your name?'

Somehow, I found the strength to reply, 'Naomi. What's yours?'

'You may call me Cedric. I have been known by many names, but I like that one the best. Now tell me, what has you so sad?'

'My horse died.'

Cedric thought a bit then said, 'You mean that beautiful pony you used to ride up here?'

'Yes.'

'I see. What a pity. She was young and strong—and fast as the wind. I used to watch you race across the meadow. What happened?'

'She broke her leg and had to be put down.'

'I see. So sad.' He paused for a bit, clearly thinking. Then he went on. 'I don't understand. She was a beautiful horse, but she was just a horse. Why all the tears?'

That remark made me mad. I forgot my fear and said, 'She may have been just a horse, but I loved her.'

'I see.' He said again. I was getting fed up with his calmness. I was about to tell him so when he said, 'What did you love about her?'

I was surprised to hear that question. I hadn't really thought about it before. Finally, I said, 'She was beautiful and gentle and fast and *she* loved *me*. I loved just being with her, but mostly I loved riding her. When she ran, it was like flying."

'I see. It seems to me that you are making yourself miserable trying to hang on to the past when Jasmine was alive. Most present moments are OK. Maybe it would help you to feel better if you fill some present moments with joy. Perhaps if you could ride again?'

'Maybe.' I replied. 'How could I do that? Dad won't let me ride the Belgians and we don't have any other horses.' This guy was really starting to bug me.

'You could ride me. However, it wouldn't be *like* flying; it would actually *be* flying.'

With that he stood up and shook like a wet dog, dirt flew everywhere. Then he opened his wings. They were huge. He was huge and his eyes started to glow red. While my fear had gone away while I was angry, I got scared again when he stood up. I backed away.

'Where are you going? You're not scared are you?' Then, I swear, he started clucking like a chicken. 'Little Naomi is a chicken. Scared of the big nasty dragon.' Then he started clucking again. I was having a rough day and I wasn't going to take that kind of crap from anyone.

I stepped forward and said, 'How would I ride you?'

'Well, you could tie a rope to my horns and sit on my head. We would have to fly at night. I'm still hiding. I must say I think I would enjoy it, I haven't flown in years. Are you up for it or are you . . . *chicken*?'

I was a bit angry at this point, so I looked him in the eye and said, 'You're on.'

'Alright, come back after dark. Bring a rope and wear a jacket. Oh, and of course you can't tell anyone.' With that he laid back down and closed his eyes—looking once again like Dragon Head Rock.

I don't mind telling you my mind was spinning as I walked back to the house. I had met an actual, real dragon—and he didn't eat me. He talked to me and even offered to take me flying. I had trouble believing it but you can bet that when the sun went down I conspicuously went to my room and not so conspicuously out the window. From there I went to the barn to get a rope out of the tack room and off to the hill and my ride.

When I got to the hill Cedric looked like he was still sleeping. I was starting to think I had imagined the whole thing when his eyes snapped open and he stood up. He stretched like one of the barn cats and yawned. That's when I realized he could swallow me whole if he wanted to and I started having second thoughts.

'That feels good, I have been lying there for hundreds of years. I might be a bit stiff.' He said, stretching again and flexing his wings. He looked at me and said, 'You look scared again.'

'Well,' I began, 'I got to thinking, dragons are supposed to be fierce and dangerous. Just now, when I saw you stretch, I thought you might eat me.'

Cedric started laughing, a quiet chuckle at first then building into a hearty guffaw. He started pounding the ground with his fist. He rolled over on his back, holding his stomach and kicking his feet. He was laughing so hard tears were rolling down his cheeks. 'That's rich.' He said. 'Me eat you? If I eat you, who will I talk to?' He laughed some more. It was over the top, really. Finally, he kicked a tree and knocked it over with a crash. 'Woops,' he said. 'Better get a grip. It just feels so good to laugh again. Just remember, you can't believe everything you hear. I have never eaten anyone who didn't deserve it.'

He got to his feet and walked to me. He put his chin on the ground and said, 'Climb aboard. Tie that rope around my horns and around your waist. Make sure you tie it good and tight. I wouldn't want you to fall.'

I did as he told me. As soon as I was ready, he flapped his mighty wings and we were flying. It was scary and exciting at the same time. We climbed higher and higher. I could see lights all down the valley. Then he roared and started laughing again.

'I haven't done that in a long time either. I love to fly, and I love to roar. Hey, do you want to see something?' he said.

I was completely dazzled so I said 'Sure."

He opened his mouth and blew a flame at least a hundred feet long. 'I bet your pony couldn't do that.' He said.

With the mention of Jasmine, I instantly felt guilty having so much fun without her. I said, 'Don't talk about her like that.'

'I'm sorry. I didn't mean to be hurtful. But if she loved you, don't you think she would want you to be happy and have fun?'

I thought about that a bit and said, 'I suppose you are right, but let's not talk about her anyway. OK?'

'Splendid. Want to do something really fun?'

'Sure.' I replied.

He folded his wings against his body, pointed his head toward the ground and plummeted like a rock. I screamed.

'Hold tight.' He said. When we were nearly to the treetops, he opened his wings and leveled out. We were flying so fast I couldn't keep my eyes open, but I had to see. So I opened them just a crack and the wind blew the tears from my eyes straight back into my ears.

Then he started flapping his wings again and said, 'That's probably enough for the first night.'

We flew back to the hill and landed. When I got to the ground, I looked up at him and said, 'Cedric, bend down here.' When he did, I threw my arms around his big, giant head and hugged him. Then I kissed him and said, 'Thank you.'

He chuckled and said, 'It is I who should be thanking you. I have been hiding here so long I forgot what a joy it is to fly—and to roar—and to laugh—and even to breathe fire. Most of all, I forgot how wonderful it is to have some company. I am very pleased to make your acquaintance Naomi. I, Sir Cedric of Britain, Ireland and the Lesser Iles, Bringer of Wisdom and Terror, friend of Merlin, Arthur and other less famous heroes am at your service. Be discrete and we shall have wonderful adventures.'"

Naomi paused her story long enough to take a bite of her roll and a sip of coffee and then went on. "And we did have wonderful adventures. Plus, he was wonderful to talk to. He was thousands of years old and had seen so much of history. I learned so much from him. I came to love him very much. I hated to admit it, but in many ways he was an improvement over my poor pony. We flew as often as we could for over a year and a half."

In spite of herself, Rebecca was starting to enjoy the story. She was still pretty sure Grandma was making it up, but she liked the story so far.

"One day Dad and I were out in the cow pasture bringing the cows in to be milked. There was a cow grazing by the edge of the woods. I went over to get her when a wolf jumped out of the bushes. He was growling and foaming at the mouth and was clearly stalking me. I screamed and froze. He was still about fifty feet away, but I knew I couldn't outrun him. We knew there were wolves in the woods but mostly they left us alone. This one clearly had rabies.

Dad shouted, 'Hold still, I'm coming.'

I could see he had picked up a stick and was running toward me. Then it happened. There was an ear-splitting roar. I looked up to see Cedric diving from the sky. He landed between me and the wolf. He roared again and picked up the wolf with his mouth. He crunched him with his teeth and swallowed him whole. Then he turned around and winked at me.

'Get away from that thing,' my dad shouted. He was panting when he got to me. He grabbed me and started pulling me away from Cedric. He brandished that stick and shouted to Cedric, 'Keep away.'

Really, I don't know what he thought he was going to do with that stick, but he was protecting his daughter. I started to protest. I tried to tell him Cedric wasn't dangerous, that he was my friend. He wasn't hearing me.

Cedric looked at us with a cold expression in his red eyes and flew away.

The next day there was a gathering at the church. Cedric had been seen, not only by my dad but some of our neighbors.

'That thing is a menace. It could have swallowed us whole just like it swallowed that wolf.' Dad told the crowd.

'What was it?'

'I say it was the Devil.'

'Devil or not, something that big has to have a big appetite. It will soon be eating our livestock or even our children.'

I tried to protest, but no one listened to me. They were scared and often fear can quickly turn to violence. Soon they developed a plan to hunt Cedric and kill him. I was heartsick. I had to warn him.

Later that day I was told to stay in the house while they hunted my friend, but as soon as I could I snuck out. I ran to the hill and Cedric was there as usual.

'Cedric, wake up.' I said. 'They are coming for you.'

'I was afraid of this.' He whispered. 'I acted rashly. I saw the wolf and was afraid you would get bitten. You would die. I couldn't allow that.'

'You must fly away.' I said.

'To what end?' He replied. 'It will be the same everywhere. People fear us, though many of us have served mankind through the ages. I'm tired of hiding—tired of running. It goes against my nature.'

'But they'll kill you.'

'I suppose they might at that. I'm pretty tough though. I don't think these farmers pose much danger. But I suppose it wouldn't end there. The army would eventually get involved. People can be pretty persistent. Then again, if I fly away, I would lose my only friend. There might me another way.'

'What do you mean?'

'Well, if you haven't already figured it out, dragons are magical creatures.'

He paused and I wasn't sure where he was going with this.

Then he went on. 'It has been said that a dragon can live in the human heart.'

'How would that work?'

My essence would enter your heart and I would stay there—away from prying eyes. We could still be friends. The only problem I see is that I wouldn't be able to leave. It would kill you.'

'Would it hurt?'

'Maybe. I don't know. I'm not even sure it would work. It could just be tall tales I've heard.'

We just looked at each other for a while. I was thinking. I didn't want to lose my friend. I didn't want anyone else to get hurt either.

'Ok,' I said. 'Let's do it.'

With that he rose into the air. I could hear the shouts of the search party. They had seen him. Whatever was going to happen had to happen fast. He started to glow. Soon he was just a glowing ball. The ball started shrinking and getting brighter. When it was about the size of my fist and so bright, I could hardly look at it, it flew at me. When it hit me in the chest I passed out.

When I woke up, I was in my bed. My whole family was there.

'She's awake.' My brother said.

My dad, who had been dozing in a chair, leaned in and said, 'Foolish girl, what were you doing out there? That thing could have killed you.'

'But it didn't,' I replied.

'Thank God for that. I don't know what I would do without my beautiful Naomi. But next time I tell you to stay in the house, you better stay in the house.'

'I'm sorry Dad.'

'Well, no harm done I guess. You're OK and we can't find that beast. Did you see where it went?'

'No, I saw it and I guess I fainted.' I felt a bit guilty about lying to Dad, but it was necessary."

Naomi took a sip of her coffee and they sat quietly for a bit. Rebecca was clearly thinking, taking it all in.

Then she said, "That was quite a story. I still don't believe it. I'm not a baby. But it was a good story. I don't understand why you thought it was so important to tell me this."

Naomi smiled and took Rebecca's hand. Naomi's hand seemed hot. Rebecca almost pulled back, but instead looked into her grandmother's eyes—which were glowing red.

"The point", my dear girl, "is that all these years Cedric has lived in my heart, just as your mother still lives in yours if you'd only look."

Rebecca tried to pull her hand away, but Naomi held tight. She stood up and pulled Rebecca into her arms and held her tight. She said, "Cedric was right, most present moments are OK. Your mother would want you to be happy. I love you girl, just as your mother did. You will see if you just look into your heart."

With that, Rebecca started to cry.

2. New Friends

It had been several weeks since Naomi revealed her little secret to Rebecca. It had been a busy time for both of them. There was garden to put in and lambs to deliver. Rebecca was expected to help and in spite of herself, she discovered she enjoyed it. Rebecca particularly liked the lambs. They were all slimy and messy when they came out and in a few minutes their mother had them all cleaned up and they were walking around, looking for their first meal. In a few days they were chasing each other around the pasture. Apparently, Naomi and Cedric had been right—most present moments are OK

The situation with Naomi and Cedric was a bit hard for Rebecca at first. She wavered between thinking her grandma was crazy and being afraid she wasn't. Sometimes she saw Naomi apparently talking to herself. Naomi said she was talking to Cedric, but it seemed a little creepy to Rebecca all the same. Just when Rebecca was sure Naomi was crazy she would see those eyes—the red glowing eyes.

One day at supper Naomi put her fork down and looked Rebecca straight in the eye. She said, "I get a sense that you are having trouble with my *situation* with Cedric."

"Well……. It is kind of weird"

"Maybe it would help if you could talk directly to Cedric."

"What do you mean?"

"Well, I can sort of step aside and let Cedric talk directly to you. Would that be OK?"

"I, well, I guess so."

With that Naomi's eyes started to glow red. Then in a deep voice, quite unlike Naomi's Cedric said, "Hello, Rebecca. Fear not. I will not hurt you."

Rebecca just sat staring into those red eyes.

After a moment of staring at each other Cedric continued. "I can see that you are still afraid. It is a pity that there are so many stories about how evil dragons are. Everyone gets scared around us. Since we seem to be stuck with each other, it would seem that we need to find a way to make you more comfortable and make this thing work. Let's see. . . . . .Maybe if you could talk to someone who is less intimidating, more. . . cuddly."

"What do you mean?"

"Maybe it would be easier to show you. Pip, show yourself." Cedric turned his head, looking at one of the empty chairs at the dining table. Rebecca turned her head in the same direction and there he was. There was a pudgy little face just barely peeking over the table and a tiny little hand waving at her.

"Hi, I'm Pipyrruqawadermurgh. You may call me Pip." He said. He then jumped down, waddled around the table, and extended his hand. "I am very pleased to meet you, Rebecca."

Rebecca stood up and shook his hand and just stared at Pip. He was short, not even as tall as the table. And he was fat. He wore a green jacket, like a sports jacket, with a matching vest, the buttons straining against his bulk. His brown pants came down barely past his knees. His calves and ankles were covered with red and white striped socks. His black shoes had pointy toes and big gaudy looking gold buckles. Then there was his hat. It was green, matching his jacket and vest, and reminded Rebecca of hats she had seen in pictures of Robin Hood—pointy with a long feather.

Finally, Rebecca said, "You're a . . . . . a"

"Gnome" Pip finished. He doffed his hat in a broad sweeping gesture and bowed at the waist, saying "Pip the gnome, at your service m'lady." He stood up and just stood there, a grin beaming from his clean-shaven face.

Rebecca started to giggle. She would later learn that it was impossible to not giggle when a gnome grins at you. She was totally caught up in the moment—and it was good. "A gnome" she said and started laughing. "Why not?" She said. "If dragons exist, why not gnomes, or unicorns, or fairies?"

Pip, still smiling, said, "Why not indeed?" Then he walked to the door, turned, and said, "Are you coming?"

Rebecca followed Pip out to the porch.

"Behold," he said, gesturing toward the garden. Rebecca didn't see anything but the garden—at first. The sun had just gone down, and twilight was starting to set in. Then a light like a candle appeared, then another, then another. Soon the garden was filed with lights flitting back and forth. Finally, one appeared right in front of her face. Up close she could see that the light was really a tiny person only with wings like dragonfly wings. Then he flew away toward the garden.

"Fairies" Pip said. "They're kind of . . . . . hyper."

Rebecca was fascinated. She had never imagined that such things were real, but here they were. Pip was right. They all seemed to be very busy. "Fairies," She said to no one in particular, then to Pip, "What are they doing?"

"They are helping the plants to grow," he explained. "All day the plants absorb sunlight. When the sun goes down, the fairies come out and make sure the energy goes where it will do the plants the most good."

"So . . . . . all plants have these things, these fairies?"

"Not exactly," he replied. "They won't go where they are not wanted. Also, they can be chased away by storms and such."

"I see. What do you do?"

He chuckled. "That is a very good question. I sort of go where I'm needed. I coordinate. I organize. I . . ."

"Sleep a lot" Naomi, who had come out onto the porch, said.

Pip laughed, then pretended to be offended. "Ouch! What do you know? Anyone who works as hard as me needs his rest." He said, still grinning.

They all chuckled a bit then Naomi said. "It's starting to get chilly out here. Let's go in and talk a bit."

They all walked in and sat by the fieldstone fireplace, where Naomi already started a fire. "I like a fire," Naomi said. "I know it isn't the most efficient way to heat, but it is so friendly." They were all quiet for a few minutes, watching the fire.

Finally, Naomi turned to Pip, who was sitting cross-legged on the hearth, and said, "I think I would like to talk to Rebecca alone."

"I know when I'm not wanted." He said and just disappeared.

"You know I can still see you," Cedric growled.

"Sorry, I forgot." Pip said from nowhere. Tiny footsteps could be heard, then the front door opened and closed seemingly on its own.

"Such a clown," Naomi said, shaking her head. "I was just wondering what you think of all this, Rebecca."

"Well . . . I admit Cedric kind of scared me."

"I get that a lot." Cedric interjected.

"Oh . . . sorry. I forgot you were here."

"No offence taken I assure you. I was just teasing you. I'm really pretty funny, but people are afraid to laugh at my jokes. Anyway, I think I'll take a little nap now so you can have some privacy."

Naomi's eyes returned to normal, and she said, "What did you think of Pip?"

"He's cute."

"That he is." Naomi said, chuckling. "Cedric and I thought letting you in on the rest of our secret might cheer you up. You know it is impossible for a human to not chuckle when a gnome grins at you. And the fairies are so cheerful."

"So, that's what happened. I was laughing but I didn't know why. Grandma, are there fairies everywhere?"

"Almost, you won't find many in the big cities. That is one of the reasons I live here. Also, you won't find many in the winter. They migrate like birds. Our fairies go to the other side of the world where their summer is our winter and vice-versa."

"Why can't we see them all the time?"

"That's kind of a long story. I won't go into details now. Suffice to say that once upon a time we could. Then people started to think that all magical beings are bad. There was some unpleasantness and the magicals decided to go invisible."

"How many kinds of magicals are there?" Rebecca queried.

"Too many to list. Just don't be surprised or afraid if you see something you don't expect. Most of them are very nice, some are playful, like Pip and even Cedric. I suppose I should tell you that there are a very few bad ones, but I don't want you to worry about them. It seems like whenever you start thinking too much about them, they have a way of showing up. You are pretty safe here. While I will caution you that you shouldn't talk about this to 'outsiders'. Either they won't believe you and think you are lying or just plain weird; or they will believe you, which could be even worse."

"I know, Grandma. I remember what happened to Cedric. So . . . now what?'

"Well . . . . Just live your life. Go to school. Make friends. Grow up and make your mark in the world. I wanted you to know because I didn't want you to be scared of me, or think I am crazy. And yes, I noticed by the way. Don't feel bad because I noticed. You feel what you feel. I won't judge you for it. Anyway, I also thought you should know your heritage. I *am* your Grandma, after all. I am what I am. Please don't judge *me* for it."

They sat quietly for a few minutes, watching the fire and listening to it crackle. Finally, Rebecca got up and walked over to Naomi. She gave her a big hug and said, "Thanks, Grandma. I'm glad you told me. I don't think you're crazy. I think you are cool. The coolest Grandma ever."

Rebecca yawned and said, "I suddenly feel really tired."

"Why don't you go to bed early tonight?" Naomi replied. "You've had kind of a big day."

"OK, goodnight, Grandma."

Rebecca slept better that night than she had for months.

* * *

The next day at school Rebecca was sitting by herself, as usual, eating lunch. She was thinking about Pip and the fairies. As usual when she thought about Pip, she was smiling. She was lost in her thoughts when a girl from her class named Heather plopped down in the chair across from her.

"So, what's your deal?" Heather said.

Rebecca was somewhat taken aback by this rather bold question. "What do you mean?" She said.

"Well, ever since you got here you have been the sourest looking person I have ever seen. Now you are sitting there with a happy look on your face. Something must have happened. Is it about a boy?"

"No!" Rebecca spat out. "It is NOT about a boy!" Rebecca could feel her cheeks turning red. She wasn't sure if it was anger or embarrassment.

"My friends over there. . . " She looked across the lunchroom to a table where three other girls were looking back. Rebecca looked too and the girls started whispering and giggling. "They think it *is* about a boy and they're trying to figure out who."

"Well, it's not." Rebecca said. Her mind had jumped into overdrive. She couldn't very well tell Heather about Cedric and Pip, but she had to tell her something. She decided to go for a version of the truth she thought Heather would believe.

"When I first got here, my mother had just been killed in a car accident. I had to move halfway across the country—away from all my friends—to live with my Grandma. She is the only relative I have. Also, it is so *cold* here. I hate the cold. . . . Anyway, if I looked sour, I guess it is because I was sad."

"Wow." Heather said. "We. . . I didn't know."

"Well, how could you? I never told anybody about that. Anyway, last night I guess I realized I was living in the past—thinking about all the stuff I lost. My Grandma helped me see that I still could have a good life; that I'm still a kid; that winter's over and maybe it is time to have a little fun. So, I guess maybe I'm not so sad today."

Heather sat thinking for a few minutes. "I thought you were kind of weird, but you're OK. You want to hang out with us?"

"Sure!" Rebecca suddenly realized that she had been lonely for friends her own age.

"Let's go" Heather said.

They picked up their lunch trays and walked over to Heather's friends where she announced, "She's cool. I've asked her to hang out with us."

Rebecca recognized the other girls as Gail, Barb, and Linda from her class. They considered themselves the "popular" girls. Rebecca had always avoided the popular girls; thinking they were too full of themselves. However, now, as they peppered her with questions about her life and seemed to accept her; she found herself enjoying their company.

When Rebecca got home that day she went to her room and found Pip sitting on her bed grinning—of course.

"Did you enjoy lunch today?" He inquired.

Rebecca started to answer, then she realized *he knew.* But how could he know? There was a lot about magicals, and Pip in particular, that she clearly did not know.

"Yes, I did." She said. "I made friends."

"I know." He stated.

There it was. He knew something.

"*How* do you know?" she asked.

"Obviously I was there, silly."

"So what? . . . . . Are you following me now?" She demanded. Rebecca didn't think she liked that idea. But as Pip just sat there grinning, she realized she could not stay mad at him.

"I wanted to get to know you better, so I followed you. There you were—just sitting there looking glum. So, I sat beside you and grinned at you—to cheer you up. My joy is contagious by the way, even if you can't see me. Then that Heather came over, so I grinned at her too. Then, you went over to those other girls, and I grinned at them. You get the idea." Pip seemed pretty pleased with himself.

Rebecca thought about this news for a minute then said, "So, it was *you*. I thought they actually liked *me.*"

For the first time since she had met him, Pip stopped grinning.

"Hey," he said. "I don't like where this conversation is headed. They absolutely did like you—the happy you. Even if you didn't tell the *whole* truth, everything you said was true; was it not?"

"Yes"

"I can't make somebody like somebody else. If they liked you, it is because you are a likeable person. I didn't make Heather approach you. She did that because for the first time since you got here you were not giving off those 'Leave me alone' vibes. Sure, maybe I had something to do with that. There might have been some tinkering. I may have been involved, but you enjoyed it. I am putting this in the 'win' column. I suggest you do the same." The grin was back.

"OK", she said. "You know I can't stay mad at you. Which isn't fair, by the way. I guess you are my friend too. Seems like I have a lot of new friends."

"Well . . . . . now that we're friends, do you want to do something?" Pip enquired.

"Sure, what?"

"I thought we could go for a walk. I think you haven't seen much of your grandmother's farm—since it was winter when you got here. There's some pretty cool stuff here."

"OK, let's go."

"We'd better let your Grandma know."

* * *

Her Grandma's house and farm buildings were nestled in a small valley, with tall hills on three sides and the long driveway leading off to the south. Rebecca had never been past that valley. Pip led her through the pasture on the hillside north of the house, through the gate at the top of the hill and on to the road that led into the woods. Calling it a road was generous, really. It was more like two-wheel tracks with grass and weeds in the middle.

As got deeper and deeper into the woods, Rebecca found herself staring up into the treetops. The trees were tall, really tall, with long straight trunks and no limbs until way at the top. She was staring up as she walked—not really looking where she was going—when she walked right smack into Pip.

"Hey, look where you're going." Pip said. He had, in fact, deliberately stepped in front of her when he noticed her looking into the treetops because he thought it would be funny. He still thought it was

"Oh, sorry."

Pip chuckled then replied, "No harm done. Magnificent, aren't they?"

Rebecca looked up too. "Yes, they're so tall."

"Yes and look at how big around they are. I bet you couldn't even reach around one. Go ahead and try. It'll be fun."

Rebecca, feeling kind of dubious about this suggestion because she clearly could not reach around any of these trees, decided to humor Pip. She stepped up to the nearest tree and wrapped her arms around it—barely reaching halfway. Then she felt it. The tree started to vibrate. She jumped back. Then she heard it. It was like a low hum, then it got louder.

"Mmmmmm . . . . . thank you." It was a deep, quiet voice.

Rebecca looked at Pip, who was cackling with laughter. She started to suspect something was up, so she asked, "What's going on?"

The deep voice again, "I was thanking you for the hug."

Pip paused his laughing long enough to say, "You're a tree hugger!"

Rebecca, who was a sharp kid by anyone's standards, stared quizzically at Pip for a moment, then said, "Was that the tree? The tree is *talking*?"

"I knew it. You *are* a smarty-pants. I don't care what anyone says. Yup, it was the tree."

"Trees can *talk*?"

"Well, obviously." Pip quipped, wiping tears from his eyes—his laughter finally subsiding. "Well, not all trees. It has to be an old one."

"What do you mean, old?" The tree rumbled.

"Oh, sorry, *mature* then—no sense of humor, really. Anyway, Rebecca, forgive me. I just couldn't resist. Opportunities to play that joke are almost nonexistent. I thought you should know. All things, living or otherwise, have Spirit. Trees, for example, can live so long that they develop personalities and the ability to talk. Although, they don't talk to many people. So, I don't want you to be surprised if you discover that babbling brook is actually *babbling*."

Rebecca, who was not only getting accustomed to amazing revelations, but actually starting to enjoy them; simply said "OK."

"We should keep going. There's more to see." Pip said.

"Good-bye Mr. Tree." Rebecca said as they resumed their journey.

They walked through the tall trees, across the hay field and down a ravine until they came to a spring of clear, cold water bubbling up out of the ground. The water formed a small rocky stream that tumbled down the slope to the pond. There were fairies everywhere. Suddenly, standing across the stream was a beautiful, blond young woman. She was wearing a white short sleeved dress that came down nearly to the ground. She was barefoot.

"Greetings, Pip," She called.

"Greetings, Amaryllis." Pip replied. Turning to Rebecca he said, "This is Amaryllis, the spirit of this spring. Her name means 'sparkling fresh'. Don't you think it suits her? She is the love of my life, though she won't have me."

"Oh Pip! What sweet lies you tell." Amaryllis said. "And this must be the famous Rebecca. Greetings to you Rebecca."

"Greetings to you, Amaryllis." Rebecca replied, giggling a bit because of the strange way of talking.

"What do you mean famous?" she went on.

"Well, in the magical world very few humans are allowed to see or hear us. Everyone is talking about it—especially this one." She said, pointing at Pip. "In fact, he won't shut up about you."

Pip perked up a bit at this. "Have I made you jealous, sweet one?" He looked positively eager.

"No, you most certainly have not," she snapped. "But you often miss perfectly good opportunities to remain silent."

Pip laughed at this. He clearly had been teasing. He loved to tease, but it was always good-natured and never hurtful or mean. Also, he was a chatterbox. He knew it and was proud of it.

"Pip," Amaryllis began. "I need to talk to you about something." She gave him a look that clearly meant "privately."

"Rebecca, why don't you go down to the pond and see what you can see. I'll be down shortly." Pip said.

Rebecca started down the path that ran along beside the stream. Pip and Amaryllis watched her go until she was out of earshot. "I have been hearing that Marid has been seen skulking around."

"Marid! What do you suppose that troublemaker wants?" Pip replied. "Let me know if you hear anything more. I'll have to warn Naomi."

"Good idea. I'll tell the fairies to keep their eyes open, too. You had better go keep an eye on Rebecca. If anything happens, you know where to find me."

* * *

Meanwhile, Rebecca had followed the path down to the pond. What she found there was a small sandy beach, with a dock and a small wooden rowboat upside down on the beach. Sitting on the boat was a small creature unlike anything she had ever seen. He looked a little like a teddy bear, except he had hands and a human-like face. In fact, his face looked a little sinister. His grin was not contagious like Pip's. It was kind of creepy.

However, in light of all the new and amazing things Rebecca had seen and heard in the last couple of days; she decided to not judge this book by its cover. She walked up to him and extended her hand.

"Hello, I'm Rebecca." She said.

"I know." He said, shaking her hand. "You may call me Marid. I am *very* pleased to make your acquaintance, Becky . . . Becca . . . the Beckster."

"I prefer Rebecca." She said.

He seemed friendly, but there was something about that grin. It was downright creepy. Rebecca was trying to think of something to say when she heard Pip from behind her.

"Rebecca, back away from that thing." He shouted. "And *you*! Marid!" He spat the name out as if it tasted bad. "What are you doing here? You know you are not welcome here."

"The Boss won't be happy about this." Marid snarled.

"I really couldn't care less what your boss thinks. Just go."

"Ok, I'll go. But before I do, I have one thing to say to Becky." He said, turning to look her straight in the eye. "Your mother's death was not an accident."

Having delivered his message, he just disappeared, but his laughter could be heard fading away into the distance.

Rebecca just stood staring at the spot where Marid had been standing. Then she turned to Pip and said, "Who was that?"

"Marid, he's more of a 'what' really." Pip said, gazing in the direction where Marid disappeared.

"Ok, so *what* was that?" Rebecca's voice had an edge to it, as she was starting to lose her patience with Pip.

"*That* was a gremlin," he began. "I suppose I better explain it to you since you are getting cross with me. Gremlins are trouble. They delight in chaos. They break things just for the fun of it. They lie and cheat and generally make a mess wherever they go. Naomi, or rather Cedric has banned them from this wood."

"So, who is this 'boss' he mentioned?"

"That would be the so-called 'Great God Pan'. He used to be one of us, but he grew to hate humans. There was some unpleasantness—I don't want to go into details—and Pan, and his followers the gremlins, trolls, and a few others, broke with us and have been causing trouble since. You should not think about them because it attracts them."

“He’s a *god*?” Rebecca asked. This was getting to be too much, really.

“Depends on how you define god.” Pip replied in his usual playful, but unclear manner, looking rather pleased with himself. Then he saw Rebecca frown and continued. “He is most definitely *not* a god. He’s just full of himself.”

Rebecca thought about this a bit then said, “What about what Marid said about my mom, about how her death wasn’t an accident.”

“You should not believe him; gremlins lie and sow discord wherever they go.” Pip replied. “We should be getting back. You’ve had a long day and Naomi will be getting worried.”

3. Preparations

When they got back to the house, they told Naomi and Cedric all about their walk, with special detail on the part with Marid. Naomi and Cedric were very concerned about this news. It had been a while since Marid had reared his smarmy little head. This definitely did not bode well.

"Well," Naomi began. "I suppose we need to take some measures just to be safe. Pip, I want you to get the word out. If anything, and I mean anything, looks out of place I want to know about it. Rebecca, I know you are going to have a hard time not thinking about Marid and what he said about your mother, but it is important. Tomorrow, I will start you on some mind training lessons, you've had enough excitement for one day. For now, just remember that trying to not think about something is the same as thinking about it."

"What?" Rebecca said, clearly confused by that last statement.

"What I mean is when thoughts about Marid pop into your head, and they will, just notice them and direct your attention somewhere else. Does that make more sense?"

"A little, I guess. Where should I direct my attention?" Rebecca asked.

"Anywhere else," Naomi said. She thought for a moment and said, "I know, I'll give you something else to think about. Your birthday is coming up. Why don't we have a little party? You could invite your new friends. Perhaps we could find some extra horses and we could all go for a ride on the trails. Does that sound like fun?"

Truthfully, Rebecca was still a bit dubious about riding and still wondered if any of her new friends would actually come to her birthday party. But she ignored that and smiled at her grandmother and said, “Sure.”

“Then it’s settled. I’ll start getting things together tomorrow. We have two weeks before your birthday. You and I will have to ride a bit before the party. I’ll call some of my riding friends to borrow horses for your friends. Don’t mention it to anyone until I say, I want to make sure things are set first. First thing when you get home tomorrow, we’ll do mindfulness training and then we’ll take a little ride.”

“OK, Grandma. It sounds like fun.”

“But it’s getting a bit late, and you’ve had a big day. Why don’t you go take a nice hot bath and get ready for bed?”

Rebecca nodded and headed upstairs. When she was gone, Naomi turned to Pip and said, “I don’t like this.”

“I absolutely don’t like this,” was Pip’s reply. “Pan is up to something, but what?”

“It’s something to do with the girl.” Cedric piped in, then continued, “I don’t understand it myself . . . . yet. But I will. In the meantime I want to hear immediately if that pusillanimous little runt Marid shows his rotten little face—or if there is any sign of his tinkering. I told him to stay out and I meant it. I may be trapped in this human body, but I still have a few tricks up my sleeve.”

“OK,” Pip responded. “I think I’ll put out a few discrete feelers and see what I can find out. I told Rebecca that Marid was lying about her mother, but I don’t know if that is correct. We’ll get to the bottom of this eventually. I want to put her mind to rest.”

Naomi, back to herself again, began, “I think you are right, Cedric, about Pan. It’s something to do with Rebecca. Pip, do you think you could find someone to stand guard on her—covertly?”

“Of course. I’m sure I could find an elf or two who have some spare time. I better get going. I have a lot to do. I wish you both good night. I'll send someone to guard right away. I'll tell him to stay out of sight. No need to alarm Rebecca. And I'll be back when I have some information." With that, he left.

When he was gone Naomi said, "Cedric, do you ever have regrets about our arrangement?"

She could hear his reply in her head, though others in the room would not be able to hear. "Never," he said.

"But you said earlier—"

"I know what I said—said in the heat of anger. I have cherished our life together. Do you have regrets?"

"No. What adventures we've had, but sometimes I miss the flying."

"So do I," he said. "So do I. But enough of this. We need to figure out what we can do if this comes to a fight. As you know, you have my strength and speed. I don't know if that will be enough. Maybe we should ask the elves about some armor and weapons."

"Good idea." she replied. "One more thing to do tomorrow. I'd better get some rest."

* * *

The next day Naomi was busy. First there was the morning chores. Then she started calling some of her riding friends. As it turned out, she was well acquainted with Heather's parents. She had been riding with them many times. Her father was a doctor, her mother a part-time social worker for the county. They lived just a mile down the road and thought the party was a great idea. They had several horses they could bring so everything was set.

Next, she set off for the woods. There was a certain tree she needed to talk to. She walked out past the spring and around the pond. She followed the small stream at the far end, past ancient oaks and basswood, past huge willows, and giant maples until she came to a particularly enormous bur oak—the King of the Forest.

"Great king," she said. "I need to speak with you"

"Aaah," he whispered. "I have expected you. I have heard rumblings."

"Yes, Marid has been sneaking around and it seems at Pan's bidding. I am worried about my granddaughter. I fear there is a fight coming and I need to prepare."

"I see," he said. "You want to talk to the elves."

"Yes, Great King."

"As you know, I have no beef with Pan. He has saved many of my brothers and sisters from the woodsman's axe. But it is also true that were it not for you, I would have been lumber long ago. So, I am indebted to you. I will get a message to the elves. They will help you. As for Marid, he is but a minor nuisance to me. But I can see how he could pose a danger to you and yours. We of the forest will watch for him and warn you if he comes."

"Thank you, Great King. May you have gentle rains and mild breezes." Naomi said. She knew that the trees of the forest—all plants, really—were connected underground. They had a very efficient communication system. She knew that even now, as she walked the path back to her house, a message was on its way to wherever the elves were currently staying.

Elves were very clever; well known among the magicals as master craftsmen. But they were shy. They tended to set up their workshops in out of the way, hard to find places. Naomi had met a few in her life and was on good terms with them. So, she wasn't surprised when she turned a corner in the wood, just past the spring, and saw an elf sitting on a big rock waiting for her.

"Greetings, Nolan" she said as he jumped down from the boulder.

"Greetings, Naomi." He replied and he extended his hand. He was nearly the same height as Naomi and slender. He was immaculately dressed from his stylish fedora to his finely crafted boots. He looked a bit out of place in the woods with his grey three-piece suit. Except for the pointy ears, Naomi thought he looked like a banker, or a mafia don. She couldn't decide. They had been friends for a long, long time. As for his clothes, he liked to say, "I'm in management."

"Thank you for coming," Naomi started. As she explained the situation, Nolan nodded at each point and made notes in small leather-bound notebook.

When she had finished, he closed the book and returned it to the inside pocket of his jacket. "I see," he began. "It seems to me you need personal protection. We've been working on something new—impenetrable fabric. In fact, my suit is made of it. Let me show you." With that he produced a dagger from inside his jacket and handed it handle first to Naomi. "Now I want you to stab me. Go for the heart." He held his jacket open to give her better access to his chest. "Go ahead. Give it your best shot."

Naomi was a bit dubious about this idea. She looked at the dagger. It was clearly sharp enough to shave with. Elf's knives were always sharp.

"I don't know, Nolan. I think I'll take your word for it."

"Nonsense," he said. "How will you know what to expect if you don't see a demonstration?"

"OK," she replied as she thrust the dagger toward the elf's heart. The blade just stopped when it hit his vest.

"What? Are you tickling me now? Come on, Ced. I know you're in there. Really lay into it."

"You asked for it." Cedric growled as Naomi plunged the dagger again. This time Nolan flew off his feet and smacked into a tree at least ten feet behind him and slid to the ground. He was chuckling as he dusted himself off and picked up his hat.

"Now that's more like it. Now check this out." He said as he gestured to his vest. There wasn't a scratch on it. Nolan, clearly enthusiastic about his new product, started unbuttoning his vest then his shirt. "Look," he said. "Not a scratch or a bruise. Didn't even hurt, really."

"Well Nolan, I have to say I am impressed." Naomi, still holding the knife, noticed the tip was bent. "I bent your knife."

"An easy fix."

"How does it work?"

"Well . . . . I can't get too specific, you understand—trade secrets and all. But, basically when something hits the fabric it becomes rigid briefly; distributes the blow over a wider area. It is absolutely puncture proof. Plus, it breathes, very comfortable really."

"I think I need a new set of clothes for myself and my granddaughter. And a bow and some arrows for me—and a sword, I think. This one might be tougher. I need to interrogate Marid when he returns. I need a way to hold him and make him tell me about Pan's plan." Naomi felt sure Nolan would come up with something.

"Excellent! Don't worry about payment. I am sure that whatever Pan has in mind bodes ill for us all in the end. I shall stop by your house tonight to get measurements. Until then I bid you adieu." With that he simply disappeared. Naomi was not surprised. She knew that elves could travel by simply "popping out". It made them impossible to follow. Nolan was already in his workshop giving orders to his workers.

* * *

When Rebecca got home Naomi told her to change her clothes and meet her at the barn for riding lessons. They rode around the barn yard for a while until Rebecca started to relax. Then they went out to the pasture.

As Sadie and Bert walked side by side until Naomi turned to Rebecca and said, "We'll run the horses now. Don't worry, just hang on and do what I do. Sadie will stay with Bert. We'll go to the far end and come back to the barn. Are you ready?"

"Yes." Rebecca said, though she wasn't entirely sure that she was.

Soon they were galloping full speed across the pasture. Rebecca copied her grandmother's posture by leaning forward, though she held tight to the saddle horn. They rode in a big circle and headed back to the barn. Halfway back Naomi slowed Bert to a trot and then to a walk.

"We need to walk a bit to cool the horses down." Naomi began. "Well, what do you think?"

"Oh Grandma, that was awesome! Can we do it again?" Rebecca was clearly over her anxiety about riding.

"I'd love to, but we have too much to do today. Plus, I think you will find that you're a bit stiff tomorrow. Riding uses different muscles than walking or running. It's best not to over-do."

After they put away the riding gear and brushed and fed the horses, they went to the house for mindfulness lessons.

They each sat in the wing-back chairs by the fireplace, though there was no fire. Naomi began, "I learned mindfulness from a great teacher, Cedric. Mindfulness is all about being in the fully in the present, without judgment. It is really very simple; but it is a skill that, like any skill, gets easier with practice. What I want you to do when I tell you to start is close your eyes, direct your attention to your breathing, and count. Count one when you breathe in, two when you breathe out, three when you breathe in and so on until you get to ten. Then start over. You will find that thoughts pop into your mind while you are counting. This is normal. This is what the mind does—generate thoughts. Just notice them and let them go. Direct your attention back to your breath counting. Don't worry if you lose count. Just start back at one. Questions?"

"No, Grandma."

"OK, begin."

Rebecca closed her eyes and began to count. Just as Naomi had said, thoughts began to pop into her mind. When she noticed she wasn't counting anymore, she started counting again. Those thoughts kept popping in. She had to re-start her counting numerous times. She was starting to get a bit frustrated. She began to think she couldn't do this—that she was somehow incapable. But she remembered Naomi's words—just notice the thoughts and let them go. It is normal for thoughts to pop in. Then she started to relax. She became so relaxed, in fact, that she fell sound asleep. She awoke with Naomi's hand on her arm, gently shaking it and calling her name.

"I'm sorry, Grandma, I fell asleep."

"Don't worry about it. It just means you haven't been getting enough sleep. One thing you want to avoid is being judgmental about yourself if your mindfulness practice isn't perfect. It will get better with practice. Speaking of which, I want you to practice once in the morning before you leave for school and once again when you get home. It's important."

"OK, Grandma. But why is it so important?"

"Well, there are a couple of reasons. First, regular mindfulness meditation will give you many benefits. It will help you to deal with stress more effectively. It will help you to sleep better, improve your concentration, and make your study easier and more effective. These are all good things, and there more benefits. But the second and I think, for the time being, the most important; is that it will make you better able to not think about Marid and Pan. They may appear anyway, but we don't want to make it too easy for them."

"OK, I'll do it. I promise."

"Good girl. Now let's make some supper. We have guests coming this evening."

* * *

After the supper dishes were done Naomi and Rebecca were once again sitting in the wing-back chairs by the fireplace, this time with a roaring fire when there was a knock on the front door. Naomi opened the door to see Pip and Nolan standing there, each with a long, narrow package.

"Come in," she said, stepping aside so they could enter.

Nolan carefully hung his hat on one of the pegs by the door and continued in by the fireplace. "You must be Rebecca." He said, holding out his hind. "I am Nolan, your tailor."

Rebecca shook his hand, but Nolan noticed she was staring at his ears.

"I see you have noticed my beautiful ears. I am an elf."

Rebecca, who had grown accustomed to meeting an assortment of characters said, "I thought elves were short."

"And I thought little girls were polite." He quipped.

"Touché." Pip interjected. "Where did you want this stuff? What's in these packages anyway?"

"Weapons. I'll take those." Naomi said. "Nolan is here to measure you for your new riding clothes. I thought you should have new clothes for your party. I'm getting some too. On second thought Pip, why don't you help me put these packages away while Nolan gets Rebecca's measurements?"

Once they were in Naomi's bedroom, Naomi turned to Pip and said, "Did you find out anything?"

"Indeed, I did," He replied. "It seems our speculation was correct. Pan, for reasons known only to him, has something against Rebecca. It also seems that there may have been some tinkering with Rebecca's mother's car just prior to the accident. Gremlins, probably Marid, were involved."

Naomi, who had been expecting this, closed her eyes and collected her thoughts. Then she opened them and looked at Pip. "What about the guards?"

"I found a small group of mercenary elves. Five guys. She will be guarded around the clock. I had to promise you would pay them, but we didn't settle on a price."

"Well done. I'm not worried about the price right now." Naomi knew that elves were fierce fighters as well as excellent craftsmen. They were the best archers in the Magical Kingdom and their swords were always sharp.

When they returned to the living room Nolan and Rebecca were finished measuring and just sitting and chatting. Soon Nolan was measuring Naomi and making notes in his little notebook.

"Before I forget," Naomi said. "What did you come up with for Marid?"

Nolan stood up and pulled a small, folded cloth from his inside jacket pocket. "I think you are going to like this." As he unfolded the cloth Naomi could see that it was a bag with a drawstring at the top. "It works like this: If you can get him in the bag and tie the drawstring, he can't get out. It is made of that indestructible material I showed you earlier today."

"Very nice," she said, taking the bag. "Thank you. I have a score to settle with that little pimple."

"OK . . ." Nolan replied, not really knowing how to respond to that last statement. "Your clothes should be ready in a couple of days. I assume, since this is riding attire, you will be wanting boots, gloves, and hats as well?"

"Of course. Thank you."

* * *

The days that followed were busy. Rebecca practiced mindfulness twice a day as Naomi suggested. She was already sleeping better. That was a good thing because the riding lessons got longer and longer. The new clothes showed up as promised. They were the most comfortable clothes she had ever worn. As she stood looking at herself in the mirror, she looked every bit the cow-girl, with her jeans, white shirt, leather vest, boots, hat and gloves. She decided she liked the look. This was going to be a great party.

4. The Party

The day of the party had finally arrived. The bright sunny mid-May morning promised a beautiful day. Rebecca was up early even though it was Saturday. She was happy and humming a tuneless melody as she thought about the party. However, she frowned as she looked down and saw the dew from the grass getting her new boots wet as she walked out to the barn to do her chores. Had she been looking up instead of down she might have noticed the large bumble bee perched on the edge of the barn roof, looking at her. What she could *not* know was that bee was none other than the gremlin Marid. Gremlins are adept shape shifters. It is a skill that serves them well when they get up to their mischief.

Marid watched her as she finished her chores and returned to the house to see if Naomi needed help with any preparations. He watched as the pickup pulling the horse trailer pulled in and unloaded. He watched as the rest of the guests arrived. He was biding his time, waiting for the perfect opportunity.

"This is going to be fun." He said to no one in particular. He didn't like humans and in particular he didn't like young girls—so emotional, so excitable, and so vocal. The terrified scream of a young girl was the sweetest music to his ears. He was planning a symphony today.

Meanwhile, the partygoers were all gathered at the corral, saddling the horses and generally getting ready for the morning ride. Rebecca felt confident. She had practiced every day and was really starting to enjoy riding. Heather had been riding for years and was looking forward to a fun day. Gail and Barb had never ridden before but were following Heather's lead. She had assured them that her family's horses were very gentle. The plan was that Naomi and Christi, Heather's mother, would accompany the girls on their ride. What could go wrong?

As the party started across the pasture with Naomi and Bert taking the lead, Marid decided the time was right. "Like shooting fish in a barrel" he thought as he flew up beside Rebecca's horse, Sadie. He buzzed around her head a bit, just to make her nervous. Sadie shook her head and snorted.

"Grandma, it's a bee. What should I do?" Rebecca asked.

"Hang on, I'm coming." Said Naomi as she turned Bert around. As soon as she got turned and saw it, she knew it was *no* bee.

Before she could get close, she watched Marid sting Sadie on her hind leg. Sadie kicked. He stung the other back leg. Sadie started to buck. Rebecca flew. She screamed, which thrilled Marid to the core. When she landed, she was kind of surprised it didn't hurt more. As she lay on the ground watching Sadie buck away from her, she saw Naomi cautiously ride Bert up beside Sadie. Quicker than Rebecca's eye could follow, Naomi's gloved hand snatched the bee from the air. With her other hand she slowly reached for Sadie's reins. When she had a secure grip, she pulled Sadie close, leaned in and whispered in Sadie's ear. Sadie immediately calmed down. It was all over in a few seconds.

As Rebecca stood up and dusted herself off, Naomi said, "Here take the reins." Rebecca did, then looked at her guests. Gail and Barb were wide-eyed, holding tightly to their saddle horns.

"Are you OK?" Heather asked as she dismounted.

"I think so," Rebecca replied.

Heather turned to Naomi, who was shaking open a cloth bag with one hand while still holding the bee with the other, and said, "Wow! That was the most amazing thing I ever saw. What did you say to her? You have to teach me that!"

Naomi carefully placed the bee in the cloth bag and pulled the drawstring tight and tied it—twice. She started to chuckle and said, "I just told her to calm down."

"It had to be more than that. Sadie was in a panic, she was going crazy and just like that," Heather snapped her fingers, "she was calm."

"Let's just say it's a family secret. Listen, why don't you folks stay here while I go back to the barn and get some ointment for those stings and dispose of this?" she said, holding up the bag.

The group watched Naomi ride toward the barn. Then the girls started peppering Rebecca with questions.

"Are you sure you're OK?"

"Did you hear what she said to the horse?"

"Your grandma is really fast for an old lady."

"What's with the bag?"

"Does she have a bee collection?"

Finally, Rebecca held up her hands and shouted, "Wait!" She didn't like *this* much attention. "I did *not* hear what she said. I don't know about the bag and yes, I'm sure I'm OK! Now can we please talk about something else?"

There was a long silence, punctuated only by an Oriole calling from the nearby woods.

* * *

Marid, who had returned to his true form, had become very verbal. "Let me out! The boss won't like this. You'll be sorry. When I get out, you're going to have so much trouble." He continued in that vein as they got to the barn.

Naomi, now Cedric, carried the bag into the barn. When she got inside, she swung the bag as hard as she could and hit the floor with a bang, cracking the concrete floor. "Shut up, you worm." Cedric growled. There was a quiet groan coming out of the bag. "I told you long ago to stay away from me and mine. I'm not going to kill you—*now*. Whether or not you live to peddle your mischief elsewhere depends on you. I'm going to lock you in this box for the time being. You will have some time to contemplate the error of your ways. When I come back, we will talk. If I am not satisfied with our talk, I will end you."

Having had his say, Cedric retreated, and Naomi became herself again. She locked the bag in a locker in the tack room, picked up the jar of ointment off the shelf and returned to the others. Marid renewed his futile efforts to get free, while promising himself he would have his revenge.

* * *

"Rebecca, you hold the reins while I put the ointment on." Naomi said.

The ointment jar caught Heather's eye. It was a half pint canning jar, much like home-made jam would be in. "What's that you're putting on?"

Naomi chuckled, "Oh . . . it's just something I made."

"Something you made?"

"It's a recipe I got . . . from a friend. Just the thing for bee stings." She had actually gotten the recipe from the fairies, but she couldn't very well tell Heather.

Apparently, the ointment *was* just the thing. The stings that were clearly inflamed started to fade as soon as the ointment was applied. When Naomi was satisfied all the stings were treated, she remounted Bert. Turning to the group she smiled and said, "Shall we continue? No need to let that bee spoil our fun."

And so, they resumed their trek single file through the woods. There were many trails—mostly they had their beginnings as deer trails, so they weren't very wide. As they walked along Rebecca thought about all she had learned in the past few weeks—about gnomes, fairies and water spirits. She wondered what the trees were thinking as they rode between them. She was tempted to think about Marid and Pan, but she remembered what Naomi had told her. She did not want them showing up, though she had her suspicions about the "bee". So, she directed her attention to the present moment. "Grandma is right," she thought. "Most present moments are OK."

She looked around and saw squirrels watching them from the treetops. Some even followed along, jumping from branch to branch. There was an Oriole calling in the distance, though she never caught a glimpse of it. A Blue Jay flew ahead, announcing their presence to one and all. A Wren cussed them out for invading her territory. They even saw a faun sleeping in a thicket where his mother left him. It was a beautiful day.

The group took a long, winding path to the pond. When they got to a picnic table on the little beach they stopped and dismounted. Naomi pulled sandwiches and chips from one saddle bag and soda from the other.

"In case you need it, there is an outhouse down that trail." Naomi pointed to a foot path that disappeared into the bushes. "Otherwise, let's have some lunch."

Since everyone seemed more interested in lunch than relief, Naomi started down the path even though she didn't really *need* to. She suspected Pip was around, and she wanted to talk to him. When she stepped in, she paused before shutting the door. Pip appeared beside her.

"Sorry about the *bee*," he began. "Apparently, he flew in here disguised as a bee. I hate gremlins. Anyway, there is no sign of Pan so far. Although you can be sure *someone* is watching. I think this little stunt was more harassment than anything."

"Rebecca could have been badly hurt." Naomi replied.

"I know, I only meant to say this was not life threatening—a scare tactic. I don't think they will try again today, but everyone is watching. I posted a guard at the barn in case they try to release Marid. When do you think you will be interrogating him?"

"I think the party will be winding down about two." She replied. "I haven't decided yet what to do with Rebecca when we do that. I'm starting to think she deserves to know what we find out. Anyway, thank you Pip. I really need your help with this."

"No problem. Rebecca is my friend now too."

"I suppose I better get back before they send a search party."

* * *

The horses grazed in the fresh grass beside the beach while the girls chatted over lunch. The chattering continued on the way back to the house for cake and ice cream. The trip back was uneventful and quite pleasant.

Later, Naomi and Rebecca waved as their guests drove off. Then Naomi turned to Rebecca and said, "Well, that was fun, but we need to talk." Naomi filled Rebecca in on the details of Marid and his capture. "What we really need is more information. We're going to interrogate him, and I warn you it will probably become unpleasant. You might want to wait in the house."

Rebecca thought a bit before responding. "No, Grandma. I need answers too. I may have some questions of my own."

"Alright," Naomi replied. "Let's get some answers."

When they got into the barn Pip and a large man who was dressed in a way that reminded Rebecca of pictures she had seen of Navy Seals were waiting for them. Pip stepped forward and said, "First, introductions. Rebecca, let me introduce Lancelot."

Lancelot removed his black stocking hat, bowed and in a crisp aristocratic British accent said, "I am very pleased to make your acquaintance, Lady Rebecca."

Rebecca, clearly staring at Lancelot's pointed ears said, "Same here. Your name is Lancelot, like in King Arthur?"

"Yes, *exactly* like that."

"You mean. . . "

"Arthur and I were well acquainted, but that is a tale for another time."

"And you're an elf?"

"Indeed."

"Now that that is settled, let's get to work." Pip interjected.

They took the bag containing Marid out of the locker and hung it on a hook on a beam over the central isle of the barn. "Time for our talk," Cedric said.

"You're all dead," Marid replied. He had given up escaping and just crouched in the bag glowering.

"My, my, what a tough one you are." Cedric began. "You're going to have to do better than that or you are never getting out of here. Why don't we start with Rebecca's mother? I believe you stated at one time that her death was not an accident. Tell us about that."

Marid was quiet, clearly thinking about his reply. Then he said, "OK, but first I want to hear what Rebecca knows about that night."

The group looked at each other quizzically.

Pip asked, "What harm could it do?"

Naomi shrugged, "Go ahead, dear."

Rebecca, who hadn't thought about that night since it happened, started. "Mom came to pick me up at the school because I had stayed late to help my friend Ginger decorate for the dance. When she got there, she got to talking with Ginger's mom. We decided I could stay at Ginger's house that night. We were having so much fun." She paused, her eyes tearing up, then continued. "I was at Ginger's house when the police found me and told me the news."

"I knew it. I said it all along." Marid shouted from his prison. "The boss blamed me, but it was you. You were supposed to be in the car. You were supposed to die. It was a fool-proof plan. The gas pedal stuck at the same time the brakes went out. Do you have any idea how hard it was to time all that with the red light and the on-coming truck? It took weeks of planning, and you ruined it! It should have been you. *It was your fault.*"

Rebecca interrupted his rant by hitting the bag again and again with a barn shovel, shouting; "YOU KILLED MY MOTHER!"

Marid was laughing. "You can't hurt me, foolish girl." His laughter continued to mock her.

Suddenly Rebecca's swing was checked by Naomi grabbing the shovel's handle. She tried to jerk it away and Naomi said, "He's right, you can't hurt him. But I can." She held up a baseball bat in her other hand. "She was my daughter you know."

Rebecca stepped back and Naomi swung, aiming for the cheap seats. The bat and the hook holding the bag both gave way. The bag hit the wall with a thud and slid to the floor.

"You are all dead." Marid moaned.

Ignoring him, Lancelot said, "Well that is half the picture, now we need to know why. Fun though it might be to torment our guest, torture has never been an effective means of getting information. I say if he doesn't cooperate, we should tie that bag to a nice big rock and drop it in the pond. Let's see how long he can hold his breath."

Cedric joined in, "Marid, I've been thinking. As much as I would like to squash you like the vermin you are, I have come to realize that destruction goes hand in hand with creation. It is all a part of the great cycle of life. While I see that such as you are necessary, I think we could get by without you in particular. So . . . I think that you will tell us what we want to know, or I will give my friend Lancelot a free hand. Or I might just kill you myself right here and now."

"OK, since my choices are few, I will answer your questions. I don't know that it matters at this point anyway, but you have to let me go after."

Cedric thought a bit before replying, "Very well, but know this: If I see you again—ever—I will kill you."

"Him too, I want Lancelot to promise."

"I, Lancelot of the Lake, do swear on my honor as a Holy Knight that I will let Marid go his way if he tells us all he knows about why Pan wishes harm to Rebecca. I, too, caution you to avoid me in future on pain of death."

"OK, I don't know everything. All I know is that it is not because of anything she has done, but rather it is something she *will* do."

"What might that be?" Pip inquired.

"All I know is that the boss went to see the Oracle and when he came back, he was obsessed with eliminating this Rebecca person. Why I don't know. He just keeps saying, 'we have to eliminate her before she ruins everything.' That's all I know. I swear."

He had barely finished when there was loud clap of thunder. Naomi picked up the bag and ran outside, followed by the others. When they looked to the west, they saw a small dark cloud. There was lightening flashing around the edges and a funnel shape starting to twist its way to the ground as it rapidly approached the barn.

"Grandma, I've never seen a cloud like that." Rebecca said.

"That's no cloud," Naomi quietly replied. "That's a fury!"

The wind had started to blow quite strongly as the twister had had reached the ground. Tree branches and other debris were swirling around the cloud. Naomi started barking orders.

"Rebecca, get in the basement. Lancelot, can you stop that thing?"

"We can try, M'lady."

"Pip . . . Oh, Pip, where have you gone?"

Rebecca went to the basement as directed, but she found a chair to stand on so she could see out the small window. She could see her grandmother chasing the livestock out of the barn, in case the barn fell she assumed. She looked at the cloud. She was somewhat surprised to see what looked like *flying horses.* There were five of them. They had long wings and were struggling to fly closer to the cloud. Atop each one was what she assumed were Lancelot and his crew, each armed with a bow.

Two months ago, this would have been quite shocking. However, in the last few weeks she had learned that her grandmother was sharing her body with a real dragon, met a gnome, fairies, a water spirit, a couple of elves and a gremlin. How shocking is a flying horse? So, she watched the flying archers and said to herself, "How cool is that?"

The mounted archers flew closer and closer to the cloud. Then they started shooting arrows into it. Rebecca wondered what they were shooting at. Then she saw it. A dark hand shape reached out and tried to grasp one of the fliers. The archer shot it at point blank range. The arrow stuck and the hand jerked back. Arrows kept flying. After a time, a large dark human shape tumbled out of the cloud and plunged toward the ground, the archers in close pursuit. "That must be the fury" Rebecca thought.

The wind started to die down almost immediately. By the time the fury hit the ground the cloud was all but gone and Rebecca was out the front door at a full run. She wanted to see the fury up close. As she rounded the corner of the barn, Naomi caught her in her arms.

"Not so fast."

"Oh, Grandma, you startled me."

"I am sorry about that, but it's best to watch the battle from a distance."

As they watched Pip came out of the woods, followed by thousands of fairies. They fell on the fallen fury. Rebecca couldn't see what they were doing, but the fury started to shrink.

"What's going on, Grandma?"

"Well, the fury is like this big reservoir of energy. Whenever you hear of a really bad storm like a tornado or a hurricane you can be sure there is a fury involved. Anyway, fairies usually deal with energy in plants. However, they can manipulate other energies as well. Right now, they are pulling energy from the fury. I think it might be safe to go over now."

As they approached the fury, they could see he had shrunk to the size of a small man and had faded to a pale grey. The fairies pulled back and hovered nearby. The Fury was like a translucent grey cloud, only shaped like a human. He opened his eyes. Pip stepped forward. "We will spare your life if you agree to deliver a message to your master."

"I agree." The fury's voice was like a breathy whisper.

"Then listen well. Rebecca is under our protection. Any attempts to cause her harm will be stopped. We are lenient today. We will not be so in the future. Rebecca's fate is her own, to shape as she will. You cannot win this foolish venture." Pip turned to the others gathered there and said, "Anything to add?"

“I couldn’t have said it better myself.” Cedric replied.

“Very well, then be gone, fury and do not come back.”

The group stepped back, and the fury rose into the air and sped off over the horizon. That left only one more task.

Naomi as Cedric stepped away from the group, still holding the bag. Held the bag up and said, “Were I my true self I might not be able to resist the urge to eat you. However, we are true to our word. I will release you, but I warn you. Do not try anything on the way out or I will consider our agreement null and void.” With that, he up ended the bag and dumped Marid unceremoniously on the ground.

He got up, dusted himself off and scowled at Cedric. “You haven’t heard the last of this.”

“Perhaps,” Cedric replied, his eyes narrow and glowing red. He folded his arms and bent down close to Marid. “But I better have seen the last of you.” With that, he puckered his lips and blew a small ball of fire that grazed the top of Marid’s furry little head—leaving a strip of singed hair in its wake.

Eyes wide, Marid turned and ran as fast as his stubby legs could carry him. He was nearly to the woods before he remembered he could shape shift. He turned into a raven and flew as fast as he could until he was out of sight.

“Well, that’s that.” Pip said, then turning to Naomi, “Cedric, I did not know you could do that.”

“In truth, I wasn’t sure it would work myself. But I thought it was worth a try.” He replied, chuckling.

The others laughed with him. When the laughter died down Pip said, “I’ll say this. Naomi throws one whopper of a party. Happy birthday, Rebecca.”

Even the fairies laughed at that one.

5. The After-party

Having defeated Marid and the fury, the band of fighters stood in the middle of the pasture as thousands of fairies flew overhead. The battle, though intense, was of short duration and left them a bit worked up with nothing else to do.

Naomi spoke first. “I think we need to celebrate our victory.”

A cheer went up. Word went out through the trees. By sundown there was a huge bonfire in the meadow and hundreds of magicals gathered around it. A small band of gnomes played music on instruments the likes of which Rebecca had never seen. The magicals were dancing. It turned into quite a party. As darkness fell, the fighters sat around the fire swapping stories. Naomi, having finished the evening chores, sat down beside Rebecca.

“How are you doing, dear?” she asked. She meant it not as a greeting, to be answered with a tossed off “fine”. She really wanted to know.

Somehow, Rebecca sensed this as she gave the question some thought before she answered. “I’m good, I think. I’m angry about my mom. I want those murders to pay.”

“Justice or revenge?”

“I don’t know, Grandma. What’s the difference?”

“That’s a good question, dear. I think revenge can consume a person. It can destroy your life and in the end be quite unsatisfying. The desire for revenge turns into hate and hate is an appetite that is never satisfied. With justice, you must be satisfied with the knowledge that in the timeless universe justice is always served. Don’t get me wrong, when the opportunity presents itself, we will see justice done here. Remember, she was my beloved daughter. But I refuse to be a slave to the desire for revenge."

Rebecca thought about that for a minute, then responded, "I think I understand. Justice then."

"Good girl. The other thing to think about revenge is that it interferes with living in the present. When you are thinking about revenge, when are you thinking about?"

"What do you mean *when*?. . . . . The future?"

"Yes, the future—and the past. With revenge, you also think about the event that you seek revenge for. What is the problem with that?"

"Well . . . since you can only think about one thing at a time, if you constantly think about the past or future you miss out on the present."

"Very good. It sounds like you have been listening to your mindfulness lessons. There is one more thing to think about regards revenge. It keeps the wounds fresh. If you are always thinking about something painful, how can you heal?"

"Wow, Grandma, you're really smart."

Naomi laughed at this and replied, "Well, I've been around a long time—and I had a great teacher."

Rebecca understood that Naomi meant Cedric. She suddenly felt very lucky. She had a very extraordinary grandmother who loved her very much. She had new friends in the human world and in the magical world. She felt especially privileged about that. She sat thinking about that, then turned to Naomi and said, "Thank you, Grandma."

This took Naomi by surprise. "Why, whatever for?" She responded.

"Well, just everything. When Mom died, I thought my life was over. Now I wouldn't trade my life with anybody's."

"You are a good girl," Naomi said. "We all depend on each other for so much. Just please, never lose that sense of gratitude. It will serve you well."

They sat quietly for a while, watching the fire. After a while Naomi got up to put more wood in the fire. Rebecca watched the sparks rise up and mingle with the stars. She was lost in the moment when she heard Naomi say, "You know . . ." She turned to face Rebecca. "We haven't seen the last of that lot."

"Really?!" Rebecca stiffened at the thought.

"You didn't think it would be that easy, did you?" Lancelot said from across the fire.

"I guess I hoped . . ."

"Do not worry," he said. "You will not face this menace alone. I and my kind are with you till the end. We have made an enemy of Pan this day and he will not forget."

Rebecca was silent for a moment, feeling guilty for bringing her wonderful new friends into her trouble. "I'm sorry." She said quietly.

"You needn't be. This day was a long time coming. Pan has long held a hatred for mankind. We knew what we were getting into. It seems as though you have the destiny of being the tipping point. I don't know what future that destiny will bring, but Pan does, and he fears it. That is an advantage to us." Lancelot thought a bit before he continued. "I don't think they will be back for a while. You should learn to defend yourself. If you agree, I volunteer to be your tutor as well as captain of your guard."

"Grandma, can I?"

"I think it is a great idea. You'll have to take it slow until school is out. But that is only a couple of weeks." Naomi replied.

"Thanks, Grandma. Can I learn to ride the flying horses too?"

“They are called pegasi after their father, Pegasus” Lancelot corrected.

“OK, pegasi. Can I”

“How about we wait until you master their earth-bound cousins?” Naomi answered. “You will have plenty on your plate for a while anyway.”

“Ok,” Rebecca replied disappointedly. “I am curious about something. Why did we let Marid and that fury go? Won’t they just come back to hurt us again?”

“They very well might.” Lancelot replied. “They have no honor. Warriors of honor do not kill defenseless young ladies, or any defenseless opponent. We gave our word to Marid so he would answer our questions. He knows the risk if he returns. The fury was only following his nature. When he was no longer a threat, he served our purpose as a messenger to Pan. Warriors of honor treat the defenseless with compassion.”

“I think I understand.” She began. “I have one more question and then I want to dance. Do you think we’ll be OK in the end?”

Cedric cleared his throat. “I’ll take this one, if you don’t mind. There are several ways to answer that question. First, since everything that happens is supposed to happen; whatever happens is OK. Another way to look at it is to say that not knowing the outcome is what gives the spice to the present moment. Think how dull it would be if we knew the outcome of every venture. Be fully present in each moment, respond wisely and hope for the best. We will all do our very best to finish this conflict and live to tell the tale—and our best is very, very good.”

“Well said,” Lancelot said. “Well said indeed.”

6. Observations

The last weeks of May were busy ones for Rebecca. She really didn't have the time to think about the excitement of her birthday party. School was winding down, which meant finals and a couple of projects that needed to be finished. She was spending more time with her new girlfriends. She continued with her mindfulness training with Naomi. If that wasn't enough, she had started self-defense training with the elf, Lancelot.

He had decided that, since she was very busy, they would start with physical conditioning. There was a lot of running. They would run on the trails through the woods. Lancelot set the pace and he was merciless. They ran a little further each day. When they returned to the barn Rebecca was shot, but Lancelot was barely breathing hard. Then he would make her do stretches and other exercises. She was asleep before her head hit the pillow every night.

The last day of school had finally arrived. Much to Rebecca's surprise, considering how much she had hated her new school when she started in November, she was actually a bit sad to see it end. She had made some tentative plans with her friends to get together over the summer. Since she had gotten a new phone for her birthday, she was sure they would. She was also sure that, since Heather only lived a mile down the road, they would spend a lot of time riding. It would be a fun summer.

When she got home, she had her mindfulness session, as usual. When she was finished, she opened her eyes to see Pip sitting on the hearth by the fireplace. He smiled. She responded in kind. She was in a pretty good mood anyway, but when a gnome smiles at you, you have to smile back. You can't help it. Plus, he was a gnome and dressed the part, complete with a pointy hat and shoes with toes that curled up at the end. He was so darn cute you just had to smile when you saw him.

"Hi Pip." She said.

"Hi." He replied. "I was wondering what your plans are for this afternoon."

"I have training with Lancelot."

"Actually, you don't. I heard he was planning to give you a break." He said then he shouted, "LANCELOT!"

Lancelot suddenly appeared. Rebecca still found it a bit unnerving when elves just popped in and out like that. Lancelot didn't fit any notions Rebecca previously had about elves. He was nearly six feet tall and dressed in casual military fatigues. Were it not for his pointy ears he could easily pass for human.

"I was just telling Rebecca that you were giving her a break today." Pip said.

"Yes, I thought that in view of the fact that today was the last day of school, and she has been doing well with her physical conditioning, she could take the day off." He replied in what Rebecca thought of as an aristocratic British accent. Then turning to Rebecca, he continued, "That way, you'll be good and rested when your *real* training starts bright and early tomorrow."

Rebeca wasn't sure she liked that last bit about the *real* training starting bright and early. But she kept that to herself. After all, *this* present moment was OK. Also, she was kind of looking forward to doing something other than working out. So, she turned to Pip and said, "I guess I don't have any plans. Why do you ask?"

"I thought we could take a walk." Pip replied, winking at Lancelot—who smirked a bit. Something was definitely up. Rebecca decided to go with it.

"OK," she said. "I'll play along. Let's go"

Soon they were walking the familiar path to the pond. It was a nice late spring day, sunny with a light breeze. Birds were singing and fairies were everywhere. It was nice just walking along, so no one spoke. Rebecca felt relief from the intensity of the last few weeks, so she just let her mind wander as she walked. When they got to the pond, they sat at the picnic table and Pip said casually, "Lovely day for a walk, don't you think?"

"I do think." Rebecca replied. She was really enjoying this break with her friends. There were ducks and geese on the pond. There were other birds flitting around. A few fairies had paused in their labors to join the group and even Amaryllis came down from her spring.

"So, what did you see on the way here?" Pip asked.

"What do you mean?" Rebecca replied.

"On—the—way—here—from—the—house, —what—did—you—see?" Pip repeated slowly and loudly, as if he was talking to someone who was hard of hearing. He even pantomimed the words as he spoke them.

"OK . . . I saw the usual trees, a lot of fairies, some flowers, ducks on the pond, and . . . the horses in the pasture."

"That's it?"

"Well . . . yeah. I didn't know there was going to be a quiz."

"Of course, of course, not really a quiz though. I was just wondering. Lancelot, what did you see?"

"I saw horses *and* sheep in the pasture, many trees of course, the fairies, an eagle, an oriole, there was a wren cursing at us, several kinds of flowers, the ducks and a fox hiding in the raspberry thicket. I could go on if you like."

"I think the point is made."

"What point would that be?" Rebecca snapped. "That I'm a ditzy girl and walk around in a fog all the time?"

Pip chuckled. "Well . . . you may be a ditzy girl, but that's not the point. The point is that you, like most humans, are not always fully present. You've got lots of stuff going on in that pretty head of yours. People often make the mistake of thinking that mindfulness is something you do for a few minutes every day and then get on about your business. Mindfulness is all about being fully in the present moment—every moment. Lancelot was trained in mindfulness as a child and in the many years since his training he has practiced constantly. Now he does it without thinking. He is always in the present moment. That is why he saw what you did not."

There was a long pause while Rebecca thought about what Pip had said. Part of her wanted to be mad. It was almost like they were making fun of her. But Pip sat there looking at her with that grin that was more of a smirk. She realized he was trying to teach her something he thought was important. Besides, she really could not stay mad at Pip.

Finally, she said, "So what's the rest of the lesson?"

"Good girl", Lancelot said. "Not everyone would have asked that question. You have realized that lessons can come at any time. The point of this whole exercise is to demonstrate that there is benefit in being mindful at all times and that anything a person can do can be done in a mindful way. There are three broad categories of mindfulness, participation—which is doing something, description—which is assigning words to an experience and observation—which is paying attention to your senses. The suggestion here is that you go through each day with the intent of being mindful as much as possible. And of course, as always, dismiss any judgmental thoughts you may have along the way. Always be fully present and your enemies will find it hard to sneak up on you. Questions?"

"Lots—but I can't quite decide where to start."

"Good. That's where we'll leave it for today. Tomorrow we'll start martial arts training at eight. I will expect you to have one good question for me by then."

"Wait, I do have a question I would like answered now. It's not about mindfulness."

"Very well, proceed."

"Well, I know it is good to be prepared for any attacks that Pan may throw at us. How long can we stay ready for him? I mean, isn't he immortal? Can't he just wait until we slip up somehow? Will he ever give up? Isn't there something we can do to resolve this so I can get on with my life?"

Pip started pacing back and forth with his hands behind his back. For once he wasn't smiling. "I thought you said *one* question." More pacing. "OK, I'll take them one at a time. It is not only good to be prepared, it is essential. If we are not constantly ready you will die. Not only you. Pan is a very vengeful character. He will go after any who helped you. However, you raise a good point. For all practical purposes Pan *is* immortal. He *can* afford to wait until we slip up. Although, I have to say that with the crowd you have helping you slip-ups are rare. We are all very good at what we do. Also, Pan is not known for his patience, so he is not likely to wait long. Anyway, he will never give up. So, you are right. We need to find some kind of resolution. At the moment, I am at a loss. I think we should have a meeting—tonight. We'll put our heads together and come up with something."

Pip sat back down and crossed his arms, looking quite pleased with himself. He was grinning again. "Well, we have a couple of hours till the meeting. What shall we do for fun?"

Lancelot spoke first. "I'm afraid I will have to excuse myself. I have a few errands. Roland will keep watch while I'm gone."

Roland, who had popped in while Pip was talking, smiled, and waved at Rebecca.

Pip turned back to Rebecca and asked, "Have you ever gone fishing with a water nymph?"

"No."

"Well, then you are in for a treat. Amaryllis, my sweet, would you be so kind as to help us with fishing?"

Amaryllis, who had been floating along next to the beach the whole time stood up and put her hands on her hips. She frowned at Pip, who gave her his biggest grin. Then she smiled. "It would have been better if you had asked me before promising my help, but I will help—provided you do not take more that you need for supper."

Pip giggled with glee as he began striping off his clothes until he was clad only in white boxers with big red polka-dots. Amaryllis waded in up to her waist, closed her eyes and began to sing. Rebecca did not understand the words, but the melody was beautiful. Pip dove into the pond and soon a fish flew out of the water and landed on the beach, flopping in the sand.

Then he poked his head out and called to Rebecca. "What are you waiting for? The water is fine."

Rebecca wasn't at all sure how she felt about fishing. After all, fish were slimy. But it was a warm day, the water looked inviting, and she was wearing shorts and a t-shirt. So, she kicked off her shoes and waded in. When she was in up to her knees, she looked down into the crystal clear water and saw the fish. There were fish as far as she could see. They all seemed to be hovering in place facing Amaryllis, who continued to sing.

Pip waded up to her. "Just reach in with both hands and grab one."

Rebecca bent over and grabbed the nearest one. The fish started squirming as she lifted it out of the water. She tried to hold it tighter, and it popped out of her grip. She grabbed it again and again it slipped free and plunged back into the pond.

Pip was laughing and clapping his hands. "Do you always play with your food? You are holding too tight! Just grab and flip, like this."

With that he bent over, grabbed a fish, and flipped it up to the beach. Rebecca tried again. This time she didn't hold it so tight but flipped it toward the beach. Soon it lay flopping in the sand with the others. Rebecca decided this was fun. They waded through the shallows looking for the biggest ones. Soon they had a dozen large sunfish tossed on the beach.

Amaryllis stopped her song. "I think that is enough even for a glutton like you Pip."

Pip, who had been thoroughly engrossed in fishing, stopped and looked at the beach and then to Amaryllis. "Oh, I didn't realize—you know it's not the fish. I just like to hear you sing."

"Oh Pip, if only that were true." Amaryllis teased.

"Amaryllis, you know you are the love of my life." Pip grinned and winked at Rebecca, then continued. "Well, I suppose we should get these up to the house and prepared for supper."

7. Meetings

In Japan, at the base of Mount Fuji is a fourteen square mile forest called Aokigahara. It is a very dense forest and as long as anyone can remember—and even longer than that—people visiting the forest experience an overwhelming feeling of doom. Sometimes these people feel so much despair they decide to end their lives. This happens so often that Aokigahara is often called "Suicide Forest".

Somewhere near the center of this forest is a secluded glen where The Great God Pan has been hanging out for centuries, His hatred of the human race has so permeated the place that people who visit begin to hate themselves. It is in this quiet, peaceful setting that Pan plots and schemes the extinction of the human race.

Pan is pacing back and forth in front of a very frightened gremlin named Marid. Marid, for his part, even though he can change his size and shape at will, is too scared of his master to be anything but his normal diminutive self. Pan is large, well over six feet. From the waist down he looks like a goat, with shaggy legs, a goat's short tail and cloven hooves. From the waist up he looks like a man, a very hairy, ugly man—except for the horns. He has short, slightly curved horns rising out of his forehead that give him a demonic look.

He paces with his hands clasped behind his back, occasionally glancing over at Marid. At length he speaks.

"So, let me get this straight. You failed to kill this human and have been hiding these last weeks for fear I would kill you. Then you decided that being dead was better than waiting to be killed, so you came here."

"Yes, Great Pan."

"You have failed me twice in this one simple thing. Tell me why I shouldn't kill you now."

"I can still be useful. I . . . I am still good at wrecking stuff. Nobody wrecks stuff like me.

"Then return and finish what you started."

Marid turns a pale shade of green. "I can't go back. Just look what they did to my hair." He bows his head toward Pan and points at the singed streak down the middle of his spiked hair. "If I go back, they will kill me. They have a dragon—and gung-ho elves. They were pretty clear. I can't go back. I mean. . . What's the big deal with this girl anyway?"

"What's the big deal?" Louder this time. "What's the big deal? I'll tell you what the big deal is. She will ruin everything. I will re-take my rightful place as the King of Nature, but only if she is out of the way. So, now you understand. She *will* die. So, you can either get on board or you're out—*all* the way out."

Marid takes a couple of steps back and holds up his hands in a "calm down" gesture. "Wait a minute, wait a minute. Let's not do anything rash. Maybe you should see for yourself. It's not such an easy job. She has help."

Pan stops his pacing and looks directly into Marid's eyes. "Maybe you're right. I *should* see for myself. Perhaps you have some value after all. I will see for myself and for the moment you will continue to live."

Marid falls to his knees and clasps his hands as if praying. "Thank you master. You won't be sorry."

"I'm sorry already. Be gone before I change my mind."

Marid bows, turns into a raven and flies away.

* * *

They had a big supper that night—fresh fish, sweet corn, and ice-cream with fresh strawberries from the garden. Conversation during supper was light. There was a lot of laughter.

Pip leaned back and rubbed his plump belly with a satisfied grin. "I do like fresh fish. What say we clear these dishes and adjourn to the porch? I don't think everyone will fit in here."

Naomi stood up and began gathering dishes. "Rebecca, why don't you gather some wood for a bonfire? The rest of us will be out in a minute."

"OK Grandma." Rebecca went to the edge of the woods content in the knowledge that there were many eyes keeping watch over her.

Soon they were all gathered around the fire, Rebecca, Naomi and Cedric, Roland, and several other elves—though noticeably not Lancelot, Pip, Amaryllis and many fairies. Even though the sun was still up, a bonfire was a good thing to sit around—plus they had marshmallows. Some had sticks to roast the marshmallows, but the fairies just tore off a handful and flew off. Apparently, fairies have quite a sweet tooth.

One of the fairies grabbed a hunk of marshmallow, flapped his wings, and rose up until he could see over the fire. Still chewing he announced, "I am Finnian. I speak for the fairies and also for the trees and other plant life. We realized that since we helped the innocent Rebecca out of compassion, we have made an enemy of Pan. We have seen what he does to his enemies. We remember the beautiful forest that grew where the Badlands are now and the fairies that tended her. We vow to stand with those who will stand with us. We will not go out without a fight."

A cheer broke out among the fairies as Finnian settled to a seat beside Pip. It sounded like very loud jingle-bells to Rebecca.

Rebecca stood next. "I just wanted to thank you all for saving my life and for being my friends. I can't tell you how much this all means to me." She had intended to say more but she was starting to tear up toward the end, so she quickly sat down beside Naomi.

Naomi hugged her and kissed her forehead. “I think I can speak for everybody when I say no thanks are necessary. We support the people we love.”

Then she spoke louder so everyone could hear. “I think we all know the purpose of this meeting. We need to come up with a plan to resolve this situation. None of us wishes to fight Pan, but we will if need be. So, we need to find some kind of resolution that keeps Pan away for good. I, for one, am open to suggestions.”

“Great, because I have one.” Pip spoke up. “It seems to me that this unpleasantness started when Pan went to visit the Oracle. Why don’t we go to her and ask her what’s up?”

Cedric said with his deep voice. “You know that the Oracle will not tell us what she divulged to Pan.”

“True enough,” Pip replied. “However, we know from that weasel Marid that Pan is upset about something Rebecca will do in the future. All we have to do is have Rebecca ask about *her* future.”

“Though it pains me to say it, he is right.” Lancelot said from across the fire where he had popped in. “In fact, I have taken the liberty of asking the Oracle if she will see Rebecca.”

Pip giggled with glee. “Great minds think alike. What did she say?”

“She agreed, of course. She doesn’t take sides, as you know. She said it was only fair that since her words put Rebecca in danger, she should tell her what the future holds for her.”

“Excellent,” Cedric said. “How soon can we arrange to meet?”

“She will see Rebecca on the next full moon—in ten days’ time. Rebecca can travel with me. If she holds tight to my hand, we can go there instantly. The Oracle prefers it that way. All things considered; she prefers that no mortals know her location. Rebecca will be allowed to ask three and only three questions. So, we must recon carefully what they will be.”

Finnian flew up to Lancelot's eye level and said, "Surely the first question must be as Pip suggested, 'What is Rebecca's destiny?'"

"Indeed," Lancelot replied. "That will at least tell us why Pan means to kill Rebecca. The next question must be 'Can Pan be defeated?'"

"Not can but *how*" Pip spoke up.

"Well, we do have three questions. We ask her destiny; can Pan be defeated and how to defeat him." Lancelot said.

"Then it is agreed, on the appointed day Rebecca will travel with Lancelot to ask the Oracle those three questions. In the meantime she will train. She must be prepared for any eventuality." Cedric said, as if the decision was his to make.

There was a pause while the group thought things over and watched the fire. At length Naomi broke the silence. "She most certainly will not! She will not go anywhere without me—no offence to you Lancelot. We don't know when or where Pan or his thugs will appear. I'm going with and that's that."

"I was planning on taking a few of the lads anyway," Lancelot replied. "I can take one human with me when I travel *our* way. I will take Rebecca. One of the lads can take you, Naomi. When we get back, we will meet again. Hopefully we can find some kind of resolution to this unfortunate situation."

There was a long pause again, punctuated by the crackling of the fire. The sun had gone down and it was getting dark. This time it was Rebecca that broke the silence. "Lancelot, I have been wondering. When we met, I asked you if you were Lancelot like in King Arthur and you said 'Exactly'. What did you mean by that?"

Pip seemed to think this was really funny—he laughed and slapped his knee. "She's got you now, Lance old buddy!"

Lancelot cleared his throat and said, “Very well. I shall tell the tale. It’s been a long while since I thought about those times. It will be good to remember.”

All eyes were on Lancelot as he began. “Fifteen or sixteen hundred years ago, or so, the land now known as England was occupied by soldiers of the Roman Empire, and it was called Britannia. The Romans, beset by barbarians on all sides and decadent beyond belief were losing power. One fine day they pulled up stakes and left. After centuries of not being allowed to defend themselves, the Britons were left defenseless. The scavengers of Europe came running. It was chaos.

Out of this chaos one man arose—Arthur. In the beginning he fought to protect his village, Camelot. He was brilliant and strong, a truly good man. He extended his protection to all who asked. Strong men came from across the Isle. Only those with integrity were accepted. The best sat at his round table. You remember, Cedric, you were there.”

“Yes, it was a glorious time. All men were equal under the law. There was a feeling of hope in the land—a harmony between the world of humans and nature, including the magicals. Pity it lasted such a short time.”

Lancelot looked wistful for a moment before going on. “Soon word spread across Europe about the wise king Arthur and his glorious realm. I came to offer my services. I won my place at the Round Table by defeating his champion at the joust.”

“What about Guinevere?” Rebecca asked.

“Ah, yes, Guinevere.” He paused a bit. “She was beautiful and smart. She strongly believed that women were the equal of men and should be treated as such. It was a radical idea in those days. She insisted that *all* the children in the kingdom be educated in reading and mathematics. She also believed that women should learn to defend themselves.”

Rebecca interrupted, "What about . . . I thought you two were . . . that you . . . "

"We were what?" There was ice in his voice.

"You know . . . The story goes that you and Guinevere had a *thing.*"

"Oh, I see. A *thing*. What kind of thing do you mean?"

"Lancelot, would you stop toying with her and tell her already?" Pip yelled from across the fire.

Lancelot chuckled. "Sorry, I couldn't resist. No, we most certainly did not have a *thing*. As I was saying, Guinevere was constantly after me to teach her self-defense. I foolishly agreed. You see Rebecca, as my student you are in pretty good company. Anyway, we knew that Arthur would not like it. He was forward thinking in every way but one. He believed that women had their place, and it was *not* on the battlefield. So I, again foolishly, agreed to train her in secret. We met daily in the wood, and I taught her hand-to-hand and weapons combat.

Of course, Arthur found out. I'm not sure how, but I suspect a certain gremlin. Anyway, Arthur thought the only reason we would meet in secret was to have a *thing*, as you put it. He was angry. We tried to convince him of the truth. He wasn't happy with our explanation either. His opinion was that women should be protected, not defend themselves. Also, I don't think he ever completely believed us. I left. It seemed that my presence was a constant reminder.

Arthur was never the same after that. He became moody and paranoid. He began to mistrust everyone—especially the magicals. Things began to fall apart. There was a coup attempt by Mordred and he was killed at the battle of Baden Hill."

"I read about that. Mordred was supposed to be his son—and Arthur's sister was Mordred's mother . . . which, eewww!!!" Rebecca made a face as if she had just stepped in a cow pie.

Lancelot chuckled, "Well, Mordred was his son. Mordred's mother was *not* Arthur's sister. Before his marriage Arthur spent much of his free time with Morgan Le Fay, Mordred's mother. She was not his sister, but they grew up together. When Arthur's power began to grow Morgan began to see Arthur as a king and herself as queen.

When she learned she was pregnant, she was overjoyed. Arthur was, at the time, visiting a neighboring nobleman to negotiate an alliance. When he returned to Camelot, Morgan went to tell him the news only to find him with his new wife, Guinevere. She was the daughter of the noble and their marriage was part of the alliance treaty. Morgan was heartbroken. She left Camelot without telling Arthur.

Her broken heart and jealousy turned to hatred. She raised Mordred to believe his rightful place was on the throne of Camelot and eventually all of England. And he came close. His army had essentially won the final battle at Baden Hill. Arthur and Mordred found each other on the battlefield and killed each other.

It was over. Camelot faded into legend. The story changed over the years, but those of us who were there remember the glory that was Camelot."

"Indeed" Cedric said. "Merlin the wizard was my friend. It was his dream come to life. He placed the sword in the stone. He made sure that Arthur was there to pull it out. He negotiated with the Lady of the Lake for the sword Excalibur. When it was over, he retreated to the hidden island of Avalon, never to be seen again. I miss him still."

"Wow! That was awesome!" Rebecca said.

"Indeed," Cedric replied. "Another chance to set the world right lost to human greed and avarice. One can almost see why Pan hates humanity so. After Camelot fell, I left England and roamed the world. I did stop by Europe a few times; most notably during the reigns of Alfred the Great and Charlemagne. I finally settled in America. The people here feared me but respected me as well. They called me the Thunderbird. I eventually found the hill where I met Naomi and there I slept until she came along. I guess it is meeting people like Naomi and Rebecca that keeps me from giving up on humanity like Pan."

Everyone was silent for a while. Pip poked at the fire with a stick. Each thinking of paradise lost and dreaming of possibilities to come.

Lancelot broke the silence. "Well, it is getting late. I know a young lady who needs her rest."

Rebecca winced.

Lancelot continued, "We have a plan, and I can't think of anything else we need to discuss right now."

Reluctantly, Rebecca stood up and said, "I can take a hint. What time do we start in the morning?"

"Eight, sharp," Lancelot replied.

"OK then, goodnight, all"

"Good night, Rebecca." The crowd said almost in unison. Rebecca went off to bed.

8. Training

Rebecca was up bright and early the next day. She had breakfast, did some chores, meditated and was in the hay mow of the barn at eight sharp as directed. Lancelot was not there when she got there but popped in at the stroke of eight.

"Good," he said. "You are punctual. I like that. First, we will discuss our plan of instruction. Each day we will begin with a brief meditation. You have a lot on your mind, and I need you to be fully present for instruction. Then we will do some warm-up exercises, followed by hand-to-hand training. Then weapons training, archery first then swords. Then lunch. After lunch if the morning goes well, I have a surprise for you—I think you'll like it. Any questions before we start?"

"What's the surprise?"

"If I tell it wouldn't be a surprise. Shame on you."

"OK, I don't understand. Why are we training with old fashioned weapons? I mean, what about guns?"

"Well, for various reasons guns do not work well against magicals. Also, accidents are more likely and deadly with guns. When I'm through with you, you won't need guns and you won't fear them."

"I see. Well, I guess we better get started."

"Very well. But first, the question."

"What question?"

"Yesterday at the pond you said you had lots of questions and I said I expected you to have one good one for this morning"

"Right. . . I . . ." Actually, she hadn't given the matter a second thought. "What about . . . We seem to be doing a lot of planning. How do you plan for the future if you are always supposed to live in the present?"

"That *is* a good question. Clearly you have given this some thought."

"Thanks, but what's the answer?"

"The answer is that planning is something you do in the present to prepare for the future. We direct our attention to the present, but we know there will be a future. We enjoy the summer but prepare for the winter we know is coming. Does that make sense?"

"I guess so." Really, she was starting to drift a bit. She didn't really care about the answer since she had just pulled the question out of the air. "Can we start the training now?"

"Of Course. Do you remember the mindfulness lesson from yesterday?"

"Yes. Be mindful all the time. Anything a person does can be done in a mindful way."

"Correct. Now I want you to sit in a lotus position and observe your breath for five minutes."

"Lotus Position?"

"Sit cross legged on the floor. That's it. Now hold your back straight and place your hands palm up on your knees. There you go. That'll do for now. Comfy?"

"Yes"

"Then begin."

She meditated. Then Lancelot slowly and meticulously took her through the steps of defense against a frontal attack, defense against a rear attack, how to punch without breaking your hand—all the while reminding her to focus, focus, focus.

Then they moved on to archery. She was a natural as it turned out. While she did not hit the bullseye every time, she never missed the target—for which Lancelot praised her highly.

Then on to sword play. They started with wooden swords. Even though she wore padding it really hurt when Lancelot poked her chest with his sword. She started to get mad, though she said nothing. Finally, after a particularly nasty blow she spoke up.

"Hey, that hurts!"

"You're angry."

"Yes!"

"Good. Now the real training can begin. Take the power of your anger and direct it to your focus."

Rebecca plunged her sword directly at Lancelot's heart. He easily deflected the thrust and said, "That's better. Again"

She attacked again and again. Each time he deflected her attack and landed a blow of his own. Soon her focus was as sharp as a dagger. She fought with a fury she had never known. Finally, she landed a blow right over Lancelot's heart.

He stepped back, rubbing his chest. "Excellent. You fight with a dragon's fury when you move beyond your emotions. It is a mindfulness thing really. Fear, anger—they can be distractions that kill in a real fight. You must channel the power of that emotion into action. You have done very well today. Go have your lunch and meet me behind the barn at one sharp for your big surprise.

* * *

At one sharp Rebecca rounded the corner as ordered. She was, in fact, greatly surprised at what she saw there. Lancelot stood between two beautiful, winged horses.

"You have shown yourself to be a very capable individual, so we thought it would be appropriate for you to learn to ride the pegasi. In a combat situation being airborne makes you a much more effective fighter. Also, it is really fun."

Rebecca was shocked—in a good way. She threw her arms around Lancelot and said, "Lancelot, thank you so much. You won't be sorry."

Unknown to either of them, Rebecca's friend Heather picked that exact moment to step around the corner. She saw the hug and smiled to herself. "Rebecca, who is your friend?"

Rebecca's heart stopped. She stepped away from Lancelot. Then Heather saw Lancelot's ears. She gasped. *Then* she saw the horses' wings. She gasped again and involuntarily took a step back and tripped over Pip, who said, "Where you going, sweetheart?"

Heather sat on the ground looking at Pip. "Who . . . w-w-what are you?"

"My name is Pip. As you can see, I am a gnome." Then he grinned.

Heather grinned back. As she grinned, she could feel her initial fear melting away. She looked from Pip to Rebecca, to Lancelot, to the pegasi then back to Rebecca. "What is going on, Rebecca?"

Pip spoke up. "Perhaps I should answer that."

Rebecca felt a wave of relief as she was truly struck speechless.

Pip went on. "Your friend Rebecca is a very special girl, with very special friends. She has had to keep this all secret because, well, you can see how people react to such revelations. The question is, what do we do now? Clearly you can't un-see us. Now that the cat is out of the bag, so to speak, perhaps full disclosure is the way to go."

Lancelot glared at Pip. "What have you done? I think we need to bring Naomi and Cedric into this." Then he just disappeared.

Rebecca finally found her voice. "So, what are you doing here?"

Heather stood up and brushed off her jeans. "I came with my mom. I tried to call you, but you didn't answer. Naomi said she didn't know where you were so I thought you might be down here monkeying around with the horses. But . . . what are you doing here? And who was that guy and what's the deal with his ears? And where did he go? And what are *those*?" She pointed at the pegasi, who were casually grazing beside Rebecca.

Rebecca was thinking of how she was going to answer when Lancelot, Naomi and Christi, Heather's mom, walked around the corner. Naomi suggested they all go to the house to discuss things and soon they were all sitting around her dining room table.

"You both have had quite a surprise," Naomi began. "Hopefully, when I explain things, you will feel better about . . . things. The first thing you need to know is that there exists, unknown to most people, another world—a magical world—beneath or behind the world we commonly see. Even though we usually can't see them, the world we know could not exist without them. Every magical creature you may have heard of probably exists. Pip is a gnome. I've never really figured out what he does. The fairies you saw in the garden take care of the plants. Lancelot here," she gestured in his direction, "is an elf. Elves are very much like humans in that each individual follows his own path. However, they live much longer than we do—long enough to get very, very good at whatever they do."

Naomi paused and looked around the table at her guests. Heather couldn't seem to take her eyes off of Lancelot. Christi eyes moved from Pip to Lancelot to Naomi and back again. She looked as if she had just swallowed a bug. Lancelot sat with his arms crossed and a somewhat disgusted look on his face. Pip, of course, sat with his biggest grin on his face. He knew that soon all the humans would be grinning too. They wouldn't be able to help it. Rebecca had already begun.

Heather noticed Rebecca's grin and asked, "What are you smiling about?"

"Wow, where do I start? First of all, Pip is smiling and when a gnome smiles at you, you have to smile."

"Then why isn't he smiling?" Heather said, pointing to Lancelot. Lancelot, for his part, didn't move or speak except to raise one eyebrow to look at her out of the corner of his eye.

"Well, because it only works on humans and Lancelot is not human. He's an elf. Anyway, I was also smiling because you two are funny. I was as shocked and surprised as you when I found out—for about *five minutes*. I mean, think about it. This is the coolest thing ever. Elves and fairies and gnomes are *real*! Magic is *real*! And there's more. Lancelot is the *real* Lancelot. He knew King Arthur!"

"Ahem!" Lancelot cleared his throat. "Perhaps it's best if we don't overwhelm our guests with a lot of needless details." He looked pointedly at Rebecca.

"Oh, sorry. I didn't think. I guess I'm so relieved to have someone to talk to about all this."

"I hadn't thought of that," Lancelot began. "I swear if I live forever, I will never understand the apparent need of teenage human females to get together with others of their kind and prattle on about absolutely everything. Then I suppose this is for the best, really. We have enough to worry about without having to keep all this secret. Perhaps full disclosure is the way to go."

"Perhaps it is," Naomi said. So, she told them everything—about Cedric, Rebecca's mother, the fight after the birthday party and about Pan. When she was finished there was a long pause.

At some length Christi spoke up. "Well . . . that's quite a story. I mean, it's obviously true. I guess I feel quite . . . honored to be let on the secret. But here's the thing. I don't feel I can keep a secret this big from my husband or my other kids. I'm just not made that way. I can see why you couldn't go to the authorities about Pan. I don't know . . . This is pretty scary stuff."

She looked at Heather. "My first thought is to take my kids and get as far away from this place as I can."

She reached across the table and took Naomi's hand. "But we've been friends a really long time. I lost count long ago how many times you have helped us out. I think we need to stick together. How can I help?"

Naomi was clearly touched by her friend's support. "At the moment I really couldn't say but thank you. I really mean that."

"You would do the same for me. But I have had enough excitement for one day. I think we should go home."

Pip jumped from his chair, walked around the table, extended his hand to Christi, beamed his biggest grin and said, "It has been a pleasure, madam. I'm sure we will become great friends."

Christi shook his hand and smiled back. Christi and Heather said their good-byes and left.

Lancelot looked to Rebecca and said, "We have riding lessons to attend to."

Rebecca leaped up. "I can't believe I forgot. I get to learn how to *fly*!"

9. Flying Lessons

"The first thing you need to know about pegasi is that they are different than horses. You will notice they have no bridle. It is not needed. They can read your thoughts. They will go where you tell them to go, except you don't have to say it—just think it. Questions?"

"I can't think of any." Rebecca replied. She was so excited about riding the pegasi she couldn't think of anything really.

"Very well," Lancelot said. "For your first lesson we will take things nice and slow. We will stay over Naomi's farm, and you will follow me. Above all, hang on. If you fall off, it is a long way down."

Lancelot helped Rebecca mount her Pegasus and swung into his saddle with the same grace he displayed in everything he did. Then he turned to Rebecca and shouted, "Hang on!"

Rebecca held tight to her saddle and clamped her legs around the Pegasus as it reared back on its hind legs and jumped. With a strong flap of its wings, they were airborne. Rebecca watched the ground fall away then turned to look at Lancelot. For the first time since she met him, he had a look of pure joy on his face.

"This is awesome!" she shouted.

"Indeed. To control your mount, you must call her by name."

"What's her name?"

"You couldn't pronounce it. You must make one up. What's the first thing that comes to mind?"

"Wildfire."

"Excellent! Wildfire it is. She has been listening to me, but I have just told her to listen to you. Tell her in your mind to turn left. Remember to call her by name. Do it now."

Rebecca did as she was told and much to her astonishment Wildfire banked into a slow left turn.

Lancelot followed. "See how easy that was? The tricky part is getting used to being so high up. But you, Rebecca, have the heart of a champion."

Rebecca hadn't looked down since they took off. She did so now. Her heart nearly leaped out of her chest. They were hundreds of feet up. But she had the heart of a champion—Lancelot said so. She took a deep breath and looked at Lancelot and suddenly felt safe.

They flew in silence for a while, enjoying the ride. Finally, Lancelot spoke up. "We'll fly around the pond and then back to the barn. We don't want to over-do on your first day."

Rebecca was enjoying the leisurely ride to the pond when she noticed an eagle soaring along right beside them. She was watching the eagle when he turned his head to look right at her. For a moment they were eye to eye, and she heard a voice in her head say, "Good day to you Rebecca." Then the eagle banked his wings and sailed away.

Rebecca turned to Lancelot and said, "Did that eagle just talk to me?"

Lancelot laughed. "I forgot to tell you. When you are riding Wildfire you can communicate with animals—because of your link with her."

"Wow! I could get used to this. Up here it is easy to believe I don't have a care in the world. It is easy to be fully in *this* moment. Plus, I can talk to animals. How cool is that?"

"You know Rebecca, I can't help but think that this has all been so unfair to you. You never asked for any of this. And yet you seem to accept it without complaint. You remind me a bit of Arthur in that way. No matter what obstacle the universe threw at him he always faced it head-on. Anyway, a girl your age should be concerned with nothing weightier than whether or not that boy she likes is going to steal a kiss."

Rebecca could feel her face flush. She was trying to think of a response when Lancelot went on.

"That's why I changed my mind about full disclosure. An old soldier like me can forget that young girls have needs not related to military advantage. You need to spend time around people your own age."

"Thank you for that. Since my birthday I've been so caught up in all this I haven't had time to think of anything else. I would like to go out with my friends. Maybe go to a movie or the beach."

"And so you shall. Of course, you'll still have to keep up on your training and we must take precautions. I see we're over the pond. What say we race back to the barn?"

In response she told Wildfire to 'Fly like the wind' back to the barn. Wildfire did not disappoint. She started flapping her wings in earnest. Rebecca bent low to catch less wind. Her hair blew back, and she had to squint to keep her eyes from tearing up. She couldn't remember when she had so much fun. In no time at all they shot over the barn—a full head in front of Lancelot. Then they circled around and touched gracefully down in the pasture behind the barn.

"You let me win. I don't care. Thank you so much. You truly are my knight in shining armor."

Lancelot bowed deeply from the waist and said, "The pleasure was all mine, Milady." They both laughed and he continued. "Now we must store our tack and give our mounts a good rubdown. It isn't really necessary, but they do love it so. Then we'll turn them loose. No fence can hold them, but they will stay around because we ask them. When we're finished, I think you should call your friends and see if you can't find something fun to do."

Later, as they were brushing their mounts Rebecca seemed lost in her thoughts. Lancelot watched her for a minute then said, "Penny for your thoughts."

Rebecca smiled a soft smile and kept brushing. "You know, Lancelot, I never knew my father. If I had a father, I would want him to be just like you."

Lancelot reached out to stop her brushing and they locked eyes for a moment. "And I would be proud to have a daughter like you." They hugged for a moment and Lancelot said, "You better go call your friends."

10. The Movie

Rebecca dialed Heather's number as she walked back to the house.

"Heather?"

"Rebecca, I'm so glad you called. It's been *quite* the scene around here."

"What do you mean?"

"Well, when we got home Mom called Dad and asked him to come home from work. He wasn't happy. Then, we got the whole family together and told them the whole story. Dad was pretty skeptical—he still is. But he hasn't seen what we've seen. Anyway, it was all pretty dramatic."

"I suppose it was. Anyway, I was calling to see if you wanted to do something tonight—go to a movie or something."

"I'd *love* to. Hey, I know. Why don't I talk to Randy, you know—my brother. He just got his license. Maybe he could take us. I think he wants to talk to you anyway."

Rebecca had met Randy only a couple of times in passing. She couldn't imagine why he would want to talk to her. "Why does he want to talk to me?"

"Oh, I don't know. Something about wanting to train with you and Lancelot. He's such a jock." She said it like it wasn't a complement. Truly, she thought he was much too full of himself. Really, he was the quarterback of the football team and had taken first at the State Wrestling Tournament last year *and* had a room full of track trophies. Still, he didn't have to be so arrogant *all* the time!

"I don't know what Lancelot will think of that." Truly, Rebecca wasn't sure what *she* thought about that. "OK, why don't you talk to him and call me back?"

"No, hang on. He's right here. *Randy, do you want to take Rebecca and me to the movie tonight? OK.* He said yes. He's going to ask Mom, but I'm sure it'll be OK. What time should we pick you up?"

"How 'bout six thirty?"

"I think the movie starts at seven, so that sounds right. See you then."

* * *

"So, what do you think, Grandma?"

"I think it's a great idea."

Then Naomi's eyes started to glow red, and Cedric spoke in a deep voice. "I think it is perhaps safer to be out in public. Pan wishes to remain hidden as much as we all do. Someone will be watching, just in case though."

"Great," Rebecca said. "I go from having no parents to having more parents than I can count." She said like it was a joke, but it sort of fell flat. "Oh, I didn't mean . . ."

"Think nothing of it," Cedric replied. Then, under his breath, "Teenagers, 'twas ever thus."

* * *

Rebecca was ready and waiting at 6:30 when Heather and Randy picked her up. As soon as she got in the car Randy started up.

"HI, Rebecca. This magic stuff is really something, isn't it?"

"Well . . . Yeah." There was something about his manner that put her off, but she couldn't put her finger on it.

"You know, I used to read a lot of fantasy stuff and Arthurian stuff. I can't wait to meet Lancelot. I had been planning to go to wrestling camp this summer, but if I could train with Lancelot . . ."

"Yeah, about that, I don't know if he will agree to train you. He's kind of particular." Truthfully, she wasn't sure she wanted to share. "But I guess I could ask if you want."

"That would be great! Thanks."

Heather cut in at this point. "Ok, now that that is out of the way, let's talk about something else. What's the deal with the winged horses? Can they really fly?"

"Yes! And I got to ride one. It was Awesome! I named him Wildfire and I control him with my mind."

"You mean like with telepathy?"

"Yes."

"Wow! I want one."

While Rebecca wasn't enthusiastic about Randy training with her, she was starting to think that it would be great fun to fly with Heather.

"I'll talk to Lancelot."

"Speaking of—that guy is hot."

This last comment had taken Rebecca by surprise. At this point in her life, she truly hadn't thought about anyone in *that* way before. She turned her head to look at Heather before she responded. "I suppose he is." She turned her gaze back to the road with a funny little smile on her face.

Heather looked at her a bit then said, "You *suppose* he is? Look at you. You have a crush on him!"

"I do not! He's more like a father to me. I never knew my father you know."

"Oh, I'm so sorry. I didn't think." Heather thought a moment before continuing. "But I still think he is hot."

They both laughed.

Randy, who had been actively *not* listening to the girls, announced, "We're here."

The trio bought their tickets and snacks without much comment. When they were seated in the theater and the lights went down Rebecca noticed that the seat to her right was no longer empty and there was a tiny hand in her popcorn.

"You don't mind sharing, do you?" Pip asked before stuffing his mouth with popcorn.

"I guess not. What are you doing here?"

"Someone had to keep an eye on things. Plus, I love movies. I never have to buy a ticket, you know."

Rebecca smiled at this and turned to her left to see her two friends both leaning forward and looking at Pip.

"It's just Pip, you guys. Don't stare, you'll attract attention."

Randy and Heather turned back to the movie and watched without further incident.

On the way home Pip sat in the back seat with Rebecca while Randy and Heather took the front. Pip and Rebecca were whispering something, and it seemed to be getting a little heated.

Heather turned around and said, "What's going on back here? I can't take you kids anywhere."

Pip and Rebecca stared at each other for a moment, then Pip motioned toward the front with his head. "Go on." He whispered.

"Pip thinks," Rebecca began, still looking at Pip, "That you two should just show up tomorrow for training. I thought I should talk to Lancelot about it first."

"How can he refuse?" Pip said. "Now that you know about *things,* he has to train you. You are in almost as much danger as Rebecca."

Randy, who seemed just a bit too eager for Rebecca's taste, quickly chimed in, "That would be great! Name the time and place and I'll be there."

Rebecca, still glaring at Pip, replied, "Eight o'clock sharp in our hay mow."

11. More Training

And so it was at eight o'clock the next morning not only Randy and Heather appeared at the barn, but their mother as well.

At the stroke of eight Lancelot appeared.

"Well, well, what do we have here?"

"Pip said it would be OK if we trained with you." Randy volunteered.

"Of course he did." Lancelot began pacing back and forth, visually appraising each would-be trainee. He stopped when he got to Christi. "And you, madam? You wish to be trained as well?"

"Not really," she replied. "I'm here to make sure my kids are going to be safe."

"I see. I wish I could guarantee that. The unfortunate truth is that even if you stay at home, living as close as you do, you are all in danger."

Christi stood quietly for a minute, clearly worried about her family. As she thought about it, she realized that Lancelot was right. "So, what can I do about it?"

"Perhaps I can answer that." Cedric's deep voice boomed from behind them.

Then Naomi spoke. "Christi, why don't you come with me? We'll have some coffee and talk things over. Meanwhile these young people can get on with it."

"I don't know if I am ever going to get used to that deep voice, but some coffee would be nice"

After Naomi and Christi left, Lancelot turned to the three kids. "Very well, I will do as you ask. You will follow my instruction without complaint or argument." He had been pacing in front of the trio, but he stopped in front of Randy and extended his hand. "We were not introduced. I am Lancelot."

Randy shook his hand and said, "I'm Randy Lund, Heather's brother."

"So I assumed. You look like an athlete."

"I was state wrestling champ last year."

"Jolly good. You must be in good condition."

"I work out every day"

"Excellent! You know Naomi's pond?"

"Yes."

"I want you and your sister to run there and back. Do it now."

Randy and Heather looked at each other and then left. When they were gone Rebecca started to apologize, but Lancelot held up his hand in a "stop" gesture.

"No apology needed. Pip is often annoying, but his heart is in the right place and in this instance he is right. Whatever is happening here is bigger than just you and me. It will affect the whole world. I suspect there is a big change coming and the more people who are prepared the better. Well, we better get started. First, a bit of meditation just like yesterday."

Lancelot were well into their hand-to-hand routine when Randy returned. He was panting heavily.

"That was quick." Lancelot observed.

Randy, used to praise, smiled, and said, "I run track."

"I see. And where is your sister?"

"I don't know. She's pretty slow. I passed her halfway to the pond; she was still going and I was coming back." He said with some pride.

Lancelot's eyes narrowed as he leaned forward into Randy's face. "Did I tell you this was a race?"

"No." Randy seemed to be losing some of his cockiness as he perceived Lancelot's irritation.

"Then why did you turn it into one?"

"I thought . . ."

"You thought to impress me? You thought this was a competition? You arrogant little buck. You will go find your sister and you will carry her back here. We act as a team and don't you forget it!"

Randy looked as if he was about to cry, but he turned and ran back to the woods. When Lancelot turned to look at Rebecca, he had a twinkle in his eyes and a slight grin. "I think we could use a little break." He strolled over to the window that looked toward the wood. "This should be good."

They watched out the window and it wasn't long before Randy appeared running toward the barn with Heather sitting piggy-back on his shoulders. Heather was beaming, but Randy appeared quite unhappy. Rebecca and Lancelot both started to laugh. They were still laughing when Randy and Heather came up the ladder to the hay mow.

Randy stood bent over with his hands on his knees, panting, sweat dripping from his nose and chin. "OK." He said between pants. "I got her." Clearly, he did not enjoy being the butt of the joke.

"Indeed," Lancelot said. "Just remember, you never, ever leave a comrade behind. You don't know when one of Pan's minions will show up. We could be planning a rescue now, or even worse, a funeral. You will take this seriously or you will be gone. I don't have time to waste on a foolish, selfish *boy.* Do you understand?"

Randy, who was more used to being praised than chewed out, straightened up and looked Lancelot in the eye. "I get it."

"Jolly good. And now to work. We start each session with mindfulness, then hand to hand, swords and archery. After lunch will be riding. I assume you have ridden a horse before?"

"Yes, we've been riding since we were little." Heather replied. "Will we get to ride the flying horses?"

Lancelot closed his eyes and shook his head. "Yes . . . I suppose."

"Hooray!!!" Heather literally jumped with joy.

* * *

Meanwhile, Naomi and Christi were discussing things in Naomi's kitchen. Naomi had explained their plan to meet with the Oracle and hope to find some resolution with Pan.

"I just don't understand what Pan could possibly have against Rebecca." Christi said. "What could her destiny possibly be that he fears so much he has to kill her?"

"That's really the question, isn't it?" Cedric replied. "We really won't know how to proceed until we know the answer to that. We know Pan has long held a hatred for humanity. Thousands of years ago Pan was revered. He was the benevolent king of Nature. He nurtured humanity when it was young, taught the first farmers how to grow their crops and domesticate animals. Then there was a falling out. Humanity started to hate and fear Pan and he responded in kind. But why this one young girl? It is a mystery. Anyway, we will try to negotiate with Pan. Perhaps we can have her *not* do what Pan thinks she *will* do. Perhaps then he would leave her in peace."

"That sounds good. I hope it works"

There was a pause while the two women sipped their coffee. Naomi broke the silence. "In the meantime, maybe it would be a good idea if I asked Pip to check things out at your house to see if there is anything you could do to make things safer there."

"OK." Christi was a bit dubious about that suggestion, but she was completely out of her element.

Naomi put her hand on Christi's and said, "I wouldn't worry too much about your kids. Lancelot is really very good and safe. I trust him with my granddaughter's life."

"I hope you're right. Well, I suppose I better get home. When should I pick up the kids?"

"Don't worry about that. I'll see they get home alright."

* * *

Later that afternoon, after hand-to-hand, archery and sword training and lunch, the kids rode the flying horses. Randy loved the combat training and Heather loved the pegasi. They flew back to the barn to find Naomi waiting for them.

"How was your first day of training?" Naomi asked as the group landed.

"Just amazingly, awesomely wonderful!" Heather said as she gave Naomi a big hug. "Thank you so much!"

"I told your mother I see you got home safely. How would you feel about taking the pegasi?"

"That would be great!" Heather replied.

"Can I go too, Grandma?" Rebecca asked.

"I was going to suggest that actually. But come straight home." Naomi watched as they remounted their steeds and flew away.

12. A Chance Meeting

The week that followed was a busy one. Rebecca and her friends trained hard all day. After a couple of days, they moved most of their training to pegasi-back. They hacked at saplings as they flew by and shot arrows into straw bales at high speeds. It was great fun, really. It was great having Heather there; and Rebecca found herself warming up to Randy once Lancelot had deflated his ego. He seemed really nice, actually. The week seemed to pass in a few moments and soon the big day approached. Tomorrow would be the big trip to see the Oracle.

After a hard day of training Rebecca was usually completely shot. But on this evening, she was so wound up about seeing the Oracle she couldn't relax. Lancelot suggested a run to burn off the extra energy.

* * *

Pan is standing concealed in the under-growth beside the path Rebecca is running on. Pan can, in fact, conceal himself from anyone he chooses without the bushes. This is why his presence has not been detected by any of the magicals—his former subjects.

He has, in fact, been lurking around the farm all day—doing as Marid suggested, gathering intelligence. He has seen the elf training the young ones. He has seen the gnome trying to keep an eye on things. He knows even the trees are watching for him or his minions. But he has not seen the dragon. He has felt something—a presence. But he has seen no dragon. He makes a mental note to discuss this with Marid.

He senses the girl's approach and soon sees her running down the path toward his position. When she gets close, he steps into her path, revealing himself for all to see.

Rebecca, unable to stop in time runs right into him. She falls down on her backside. When she looks at Pan, with his horns and goat legs, she screams. She gets up and runs as fast as her legs can carry her back to the safety of her home. Pan begins to laugh.

"Run little rabbit, run!" He shouts after her. "Run as fast as you can. Your time will come. I will kill you no matter where you hide." He continues to laugh as elves and fairies appear to protect Rebecca. "You cannot protect her. I will be lenient with you if you leave her to me."

In response the elves fire a volley of arrows at him. He disappears before they hit him, but they can still hear him laughing. "You have chosen. So be it. I *will* be back."

* * *

Rebecca had never been so scared in her life or run so fast. When she got to the first clearing Wildfire was waiting for her. She jumped on his back, and they flew straight up over the wood and back to the house. Naomi met her on the front porch.

"What is it child?" she said.

"Grandma, I saw . . . I saw the Devil!"

"I hardly think so." Pip, who had just appeared from nowhere, said.

"I know what I saw." Rebecca replied.

"What exactly did you see? Was it a tall ugly guy, with horns and goat legs?"

"Well . . . yes."

"An understandable mistake, really. That, my dear, was the great god Pan." Pip said, looking quite pleased with himself.

"Are you sure?"

"What, now I don't know Pan when I see him? That was Pan alright. I should explain. Funny story, really. But let's get inside where it is comfortable." Pan said as he opened the door and walked in, followed by the others. They sat in the living room as Pip began his tale.

"I really don't know why nobody wants to talk about this. It's just history. Anyway, long ago Pan was the King of Nature. He helped humans survive the ice age. He taught farming and animal husbandry to the first farmers. He was the benevolent leader to us all.

Things really started to go sour when the emperor Constantine declared Christianity to be the official religion of the Roman Empire. Before then, Christians were the nicest people—went around talking about peace and love all the time. First century hippies, but without the drugs.

But then, the church became entwined with the government. Most people lived closer to nature back then and it was only natural that they would give thanks to Pan for his help and support. The newly Christianized government decided this was somehow against the government.

It wasn't long before they were calling Pan 'the Devil' and saying he was evil. As you might guess, Pan was quite unhappy. There was a lot of pacing and ranting—'How dare they' *this* and 'After all I've done for them' *that.* He got so angry he decided humanity should be eradicated—wiped out."

Rebecca stared at Pip wide-eyed while Pip paused for effect. He pulled an apple out of his pocked and started polishing it on his vest. Finally, Rebecca blurted out "So what happened?"

He took a bite out of the apple before continuing. "Well. . . There was a big split in the magical world. The magicals who specialize in destruction—the gremlins, trolls, and such—sided with Pan. The magicals who honor life and build things split from him. He was no longer king. His kingdom was shattered. He blamed humans for that too.

Things got bad. There were barbarian attacks, plagues, famine, the Dark Ages. The humans blamed all magicals. We were chased and persecuted. Most of us decided to go invisible and just go on about our business.

As for the rest, tales of 'the Devil' became so accepted and common that even in this day and age the first thing a girl thinks when she sees a guy with horns and goat legs is 'Devil'."

Rebecca sat quietly, thinking about what she had just heard. She was still stirred up from her encounter with Pan and a bit worried that he would come bursting in any minute. When Lancelot popped in, she almost jumped out the window.

"Oh, Lancelot, you startled me!" she said.

"I am sorry M'lady. That was not my intent. I thought you would like to know that we are almost certain Pan is gone. We think this was a reconnaissance mission."

"You're *almost* certain?" Pip asked. "How certain are you?"

"Ninety nine-percent."

"That's *all*? Ninety-nine percent? So, there is a one percent chance he could pop in here and kill us all?"

"Ninety-nine point nine-nine then. We're pretty sure."

Pip cracked a huge smile. "Great! I was just pulling your chain. I thought a little humor could ease the tension."

"Be sure and let us know when that happens, alright?" Lancelot quipped.

"Ouch! You're not as dull as I thought."

"Alright you two." Cedric said. "Less squabbling and more planning."

"Actually, I have already formulated a plan." Lancelot began. "We leave tonight—as soon as possible. We spend the night by the Oracle's cave. Meanwhile, Pip, if you can quit joking around long enough, you will attend to tightening up security around here. We need better intelligence and more firepower."

"Oh, is that all? Better intelligence and more firepower. Is that all? Maybe a little world peace while I'm at it?"

"I'm sure you'll do your best." Lancelot stood and extended his hand to Pip and said, "Wish us luck, old man."

Pip shook his hand and replied, "I will repeat to you something you once said to me. 'Luck is not a factor.' Come home safe—all of you."

Having said his peace, Pip left. The others set about preparing for the trip.

13. The Oracle

Less than an hour after Pip left a small group gathered in Naomi's dining room. Naomi and Rebecca were there, dressed in their elfin riding clothes—modern day armor. Lancelot, Roland and three other elves were present—armed to the teeth. They each had knives, swords, and bows. There were even a couple of short-handled battle-axes. They all had packs with blankets and provisions for a week, just in case.

"Alright everyone," Lancelot began. "Are we ready?"

Roland cleared his throat and held up two swords.

"Oh, I almost forgot," Lancelot said. "These are for Rebecca and Naomi. You probably won't need them, but it is better to have them and not need them than the other way around. Be careful with this Rebecca. It is very, very sharp."

Rebecca pulled the sword from the scabbard. It was lighter than she expected, shorter than the elves' swords—just right for her. It was perfectly balanced, and she could tell that with a little practice it would be like an extension of her arm. She replaced the sword in the scabbard and buckled it around her waist.

"Ready." She said.

"Very well, load up everyone and we go on my signal. You three first. Secure the destination. Roland and I will follow with the women in one minute. If anything looks off, I want you back here to warn us. Questions?"

There were none.

"Very well, go."

The three elves popped out. Lancelot took Rebecca's hand and Roland took Naomi's. As the seconds counted down, Rebecca started to get tense. She started to think Lancelot's watch was broken. Lancelot leaned down and whispered in her ear, "You'll be fine."

Rebecca looked into his eyes and then everything went white. Then everything went black.

It took Rebecca a few moments to realize it was black because she was outside, and it was night. As her eyes adjusted to the darkness, she could see the three elves that left first standing in a circle, facing outwards, with swords drawn. The cool breeze smelled of fish and she could hear the surf some distance away. She was still holding Lancelot's hand.

He leaned down and whispered in her ear, "You can let go now."

Rebecca let go of Lancelot's hand and started looking around. They were clearly on a tall cliff overlooking the sea. A few yards behind them stood what appeared to be ancient stone buildings.

"What are those?" she said, pointing at the ruins.

"In ancient times there was a city here. Lancelot began. "People came from all over the world to consult the Oracle. When the split between the magical world and humans happened, the Oracle had to go into hiding and the city withered away. Ironically, she didn't go far. She dwells in a cave below us. We'll make camp in one of those buildings."

The group made their way around toppled houses until they came to one that was still mostly intact. They unpacked their gear and had a small supper before finding placed to sleep. The elves would take turns standing watch.

When Rebecca awoke the sun was already high in the sky. Naomi was stirring the contents of a large pot that was suspended over a crackling fire.

Rebecca sat up and rubbed the sleep from her eyes. "What time is it, Grandma?"

“It’s about six a.m. back home. I’m not sure what time it is here. It’s still morning I think.”

“Where are the elves?”

“They said they were going on patrol, whatever that means. I’m sure they are not far. Well, I think this stew is ready.”

Right on-cue, one by one, five elves appeared. Naomi filled their plates and Roland went to eat just outside the door.

“I don’t think any of Pan’s lot followed us.” Lancelot said between bites. “Besides, not even Pan would desecrate this place—not if he ever wanted to consult the Oracle again. Rebecca, I think you might enjoy exploring the ruins a bit while we wait. The Oracle won’t meet with us until the full moon sits on the horizon.”

“That sounds like fun.” Rebecca said.

“It does.” Naomi said. “I think I’ll go too.”

“Very well. It’s settled. After lunch we’ll all go exploring.” Lancelot said as he dished himself seconds.

After lunch the group of seven set out to explore the ancient city. They had spent the night in the residential area on the edge of town. There were larger buildings as they worked their way toward the city center. There they found what appeared to be a large temple. There was a large courtyard in front of the temple with numerous broken statues. It was clear from looking at the statues and relief carvings on the temple wall that more than humans had lived here.

“Lancelot, what do all these carvings mean? I mean, did all races live here?” Rebecca asked.

“Indeed they did.” He replied. “Once this place was bustling with all races, from all over. As tension rose between the races people drifted away.”

"What was it like back then?"

"Well, if you go back far enough it was wonderful. Humans worked with the forces of nature. Everyone knew fairies, elves and all the magical creatures. We worked together to make the earth bloom. If you go back far enough there was no fighting, no poverty. Everyone was healthy and happy. There was no pollution or strife. It is the paradise referred to when people talk of the Garden of Eden."

"That sounds wonderful. I wish it could be that way again—that everyone could know you magicals the way I do."

"That would be nice, but what's done is done. Remember that not all magicals want to help humans. Some, like Pan, would kill you all. Perhaps we'll just have to content ourselves with individual cases, like your friends Randy and Heather."

They had been walking through the courtyard as they talked. Naomi and some of the others had gone directly to the temple. She poked her head out the door and called to Rebecca. "You need to see this!"

Rebecca ran through the door. "What is . . ." Then she saw it. There was a huge dragon painted on the wall. Protected from the elements it was as vivid as the day it was painted.

"Meet Cedric," Naomi said. "He told me they painted his portrait to commemorate a service he performed for the Oracle, though he wouldn't say what. I thought you would like to know what he looked like—though he is *much* bigger than this."

"Wow! He's beautiful! I didn't realize he was so colorful, or so big." Rebecca said as she looked up at his head. "And you got to ride him?"

"I did. And it was really something."

"I bet. Like riding Wildfire only bigger. I wish I could have had a chance to ride him."

Lancelot interrupted them. "There are many more sights to see. We'd best keep moving."

They spent the rest of the day exploring and there were indeed many sights to see. As the sun set behind the forest, they made their way back to the cliff. There was a glow on the horizon that indicated the moon would soon be rising. As they watched the moon rise Rebecca became aware of a hooded figure standing off to their right.

"Greetings," the figure said. "I am Alcmene, attendant to the Oracle. Is the girl Rebecca present?"

Rebecca stepped forward. "I'm Rebecca."

"Are you prepared to meet the Oracle?"

"Yes" Her brave response did not reflect the fear she held deep inside. She did not know what to expect.

"Then follow me." Alcmene said as she turned and stepped off the cliff. She did not fall, however, but started down a stairway Rebecca hadn't noticed before—probably because she did *not* like going close to the edge of the cliff. Rebecca followed.

"Be careful." Naomi said as she watched Rebecca disappear below the cliff.

Lancelot turned to Naomi and said, "Now we wait."

* * *

The stairway was narrow, and Rebecca had to keep her eyes on her feet, mostly to avoid looking at the crashing waves hundreds of feet below. She ran her hand along the face of the cliff, even though there was nothing to hang on to. Just feeling the substantial rock on her left somehow made her feel better about the empty space on her right. Just when she was starting to believe the stairs would never end, she saw an arched opening just ahead on her left. She felt a wave of relief as she stepped into the passageway—happy to have walls on *both* sides.

Alcmene turned to face Rebecca and pulled back her hood. Rebecca saw for the first time that she was an elf.

"I will wait here." She said. "You will approach the Oracle there." She gestured further down the dark passageway. "You may ask three and only three questions. The Oracle will let you know when you are finished. You will then return to me."

"I understand." Rebecca said as she started down the passageway.

While it was dark, Rebecca noticed the light of the full moon shown all the way down the tunnel to the end. Rebecca could barely make out a figure sitting there. As she drew closer details started to appear. The figure appeared to be sitting on a large armchair that was carved out of the rock of the cave. She wore a crown of some kind and a long robe similar to Alcmene's. "This must be the Oracle," Rebecca thought. She was disappointed as she got closer because the closer she got, the more her own shadow cast by the full moon behind her obscured the figure.

"Rebecca, you may sit." The Oracle gestured with her hand to a stone bench off to Rebecca's right.

When she had settled on the bench the looked back to the Oracle. She saw that when the full force of the moon hit her the jewels in her crown started to glow. There was an especially large one glowing with a white light suspended in the center of her forehead. It lit up the cave. Rebecca noticed the cave was much larger than she originally had thought, with numerous openings leading back further into the cliff.

The Oracle did not look at Rebecca but straight ahead when she said, "You may ask your first question."

"I would like to know: what is my destiny?" Though she was scared beyond thinking she had rehearsed the questions so much that she spoke without hesitation and more bravado than she really felt. She noticed that her words echoed as she spoke. The Oracle's crown started to glow so much brighter that Rebecca had to shield her eyes with her hand. She sat quietly for a few minutes until the Oracle began to speak.

"Rebecca, you are the nexus, or center around which a new order will be built. You will re-unite the magical world and the human world. You will see much strife and will suffer many losses. But you will also gain much. You have already begun. Events are already in motion that will reveal the magical world to all, and you will be at the center of it. I must warn you. You have a powerful enemy, and you may fail. You may die. If you survive, it will be the strength of love that saves you and brings about this destiny. You may ask your second question."

Rebecca hesitated before she responded. She had questions about the Oracle's answer, but she knew if she asked them, she wouldn't be able to ask the questions she planned to. But on the other hand, she couldn't see how uniting the human and magical worlds would make Pan want to kill her. It was all so confusing. She realized the Oracle was waiting for her question. She decided.

"Can Pan be killed?"

"Not in the way you think of death. You may ask your third and final question."

"Wow that was quick." Rebecca thought. And what did that really mean. This was so frustrating. She was getting answers, but they were not very specific. She didn't feel like she was much better off than before. But she couldn't think of anything else to do but ask the question they had planned.

"How can Pan be defeated?"

"Nothing in nature is as hard as stone. Nothing is as soft as water, yet water can prevail against the stone."

Rebecca wanted to shout, "What does that mean? What does any of this mean?" It was all so cryptic. But what could she do? She had used all of her allotted questions. Feeling very frustrated she stood up to go, even though she had not been dismissed.

"Thank you, great Oracle." She said as she got up to leave.

"Rebecca, wait!" the Oracle almost shouted. "I have more to say."

Rebecca sat back down, hoping for some clarification.

"I do not formulate the answers. I am only the conduit. I know you are frustrated, but you can reason it out. Or perhaps the answers will come from your own intuition. While I cannot take sides, I wish you luck. Like many other magicals I yearn for the time when humans and magicals worked together. I hope you succeed. Now you may go."

Rebecca almost cried. While the Oracle's message felt nice, it didn't really clear up anything. She hoped that her grandma or some of the others could figure this out. When she appeared at the cave entrance Alcmene stopped her before starting back up the stairs.

"I have served the Oracle for over a thousand years, and I have never known the Oracle to speak to seekers other than to answer the questions. You should know what a privilege it is. I know nothing of you, but you must be important to have received such an honor."

Rebecca didn't quite know what to think about this. She said, "Thank you". But she wasn't sure she felt much gratitude. It felt more like a burden. She hadn't really asked for any of this, and it felt like almost more than she could bear. The stairs seemed much longer going up than they did going down. It wouldn't be so bad if she felt like she had accomplished anything.

When she got to the top only Lancelot was waiting for her, which wasn't what she expected. She ran to him, threw her arms around him, and burst into tears.

"What's this?" He asked. "What happened down there?"

"I blew it." She said between sobs.

"What do you mean? Didn't you ask the questions?"

"Yes, but I didn't understand any of the answers."

"Don't worry about that. The Oracle is well known for her cryptic answers. Can you remember exactly what she said?"

"Yes, I think so." She stepped back and wiped her tears with her hands and her nose on her sleeve.

"Well then, you haven't blown anything. We'll go back to camp, have supper, and get some rest. We'll talk it over. We'll figure it out."

"Do you really think so?" She was starting to feel better already.

"I know so. What choice do we have, really?"

"Well, you didn't have to put it like that. You should have stopped after 'I know so'" Rebecca's mood was starting to lift a bit as they started to walk to the camp.

"You know I had a feeling, but I was on a roll. Goodness, I'm starting to sound a bit like Pip. Someone had to fill-in for him I guess."

Rebecca laughed. They continued to joke back and forth until they arrived at the house they were camping in. Rebecca noticed there was an actual door in the doorway now where before there was none. As Lancelot opened the door he said, "Elves with too much time on their hands."

The despair she had felt on the stairway back up the cliff had all but gone. The house was warm, and the stew was good. When she had finished eating, she leaned back and looked into the fire.

"Before we start talking about the Oracle, I'm just curious. Why did we not go home?"

"I'll take this one." Cedric began. "This ancient city is holy ground to us. No magical, including Pan would desecrate it by violence. Also, I thought it might be a good idea to discuss things before we bring the others into it. Plus, I was having fun and wanted one more night. So, Rebecca, we are all dying to know. What is your destiny?"

"Well . . . She said I was the nexus or center around which a new order would be built, that I would reunite the magical and human worlds. She said it had already begun and that I would see strife and suffer losses but would also gain much. She also said I had a powerful enemy—Pan, I figure—and that I might not survive. If I do survive, she said that the 'strength of love' would save me. So, what does that mean?"

"Well, the first part is obvious." Naomi said. "Just look at us—five elves, two humans and a dragon. It has already begun." There were murmurs of agreement from the group. She continued, "As far as the losses and gains, any conflict of this magnitude has those. And of course, the powerful enemy is Pan. As for the strength of love, that could mean many things. But I think we don't need to know that now."

"You'll have to explain that to me." Rebecca said. "Why don't we need to know that now?"

"Did you ever find yourself looking for something in a store, let's say, like some new clothes—a new top, let's say—and you can't really tell anyone exactly what you are looking for; but you'll know it when you see it?"

Rebecca nodded.

"This is like that. When you see it, you'll know. Besides, 'strength of love', that sounds like a good thing, right?"

"Alright," Roland began, "But why does this make Pan want to kill Rebecca? Doesn't he *want* things back the way they used to be?"

"Well yes," Lancelot replied. "Except without the humans. His pride has been hurt. He won't let bygones be bygones."

"So, that's it? He wants to prevent me from bringing humans and magicals together so he can wipe humans out and what? Go back to being king? What about all the magicals who don't follow him now?" Rebecca was almost shouting.

"That's a good question that I don't know the answer to, but it can't be good." Cedric replied. "Let's move on to the second question."

"OK, I asked her if Pan could be killed and she said, 'Not in the way you think about death.' What does that mean?"

Lancelot rubbed his chin, looking like he had something to say, but didn't want to say it. Finally, he did. "The question was supposed to be 'Can Pan be defeated?' We already knew the answer to *your* question. He can't."

Rebecca gasped and said, "What did I do?"

Cedric chimed in, "Don't be so hard on the girl. She may have done us a favor."

"Alright," Lancelot said. "You'll have to explain that to me."

"We already knew Pan cannot be killed, but this lets us know that he does have a weakness of some kind. All we have to do is figure out what that is and how to exploit it. Even though we can't kill him perhaps we can eliminate him as a threat.

"Yes, of course! Brilliant!" Lancelot exclaimed. "That gives us something to think about anyway." Turning back to Rebecca he continued. "What was the third answer?"

"Well, I asked her how Pan can be defeated. That was right—right?"

"Yes, very good."

"I thought her answer to this one was really weird. She said, 'Nothing in Nature is as hard as stone, nothing is as soft as water, yet water can prevail against the stone.' What on earth does that mean?"

“Well, isn’t she a clever old girl? She is quoting an ancient Chinese philosopher, Lao Tsu.” Lancelot said.

“OK, but what does it mean?”

“It means that we can’t overpower him. He is the rock, and we must be the water. I must admit I’m not sure on the specifics of how that would work. But the overall gist of things at this point is that Pan can be defeated. You have done well, Rebecca. I think that we should all get some rest and go home.”

“I guess I am pretty tired.” Rebecca said. “I just thought we would know more than this after meeting the Oracle.”

“Remember your mindfulness, Rebecca. We know more than we did. Be grateful. She has given us tools; we must endeavor to respond wisely when the time comes to use them.” Lancelot began. “Just look at the present moment. We are safe here, good friends around a campfire. Who could ask for more?”

He looked to Rebecca for response, but she was sound asleep.

14. A Homecoming Surprise

Rebecca decided traveling with elves by just popping in and out was not her preferred method of travel—a little too disorienting. One minute she was on a cliff overlooking the ocean and the next they were all standing in her grandmother's dining room. She looked at the clock. It said two o'clock. She was trying to figure out what day it was. They had spent two nights away—so it must be Saturday.

Her next thought was to call Heather. She had left her phone charging on the sideboard. Heather answered with "You're back!"

"Yes."

"Where are you?"

"My grandma's dining room."

"I'll be right there."

Astonished by the abrupt end of her conversation, Rebecca looked first at her phone and then at Naomi. "That was weird." She said.

"What's that, dear?"

Naomi had barely finished her question when Heather burst through the front door followed by Pip and Randy. The elves, always on alert, already had their swords drawn. The trio stopped in their tracks.

Pip threw his hands up and said, "Hey, hey, it's just us guys!"

"Sorry old man," Lancelot said as he put away his sword. "You startled us."

"OK, note to self—do not startle the elves. What took you guys so long? Its nuts here, just nuts."

"What are you talking about?" Lancelot asked.

"There's trolls gathering beyond the woods. I recruited as much help as I could."

"What on earth do you mean?"

"Maybe I better show you." Pip said, heading for the door.

When the group had gathered on the front porch, they could hardly believe their eyes. The front yard all the way down to the barn and beyond into the pasture were people and magical creatures of every kind. There were tents, gnomes cooking in large pots, elves measuring people for protective clothing, just about anything you could imagine. Pip was right—it was nuts, chaos really.

Naomi recognized most of the people she could see as neighbors and friends she had known for years. There were farmers, some former-hippie back-to-the-landers, a few people that worked in town but liked the country life, and one survivalist. Naomi had only met him once and he kind of gave her the creeps, but he was clearly here to fight. He had an assault rifle slung over his back, three knives that she could see, a pistol on each hip and under each arm and hand grenades on his belt.

As Naomi looked him over, he turned and met her gaze. His face lit up. "Naomi," he said. "I'm so glad to see you again." He walked up to her and extended his hand. "Jacob Hanson, call me Jake."

Shaking his hand she said, "I remember. Good to see you again."

Pip turned to Lancelot. "Now, before you get mad just hear me out. We weren't sure when or even if you would be back and those trolls started gathering right after you left. I had to do . . ."

Lancelot interrupted him. "You have done well, old friend."

For once in his life Pip was speechless—but not for long. "I *did?*"

"Yes. Rebecca's destiny is to re-unite the humans and the magicals. You've got a good start here. Now all we need is some organization."

"My thought exactly. Great minds *do* think alike." Pip was grinning again.

"Which one of you is the head honcho?" Jake asked.

"I command this team, if that's what you're asking." Lancelot answered.

Jake extended his hand. "Jake Hanson, Navy Seal retired, at your service."

Lancelot shook his hand, "Lancelot."

"I am really happy to meet you, Lancelot. I've heard a lot about you. I'm something of an Arthurian aficionado."

Lancelot chuckled, "You can't believe everything you read. Pardon my asking, but what do you hope to accomplish here?"

"I joined the Service to protect my country. When Christi showed up with this little guy here," he said, pointing at Pip. "Talking about a gathering of trolls, I did a little recon. I didn't spend all that time defending this country to let some monsters take over. Also, I'd just like to say that since I left the Service, I have been preparing for something like this. They said I was paranoid, but I knew it was going to hit the fan someday. I have a full arsenal at your disposal."

"Glad to have you. I may take you up on your offer. I think we need a meeting to organize things. What say you make sure everyone knows to meet here in . . . let's say an hour?"

"Roger that." Jake said before trotting off to gather the troops.

* * *

Rebecca, Naomi, Lancelot, and Pip stood on Naomi's porch looking out over the crowd. Jake had provided a public address system and Naomi stepped up to the microphone.

"I want to thank you all for coming. It means a lot to me, and I know it means a lot to Rebecca. First, I want to share with you what we learned from the Oracle. My lovely granddaughter Rebecca apparently is destined to reunite the human world with the magical." A cheer went up from the crowd. Naomi held up her hands to quiet them. "I, for one, welcome this change. As you now know, I have lived with the magical world most of my life. If we win this fight, we can transform this world into a paradise. Now I'd like to introduce you to my oldest friend, Cedric."

Naomi's eyes started to glow red and when she started to speak again it was Cedric's voice that came out.

"Greetings, I am happy to no longer be a secret. If it is alright with everyone, I will take charge of this operation and Lancelot here will be my second. My first question is how many of you have had military experience?" Numerous hands went up. "Excellent. After the meeting I want you all to gather in the barn. Now, how many of you have had medical training?" Several hands went up. "I want you to gather in the house. I see a couple of you raised your hands both times. I want you to go with the medical group.

I see Nolan standing there" He pointed, and Nolan waved. "He has agreed to provide us with protective clothing, starting with the two groups I just mentioned. If you think you will be in the fighting, please talk to him.

I will need volunteers with pickups to accompany Jake here," Jake waved, "to his bunker and retrieve supplies.

At this point we know there are over a hundred trolls gathered in the swamp on the game refuge land bordering the farm, with more arriving as we speak. We can only assume they will attack when they have gathered what they think is sufficient numbers. The fairies are our eyes and ears and will notify us if there is any change in status. The trees and plants, while usually neutral in these kinds of things, have agreed that this place must be defended and will help when they can.

We need to get organized quickly, so I'll keep my remarks short. We all have work to do."

When he finished speaking, the group started to break up as he had directed them. Lancelot went to the barn with the military people. Pip and Finnian followed the medical people into the house. Rebecca didn't really know what to do with herself. She hadn't really been given an assignment. She turned to talk to Naomi, but Naomi was walking away with that Jake guy. She found herself alone on the porch, so she just sat down.

As she sat on the steps with her elbows on her knees and her face in her hands, she started just staring at the ground. Suddenly a wave of despair swept over her. Then it was like a little voice in her head started saying things like, "You're going to die. Your friends are going to die, and it will be your fault—just like it was your fault your mother died."

She just wanted to hide—she could feel the tears coming. She got up and ran into the house, the screen door banging behind her. She ran past the medical meeting, up the stairs and into her room—slamming the door behind her. She threw herself on the bed and started to cry.

* * *

Pip looked over the crowd that had gathered in the living room. There were a dozen humans, a couple of elves, and dozens of fairies.

"OK," Pip began. "We need to create a combat field hospital. I think the first order of business is to select a leader." A hand went up. Pip recognized him as Steve Lund, Heather's father. "Yes?" Pip said.

"I am a doctor—a GP, but I have worked in several emergency rooms. I volunteer to lead this project."

"Excellent," Pip replied. "Are there any objections?" There were none. "Very well. I officially turn this meeting over to you." He had barely finished when Rebecca ran past and up the stairs. Then he heard the door slam. He surveyed the surprised looks on the group and said, "And with that I will take my leave."

Soon he was standing in front of Rebeca's door, knocking. There was no answer. He knocked again.

"Go away," was the response.

"Rebecca, it's me, Pip. I would go away, but I have to talk to you about something."

"OK, come in."

Pip opened the door and saw Rebecca lying on the bed. She sat up. Her eyes were red and puffy. Pip gave her his best grin. "What's wrong?"

The magic of his grin did not seem to be working. Rebecca's eyes were puffy, and tears still trickled down her cheeks. She wiped her nose on her sleeve and said "Everything."

Pip couldn't understand why his grin was not working, unless . . . He put a hand on each side of her head and turned it so he could see into her eyes. "Rebecca," he said. "You must come with me immediately." She refused. Pip yelled down the hallway, "Finnian, I need you right now!"

Finnian soon appeared in the doorway. "What is so important? We were busy."

"I think we've got a goblin, possibly a *hob*goblin. Look."

Finnian flew down right in front of Rebecca and looked in her eyes. "It's a hobgoblin alright—and a nasty one. There's only one thing to do. Pip, you keep an eye on her. I'll be right back." With that, he flew out the window.

He soon returned with an armload of leaves of some kind. There was a glass half full of water on the bedside stand. He dumped the leaves into it. He held his hands over the glass, closed his eyes and started to chant. The leaves started to crumble and the whole contents of the glass started to spin and give off a greenish glow. After a few seconds of this he stopped chanting and turned to Pip.

"It's ready. Make sure she drinks it all."

Pip picked up the glass and held it out to Rebecca. "I know you feel terrible right now, Rebecca. But if you have ever trusted me, trust me now when I say you must drink this."

For a time, Rebecca just stared at Pip. She wanted to slap that glass out of his hands. She wanted to lash out then curl up and die. But she did trust Pip. She slowly reached out for the glass and its glowing contents. She took a sip. It tasted like warmed over puke. She drank it anyway and handed the glass back to Pip. Then she started to cough.

She coughed like she had never coughed before. She coughed until her vision started to fade and her ears started to buzz. She coughed until something flew out of her mouth and hit the floor. Then she stopped. There on the floor was what looked like a tiny little man. Pip stomped on it and a bright light briefly came from under his heel.

When Rebecca's breathing was back to normal, she said, "What was that thing?"

"That, my dear, was a hobgoblin. If a person starts to feel down, conditions are right for a goblin or hobgoblin to take up residence in your brain. Then the fun starts. He tells you things that are not true until you start believing they are true. He tells you you're no good, or evil, or nobody loves you. . ."

"Or all your friends are going to die, and it will be your fault?"

"Yes, like that. Don't you believe any of it. Call it destiny, or fate, but this situation was not your making. You just happened to be in the right place at the right time. It's like being the millionth shopper and getting a prize for it. Anyway, back to this hobgoblin thing; I imagine

Pan, clever fellow that he is, sent this one. There may be more lurking, so try to stay upbeat." He grinned and she grinned back. "Oh, and it goes without saying, but I'm going to say it anyway. You know me. If you ever start thinking those kinds of things again, talk to someone right away—someone you trust. Humans are social creatures and need to support each other.

"So, what did I drink?"

Finnian joined the conversation. "Just think of it as super anti-depressant. It's an old family recipe. It turns goblins in to a physical being so you can kill it. Goblins hate it."

"I didn't care much for it myself."

"Even so, you had to drink it. If we hadn't gotten that thing out you would have fallen into a serious, life-threatening depression. Pretty much anything humans call mental illness has something to do with goblins of some sort. Makes it even more disgraceful how humans pass judgment on folks with mental illness when you know what's really going on. The person is good, the goblin is bad."

"Wow! OK, so what happened to it?"

"I killed it." Pip said proudly.

"What was that light when you stomped on it?"

"Magical creatures are mostly made of energy. When a magical dies that energy is released, and we see it as light. There is no body to dispose of. Very handy, really. So, when did you first start feeling bad?"

"Right after the meeting. Everybody rushed off and I didn't have anything to do. Then I started to think 'this is all my fault.' Then it felt like the world caved in on me."

"That just goes to show you. Stay positive, stay in the present, look for things to feel gratitude for, and above all, do not attach labels of good or bad to things. Mindfulness will keep you sane. If that doesn't work, talk to someone about it."

"I feel so much better now. Thanks Pip. And a special thanks to you Finnian."

"Think nothing of it." Finnian said as he settled on the bed beside Rebecca. "You're pretty nice for a human."

* * *

Naomi was driving her pickup slowly down Jake's driveway, which was very narrow, crooked, and lined with thick bushes and trees. Several other pickups followed closely.

"Now, when you round the next bend stop the truck. I need to disable a couple of things." Jake said from the passenger side. "When I came over, I went on foot so I could do some recon. I left a few booby traps."

When the truck stopped, he jumped out and disappeared into the brush. He was soon back, "Can't be too careful. I've known society was crumbling for a long time. This whole magical thing is a twist that I didn't expect though. What about those elves, eh? I gotta get to know that Lancelot. Imagine, the real Lancelot. He must have some stories . . ."

Naomi glanced at him as he prattled on and on. His wide-eyed expression and rambling speech did not inspire confidence. However, if he had any of the weapons he claimed to, he was going to come in pretty handy—crazy or not.

Suddenly he stopped in mid-rant and shouted, "Stop here!"

Naomi stomped on the brakes, bracing her hands on the steering wheel to keep from banging into it. The truck skidded on the loose gravel a bit. "Why are we stopping?"

"Behold," he said, holding up a garage door opener remote. His expression seemed even crazier than before. Clearly, he was enjoying playing the hero. He pushed the button and Naomi heard a humming sound. Ahead and to the right of the trail a large brush pile started tipping up. It revealed a lighted tunnel leading into the hill.

"My bunker," he said. "Come on. We're burning daylight."

Soon the group was loading cases of all manner of weapons and ammunition, as well as medical supplies. When the trucks were all loaded Jake called everyone together.

"I wanted you all to see my masterpiece, Big Lena." He pushed another button on his remote and another door opened up on the hillside. "I customized her myself. Started with a Humvee, added rocket launchers, and a mortar and remote controlled fifty caliber machine gun on the roof. She has an inch of armor plating and bullet proof windows. She can go anywhere and she's indestructible."

He had a look of pure mania on his face. Naomi thought he was enjoying this just a bit too much. Soon Big Lena was leading the small convoy back to the farm.

* * *

It is a little-known fact about gnomes that they love to cook and are really good at it. That is why they have that plump appearance. That is also why they volunteered to feed the small army that had gathered at Naomi's farm. Pip, a well-known lover of crowds, seemed to be in his element gathering everyone to get in the food line.

Supper was a bit late—eight thirty. But, since it was the middle of June, there was still a couple hours of daylight left. At Cedric's request. Pip had invited several people to dine in his tent. He called it a command staff meeting.

Present at the meeting were Naomi/Cedric, Steve Lund, Lancelot, Roland, Pip, Jake, and Rebecca. Pip and Rebecca sat on his little bed and everyone else sat in the floor.

Cedric began the meeting. "Let's start with status reports. Dr. Lund?

"Well, I brought as much medical supplies as I could from the clinic. And Jake was able to supply us with a few cases of bandages and antibiotics. We have some room for wounded in the house. We also have a few tents if need be. As far as personnel, we have two former army medics with combat experience, an EMT, six nurses, myself and two elf healers. Also, we have quite a few fairies, though I'm still now sure what they will do. The biggest problem we have now is how to get the wounded back to the house."

"I believe I have the answer to that, Doctor Lund," Lancelot said. "We elves can travel instantly from place to place and take one human with us. Your medics can call us in, we pop in, pop back with the patient—easy peasy. I'll assign a couple. Also, you'll be surprised how useful the fairies can be. A little magic can go a long way."

"That is amazing! Thanks. I can see that this is going to take some getting used to. That's about it for me. Oh, and call me Steve."

"Alright Steve. I'll go next, shall I?" Lancelot began. "There seems to be a portal in the swamp. Trolls are coming from everywhere it seems. At last count we estimate over two hundred and fifty. The real bugger here is that they keep coming. What we really need is a way to close that portal. I wish my old friend Merlin was here."

Jake spoke up, "What would it take to close the portal?"

"Well, the best way is by magical means. However, a large enough explosion might do it," Lancelot replied.

"Great, I have enough C4 to blow up a small planet. We could rig a charge with a timer and one of you guys with the flying horses could just fly over the portal and drop it in. Boom, no more portal; and we might just take out a few of those monsters in the bargain. What do you think?" The enthusiasm evident in Jakes face when he talked about blowing things up kind of put the others off a bit. But the idea seemed sound. "I'd volunteer to drop it myself, but I don't know how to fly one of those things. I would be happy to back you up in Big Lena."

“I like this plan,” Cedric said. “We should carry it out as quickly as possible to prevent the arrival of more trolls. Jake, why don’t you go prepare your charge while we finish this meeting?”

Jake nodded and left.

“I hope this works,” Cedric began. “It is likely this will trigger the trolls to attack so we should get ready for that. I think our first line of defense should be right at the swamp edge. The lack of trees in the swamp will provide maximum effectiveness for our flying cavalry.”

Pip interrupted. “I have a great idea. I think Amaryllis could help us. She can do amazing things with water, you know. Shall I go talk to her?”

“By all means, Pip. Let us know what you find out.” Cedric replied. I think the best plan is to hold them at the swamp as long as possible, then retreat past the pond. I think our only chance is a series of planned retreats. Take out as many as we can and hope they give up. Lancelot, I think you hit the nail on the head when you wished Merlin was here.”

“I think I may know where he is,” Lancelot said. “The problem isn’t necessarily finding him; it’s convincing him to get involved. He sort of gave up on humanity after Camelot fell. I think I know where the island of Avalon is. Worst case scenario would be I materialize in the middle of the ocean and get a little wet. I could seek his help. Roland could take my place here. If I were to leave right now, I might be able to be back before the fighting is over.”

Cedric was plainly stunned by this revelation. “Why didn’t you mention before that you knew where Avalon is?”

“I wasn’t sure. I was only there once as a boy, and that was a very long time ago. I think it is worth a try though.”

“As do I,” Cedric responded.

With that, Lancelot stood up and popped out.

Rebecca, who had been silent until now spoke up. "It looks like everyone has a job to do but me. What will I be doing while all this is going on?"

"You will be staying well out of it." Replied Cedric. "I have spoken to Jake about the possibility of you and Heather staying in his bunker. He agreed."

"I won't do it. If I'm just going to hide, why have I been training all this time?"

"I suspected you would feel this way. Would you agree to help Steve with the wounded and defend against any trolls that get past the main force?"

"I guess that would be OK. I just needed to feel useful. Thanks"

"Very well, I think we have a plan." Cedric said. The group left the tent, each to pursue their own part of the plan.

15. The Battle

Jake and Big Lena sat in a big hill overlooking the swamp where the trolls were gathering. There seemed to be hundreds of them milling around down there. He couldn't see them well however, because the cattails where they were hiding were too tall. The sun was finally getting near the horizon and shadows were growing long. He could just make out Roland and his flying horse approaching from the barn. He grabbed his binoculars for a better view.

It had been a simple matter to rig up the charges and show Roland how to set the timer. All Roland had to do was start the timer and drop it in the portal. Ten seconds later, no more portal—hopefully. Then he and the two mortar teams would rain death on that swamp. Hopefully that would scare them off. If not, they had a few more surprises for these monsters.

Roland was getting close now. Jake watched him start the timer and drop the charge and fly off at amazing speed. Jake started counting down from ten. Ten—nine—eight—seven—six—five—four—three—two—BOOM!!!

The ground shook and a bright light shot straight up from the portal, then was gone—along with the portal.

It took a few seconds for Jake's eyes to adjust. It was like he had looked right at the sun. As soon as he could see again, he dropped the first mortar bomb in the tube and poom! It flew in a high arc over the swamp and came down right in the middle of the trolls—boom! Debris and trolls flew. A couple of them disappeared in a bright flash of light.

"Interesting," Jake said to no one as he dropped another bomb. The other teams joined in. Soon there were explosions and trolls flashing out everywhere. Then the cavalry showed up—the flying cavalry.

There were at least a dozen elves on flying horses shooting arrows of all things! Jake was surprised to see that those guys never missed! And when they hit, a troll flashed out! Amazing!

“This can’t last long,” he thought. “Even dumb animals like trolls know enough to run from this kind of punishment.”

Sure enough, the trolls figured out what direction the fire was coming from and charged out of the swamp and up the stream toward the wood where an ambush waited.

Jake finally got a good look at the trolls and was amazed how fast they were—and ugly. What they reminded him of most was the Tasmanian Devil from cartoons, only huge. They had to be eight feet tall. The only weapons they carried were clubs and stones for throwing.

When they came out of the cattails, he started to work on them with the fifty caliber. These guys were tough! Jake had to hit them with at least a hundred rounds before they flashed out. They swatted at the bullets like they were a swarm of bees stinging them. He noticed when the elves hit them with an arrow it only took one. He’d have to ask them about that.

As the trolls approached the woods, Naomi’s fire team opened up. The plan was for her team to fight an orderly retreat, leading the trolls past the pond. Apparently, the water nymph Amaryllis had some kind of surprise for them. Jake couldn’t wait to see that—mostly to satisfy his curiosity.

When the last of the trolls entered the woods the elves dismounted, pulled their swords, and gave chase. Those guys are amazing! They could make short work of a troll. Then he got to see how the fairies fought. They would land on a troll in a huge mob. He couldn’t really see what they were doing but the afflicted troll would slowly come to a halt, fall over and flash out. He’d have to ask about that too.

"Oh well, time to be among them." He thought as he sped Big Lena toward the melee.

* * *

At first there was nothing for the medical team to do but wait. After the initial big boom, they anxiously looked at each other, rechecked supplies and generally tried to find something to do besides wait. They could hear the mortar shells and machine gun fire, but still no casualties. Finally, an elf popped in with Ray Nelson.

Ray was Naomi's neighbor, a farmer, and a veteran. He had volunteered for Naomi's fire team. He was fine with the shooting, but when it came time to retreat his age got in his way—he was in his sixties. He had been cracked in the back of the head and left for dead. He was unconscious.

Steve Lund rushed to his side followed by an elf healer and some fairies. Steve took one look and said, "What I wouldn't give for an x-ray machine right now."

"There is no need." Celestine, the elf healer said. "I can see it all here." She tapped on her temple. "The back of his skull is fractured and there is internal bleeding."

"Wow, that is not good," Steve replied. "If that bleeding isn't stopped, it will put pressure on his brain until it kills him. He really needs surgery, but we just don't have the facilities here."

"Again, no need. Let me show you how we do things." Celestine said.

She spoke with the fairies and stepped back. The fairies joined hands, forming a circle around Ray's head. Then they started to sing in a language Steve didn't recognize and the circle started to spin. They looked like they were dancing!

"What on earth?" Steve was shocked.

"First, we put the blood back in the vessels. Then we repair them. Then we mend the bones. Why don't you get your supplies and clean the external wound?"

Steve couldn't believe it. He was used to being in charge, but Celestine was speaking to him like he was a first-year intern. He was thinking of a response when two things happened. First, Ray's eyes opened, and he sat up. Second Celestine started speaking again.

"I meant no offence, Doctor Lund. I respect your years of training and experience. But the welfare of the patient was at stake. I think there is much we can learn from each other."

"Yes . . . of course." Steve replied before getting what he needed to clean the wound.

As more wounded started to come in Rebecca and Heather were starting to feel sidelined. They saw their chance when Steve stopped to sip some coffee.

"We need something to do," Heather said.

"I suppose you do." Steve replied. "Why don't you go around and ask the patients that have been treated if they need anything?"

"Ok, thanks." Rebecca said as she sped off to do just that. She was worried about everyone, but especially about Naomi and oddly enough about Randy. She didn't want to think about what that may mean so she threw herself into her task.

* * *

This was, bar none, the weirdest firefight Jake had ever been in or heard about. Even the trees got involved. As the trolls got into the woods, branches and roots reached out to slow them down. At one point he saw a troll hanging by his ankle from a large oak until an elf ran by and ended him with his sword. The troll's numbers were dwindling, but there were still hundreds remaining.

Jake found that his rocket propelled grenades were his most effective weapon. They could flash out a troll with one hit. But he had to be careful there were no friendlies nearby. So, he eased Big Lena forward, carefully picking his targets.

The running firefight continued until Jake could see the pond in the distance. The elves popped ahead of the trolls, and each grabbed one of Naomi's team and popped ahead to the beach area where pickups waited to transport them to the next fallback position.

When the first trolls got almost to the beach, Jake saw the most amazing thing yet. A wave swept up from the pond. It had to be at least fifty feet tall. It fell on the trolls and swept most of them into the pond. He noticed the water actually reach out to wrap around trolls that the wave had missed and pull them under. The water churned and swirled. For a few moments not a troll could be seen.

Then slowly, one by one, trolls started crawling out. When they stopped emerging Jake noticed there were far fewer than before. There were flashes of light deep in the pond. Apparently, trolls needed air just like everyone else.

He was so entranced by watching this scene that he didn't notice the troll approaching from his left side. The troll punched through the side window and pulled the driver's side door right off its hinges. Before Jake could react, the troll grabbed his arm and pulled him out and slammed him against a tree. Jake slumped to the ground unconscious, and the troll moved on. When Jake woke up, the first thing he saw was the face of the most beautiful woman he had ever seen.

"Are you an angel?" he asked.

The face smiled. "No, you're still with us. I am Celestine, an elf healer. What is your name?"

"Jake."

"Jake, you are at the field hospital. You have been badly injured. When we have healed your broken bones, we'll take care of that goblin too."

"Goblin?"

"Yes. You didn't think your emotional distress was natural, did you?"

"They said it was 'post-traumatic stress syndrome' from my combat experience."

"But of course they did. We can fix that."

Jake could hardly believe his ears, but replied, "Thanks, you really *are* an angel."

* * *

Rebecca and Heather busied themselves tending to the wounded, bringing food and beverages, or just talking with them. They paid little attention to the new arrivals until an elf popped in with Randy. Heather, Steve, and Rebecca rushed to him. His arm was clearly broken.

"Son, do you hurt anywhere else?" Steve asked.

"No, but I could use a rest."

"How's it going out there?" Rebecca asked.

"It's tough. Those trolls can really take a beating. We're cutting them down, though. I think there's somewhere between fifty and a hundred left. Your grandma is fine. I think it must be the dragon inside her. She sure doesn't fight like an old lady. She has more stamina than me."

"That's enough chatting for now," Celestine started. "We need to get you fixed up."

Heather and Steve stayed with Randy, but Rebecca was too keyed up. She stepped out onto the porch. She could hear the battle and see flashes of light as a magicals flashed out. She hoped those were trolls. She paced back and forth. She was worried about Naomi and really angry about Randy. The fight moved out into the pasture. The elves were remounting and resuming their aerial attack. She heard a noise off to her left and turned to see Wildfire standing there.

Without thinking she reached into the doorway, grabbed her weapons, and ran to Wildfire. She leaped on his back and flew off. From the air she could see the whole battle. The elves were circling around picking off trolls one by one. She flew to join them. Roland saw her approach and flew to meet her.

"You shouldn't be here," he shouted.

"I can't be anywhere else." She responded as she loosed an arrow. She watched her target flash out and felt a deep satisfaction.

"So be it." Roland said as he turned back to the battle.

As Rebecca surveyed the battle, she noticed the trolls seemed to be trying to separate Naomi from her team. Several surrounded her and though she fought fiercely, Rebecca feared she couldn't defeat them all. Again, without thinking she rushed to her defense. She flew in ever smaller circles, picking off trolls as she went. Soon she was firing at point blank range.

Suddenly, something grabbed her ankle. A troll had jumped up, grabbed her, and pulled her off Wildfire. He slammed her into the ground, and she felt her ankle snap. Then she was flying again.

She really couldn't understand. She was above the fray, but she was not on Wildfire. Then she noticed her body below. The troll smashed it again and again into the ground until several arrows hit the troll and he flashed out. The fighting stopped. A troll near her body tipped his head back and gave a thunderous roar. The trolls all turned and headed back to the woods.

Was she dead? The thought frightened her. She saw Naomi run to her body and kneel down. She was crying. Rebeca moved down beside her.

"Rebecca." Someone called her name. It sounded like . . . she turned to see her mother standing with her father. She recognized him from pictures. She threw her arms around her mother.

"Mom, I missed you so much!"

"Me too."

"So, I'm dead?"

"Not yet," her father said. "This is not your time. You have a destiny to fulfill. I want you to know how very proud of you I am."

"Both of us," her mother said. "But you must go back now. Don't worry, you will see us again."

With that, they faded away. She turned her attention to Naomi once more.

Naomi held Rebecca's hand and kept repeating, "No, no, no." Tears ran down her cheeks. She gently brushed the hair from Rebecca's face. "Cedric, can you save her?"

"I don't know," Cedric replied. "She is near death."

"You must try. If you leave me and enter her, would it save her?"

"It might, but you know if I leave you, you will die. You want to sacrifice yourself to save her?"

"Yes, Cedric, with you I have lived much longer than I would have without you. And it's been a glorious life. I can't bear to think of going on without her. You must save her. She is the hope of the world."

"No, Grandma!" Rebecca shouted, but Naomi clearly did not hear.

"Very well," Cedric said. "I love you, Naomi. You will live in my heart forever."

Rebecca watched as a baseball-sized ball of light flew from Naomi's chest. Clearly weakened, Naomi braced herself on one arm. The ball flew up about twenty feet. Then Rebecca heard a shout from somewhere.

"DRAGON HOLD!!!"

Rebecca looked and saw Lancelot with a stranger. He looked like an old hippy, complete with a grey ponytail, neatly trimmed beard, jeans, flannel shirt and fanny pack. He rushed to Naomi, laid her on her back and placed a thumb-sized crystal on her forehead. The crystal started to glow. Then he turned to Rebecca and placed a similar crystal on her forehead. He reached in his fanny pack and pulled out a small cloth bag, took a pinch of something from it and placed it under her tongue. Then he started to chant. Rebecca started to feel herself being pulled downward into her body.

Pain. Pain everywhere. She opened her eyes. "Everything hurts," she said.

"Shush," the hippy said curtly. "You've been dead for several minutes. Of course everything hurts. We'll do something about that in good time." Then he shouted, "I need fairies!"

In an instant fairies covered her, and she started to feel better. She could feel bones being set, then a mild burning as they were mended. She could feel other things too. She thought it must be her internal injuries being healed.

Soon the fairies moved off. She felt better and tried to sit up. The hippy gently laid his hand on her shoulder.

"Not so fast. You need rest." He said.

Naomi soon came into view. "You foolish girl, you really had me scared. I thought I lost you."

Lancelot knelt beside her. "I heard you fought well. I'm very proud of you."

Tears filled Rebeca's eyes as she said, "Thank you."

The hippy removed the crystal from her forehead and looked at it. "That should be enough. Let's help her up."

Hands helped her gently to her feet. A cheer went up from the crowd that had gathered around her. She could see Heather and Randy running from the house. And . . . there was a very large dragon circling overhead. She waved at him.

"Hello, Rebecca," Cedric's voice boomed over the pasture. "It is good to see you on the mend."

"Let me introduce myself," the hippy said, extending his hand. "Merlin, wizard extraordinaire."

16. Queen Rebecca

Rebecca took his hand. Suddenly there was a burning in her palm. She tried to pull away, but Merlin held tight. Then he released her. She looked at her palm. She saw what looked like a sword shaped scar.

"Let me see," Merlin said.

She hesitated at first, but then held out her hand and he took it.

"Just as I suspected," he said, scrutinizing the scar.

"What?" Rebecca asked.

"You are the last Pendragon. The last descendent of Arthur. Look at that scar and think 'Sword'."

She did as instructed and instantly a long sword appeared in her hand. It seemed to spring from the scar. It felt light as a feather and gave off a slight glow.

"Behold Excalibur!" Merlin proclaimed.

"Hail Queen Rebecca!" the hundreds of magicals surrounding her shouted.

She looked around her and saw every last magical on one knee with head bowed, even Lancelot. She bent down and whispered to him. "What are you doing?"

"Paying homage to my queen," he relied.

She felt a panic creeping up from her gut. This scared her more than the trolls. Suddenly she felt the need to flee. "Lancelot, get me out of here!"

He took her left hand in his and said, "As you wish my queen."

Suddenly she was back in her room. "How do I get rid of this sword?"

"Just picture your empty hand."

She did as instructed, and the sword disappeared.

"Lancelot, what is going on?"

"First, let me tell you of Excalibur. It is always with you. You can summon it when needed with a thought and return it the same way. It cannot be broken and is always razor sharp. You may have already noticed that it is light. It is actually an extension of you. It can only be wielded by a Pendragon, a descendent of Arthur. That is how we know you are a Pendragon and inheritor of Arthur's legacy—therefore our queen."

"What do you mean, your queen? What do I have to do?"

"Just continue as you are. We know America does not have royalty. You will not be expected to rule anyone. However, your subjects are honor bound to protect you and help you as we can. Your destiny to reunite the human and magical world makes sense now. Don't you see? Arthur tried to do the same thing but was defeated by his own pride. We, your tutors, and advisors, will help you to avoid that and any other pitfalls."

Rebecca sat quietly thinking about things for a minute. Then she said, "What do I do now?"

"That's an easy one—address your subjects. They have just fought a hard-won victory. Many were injured and some fairies were lost. You must thank them and give them hope for the future. Do you think you are ready?"

"Not really . . . but I guess I'm as ready as I'll ever be."

They walked down the stairs and out to the front porch. The sun had gone down and fires were starting up across the yard and pasture. Humans and magicals were gathered in small groups, congratulating, and getting to know each other—paying no attention to the house.

Lancelot whispered in her ear, "Show them your sword."

She held Excalibur over her head and Lancelot shouted, "If I could have your attention, please. Your queen wishes to speak."

Rebecca retracted Excalibur and said, "First, I wanted to thank you all."

"Louder!" Someone shouted from the back as the crowd gathered nearer.

She cleared her throat and started again—louder this time. "First, I wanted to thank you all. You all fought bravely, and I understand some of the fairies did not make it. I don't know how I can ever repay their sacrifice. We've all made new friends here and it is my hope that this is the beginning of a new era of understanding and cooperation between our peoples." She paused, looking out over the crowd. She saw Naomi, Merlin, the Lund family, Pip elbowing his way through the crowd and way in the back Cedric sat, taking it all in. "I don't really know what else to say. It has all been a lot to take in. Thank you again."

There was another pause. Finally Pip shouted, "Rebecca" Then he repeated, "Re-bec-ca." Soon others joined in. "Re-bec-ca, Re-bec-ca, Re-bec-ca," The chant continued louder and louder. Rebecca held Excalibur aloft once again and the chanting turned to wild cheers. Cedric let go a roar that rattled the windows in the house, then shot a column of flame high into the night.

* * *

After the speech Merlin approached Rebecca on the porch.

"You should rest," He said.

"I don't think I could sleep, but I would like to sit down." She turned and went into the house to find the couch. The others followed.

Soon the house was full. Naomi sat next to Rebecca on the couch holding her hand, Lancelot next to Naomi. Heather and Randy sat cross-legged on the floor. Their parents sat on the hearth. Pip took one of the wing-back chairs and Merlin the other. Fairies occupied nearly every other surface—Finnian sat on the center of the mantle, overlooking all.

They sat quietly for a while. Finally, it was Pip that broke the silence—of course.

"What a day! Things looked pretty bad there for a while. Boy, what timing Lancelot! I couldn't have planned it better! And to find out that Rebecca is the last Pendragon! Imagine!" Pip took a deep breath to continue, but he noticed that Rebecca had been staring at Finnian the whole time. He paused.

Rebecca spoke up. "Finnian, how many people did you lose?"

"Twenty-seven, and thank you for asking, Your Highness."

"Will you have a memorial service?"

"Yes. At dawn tomorrow we will gather as the sun rises and speak their names. Then we will recall their deeds and bid them farewell."

"May I attend?"

"By all means. We would be honored. In fact, you are all invited. We are comrades-in-arms now."

"Thank you, Finnian. I don't know how I can ever repay your sacrifice."

"That part is easy. Fulfill your destiny. We have been waiting for a very long time for this day."

"Here, here!" Merlin exclaimed. "We *have* been waiting a long time. I actually thought this day would never come. I hid out on my island, thinking to live out my days there. Of course, I have figured out how to live a very long time—indefinitely, really. Once you figure it out it is easy, really. Of course, I had company. Fairies and gnomes and such. But one misses the company of his own kind—no disrespect intended. Anyway, I seem to be rambling. And I see our new queen has fallen asleep."

Rebecca had indeed fallen asleep. Lancelot picked her up and said, "I'll take her to bed." And popped out.

Naomi stood up, stretched, said, "I'm going to find Cedric," and left.

The others looked at each other for a few minutes. Finally, Merlin said, "Is anyone planning to sleep on this sofa?"

He moved to the couch and the others filed out.

Naomi soon found Cedric. He was hard to miss.

"Naomi, I am so glad you still live." He said. "But, how?"

"It was that crystal Merlin put on my forehead. He said it was like a 'life-force battery'. Apparently, it kept me alive while my system stabilized, as well as pumping me full of energy. So . . . How about a ride for old time's sake?"

“I thought you’d never ask.”

Cedric lowered his head, Naomi climbed on, and they were airborne.

“I missed this!” Naomi shouted.

“As did I,” Cedric replied. “But perhaps we should keep this short. You almost died tonight.”

“Yes, of course. But I am spending the night with you.”

“I wouldn’t have it any other way.”

Cedric landed in the pasture and Naomi curled up against him and fell asleep.

17. The Memorial

Dawn comes early in June. The rooster woke Naomi when the eastern horizon was just showing the first signs of light. She woke Rebecca. Rebecca was still a bit sore from her ordeal the previous day. She put on her best dress as a token of respect to the families of the fairies who gave their lives defending her.

When she got to the porch, she saw that the fairies had all gathered in a big circle in the pasture. The gnomes and elves stood around the outside, even Amaryllis was there. Way in the back Cedric stood in all his glory.

Amaryllis made her way into the center of the circle and as the sun broke the horizon she began to sing. The song was so beautiful even the farm animals stopped their eating to listen. As she sang tears started rolling down Rebeca's cheeks. She sang until the sun was fully up. When she was finished Finnian rose up into the air and started to speak.

"Sean was my son. He lived a good life. He worked hard and was selfless to the last. He died bravely defending an ideal that we all believe in. He will live in our hearts forever."

Then he settled back to his place in the circle and the next family head rose and spoke of their loss. This continued until all twenty-seven families had spoken. Rebecca couldn't remember when she had cried so much. It was almost ten o'clock when they were finished.

When the speaking was over, she walked off the porch, right at Finnian. All eyes were on her. The circle parted and let her into the center. She walked up to Finnian and knelt down. She gently took his tiny hand and looked him in the eyes.

"I'm so sorry for your loss. I promise you that I will honor Sean's sacrifice by working as hard as I can to bring our worlds together." She said quietly. She went to each family in turn and repeated the message. She did this without thinking. If she had thought about it, she would have been surprised that she remembered the name of each family's lost member.

Lancelot watched from the porch. Rebecca's actions greatly surprised him. He leaned over and whispered in Naomi's ear. "Did you tell her to do that?"

"No," was the reply. They both looked quizzically at Pip who smiled and shrugged.

"She really *is* our queen."

"What did you expect?" Merlin, who had clearly been eavesdropping, chimed in. "She is a Pendragon. You will see her do some amazing things as her power develops."

Their attention went back to Rebecca as she made her way around the circle. When she was finished, she made her way back to the porch. Her fancy dress was covered with grass stains. When she turned to face the crowd again, she noticed Finnian had risen into the air again.

He began to speak. "Thank you, friends, for sharing this remembering. The gnomes have prepared a marvelous breakfast for us all. As you all know, tonight is Midsummer Eve. I say we put this unpleasantness behind us and celebrate life. I say we have a Midsummer celebration to remember—with our queen's permission, of course."

All eyes turned to Rebecca. Her surprise at being deferred to caused her to hesitate a moment before replying. "Yes . . . Of course. Let's celebrate Midsummer . . . And our victory over the trolls."

A cheer went up from the crowd and they all started moving to the tents where the gnomes had breakfast ready.

"Grandma?" Rebecca said, still watching the crowd. "What's Midsummer Eve?"

Naomi chuckled a bit before replying. “It’s the summer solstice. Magicals and pagans have celebrated the longest day for thousands of years. The winter solstice too, by the way. That’s why Christmas is in December. It can be quite a party. In fact, I met your grandfather at a Midsummer celebration. You’ll have fun. I think we better get going, though. They expect the queen to be served first.”

Rebecca rolled her eyes. This queen business was going to take some getting used to.

Rebecca and Naomi were guided to Naomi’s picnic table and patters of bacon, eggs, pancakes, muffins, French toast, you name it, were place before them. When their plates were full, the platters moved on. Gradually, Pip, Lancelot, Jake, Merlin, and the Lunds joined them. Room had been made for Cedric to sit nearby so he could join in the conversation.

Naomi started. “Rebecca, how did you know to talk to each family?”

“Well . . . I don’t know. I was just in the moment, and it seemed . . . right.”

Lancelot joined in. “Your Highness, it was. For a queen to show such individual attention, especially to fairies, is a great sign of respect. You impressed everyone. You are a natural leader.”

“I *do* respect them. I appreciate what they, what you all did for me.”

“This is bigger than just one person. It is a movement now. However, you are the symbol of that movement. You must stay safe. That was a very foolish thing you did—rushing headlong into battle. Please do not do that again” Lancelot replied.

“I know. I won’t. I didn’t think.”

“Of course. You have the heart of a warrior. However, even in times like that, *especially* in times like that you must remember to use your wise mind. Mistakes can cost lives.”

"Wise mind?"

"When logic and emotion work together."

"I see. I'll have to think about that. I know mistakes can cost lives. I'll do better next time."

"Of that I have no doubt, Your Majesty."

"Do you have to call me that? I don't feel like a queen."

"But queen you are. Proprieties must be observed." Lancelot said.

Merlin joined the conversation. "I may have a solution. It would be permissible for those you choose to call you by your given name in private."

"Ok, I give permission to everyone at this table to call me Rebecca in private, in fact I command it."

Pip laughed at that. "Seems like you are feeling more like a queen all the time." Everyone laughed. Pip went on, continuing to chew his breakfast as he did. "You know, we have an opportunity here. The trolls left because they thought Rebecca dead. It should be some time before he finds out different. We have time to decide what our little state will look like—to organize. We should build a fortress as soon as possible. Also, we should make a plan as to how this *reuniting* is going to happen."

There was a pause while the group thought over his words, then Jake quipped, "Ok, but what will we do tomorrow?"

They laughed again. As the truth of Pip's words sunk in, something inside Rebecca relaxed—something that hadn't relaxed since before her mother's death. In fact, she continued to laugh until long after the others quit. They all started staring at her.

Finally, Heather asked, "Are you ok?"

Rebecca was able to stifle her laughter enough to answer. "Yes, very alright. I think that for the first time in months I'm not afraid. It feels good."

The conversation was lighter after that, with people joking back and forth. At length they had all finished their meal except for Pip. Rebecca marveled at how much food he could pack away. Eventually, even Pip had to stop. He wiped his mouth with a napkin and said, "That was good." He burped loudly. "That was a good one!"

"Really, old man," Lancelot said. "Your table manners are simply atrocious."

"Oh, sorry, I didn't think. Anyway, I have noticed, Rebecca . . . that you seem to have something on your mind."

Well . . . I was thinking . . . Isn't all this *stuff* that we are going to do going to cost a lot of money?"

Merlin spoke up. "Money is not a problem. Let me show you."

Merlin held up his fork and closed his eyes. Rebecca watched, transfixed, as the stainless-steel fork turned from its silver color to a golden one. He threw it on the table in front of Rebecca. "There you go, solid gold. Plain old rocks work just as well. Being a wizard has its advantages."

Rebecca picked up the fork and examined it. "Wow! Maybe being a queen isn't going to be so bad."

"There's more, Rebecca. I can pull stone from the bedrock to build your fortress. I can do it in such a way as to create a tunnel for escaping, or whatever. Also, Naomi, I can fix it so your age won't be an issue. We should talk later. Anyway, I'm so glad to be useful again."

"And we're glad to have you," Naomi said. "Thank you again for saving Rebecca. I think maybe it's time to start putting together a Midsummer celebration."

When the group started to drift away Jake trailed after Lancelot. "Have you got a minute, sir?"

Lancelot stopped. "Of course, but you don't have to call me sir."

"It's a token of respect. Honestly, it always bugged me a bit to call some of those jerks that called themselves officers 'sir'. But I really respect you . . . sir."

"Very well, what did you want?"

"It's about the battle. How is it that I had to hit those trolls like a hundred times with my fifty caliber before they flashed out and one arrow from you elves did the trick?"

Lancelot chuckled. "Magic."

"I wondered. So, like . . . the arrows had some kind of . . . enchantment that killed the trolls?"

"Exactly so."

"So, what about the fairies? How did they kill the trolls? I didn't see any weapons at all."

"They carry none. Fairies are movers of energy. They basically suck the life-force from the troll until there is none left. They may be small, but they pack a punch. Very few creatures can stand up against them."

"One more thing, what happened at the pond? I've never seen water act like that."

"As I understand it, we have the water nymph Amaryllis to thank for that. She can do amazing things with water."

"Wow! I can see I have a lot to learn. Could you teach me to shoot the bow?"

"It would be my pleasure."

"Great! Thanks."

"But not today—it's a Midsummer." Lancelot started to walk away, then he stopped and turned back. "Jake, I almost forgot. Celestine wants to talk to you."

"Did she say what for?"

"She did not."

"Do you know where she is?"

"Can't help you there either, I'm afraid."

"Ok . . . I guess I'll go look for her. Can I ask you something . . . personal?"

Lancelot thought a bit before asking. He decided if he didn't like the question, he didn't *have* to answer it. "By all means."

"It's about Celestine. Is she . . . Does she have . . . Is she married, or whatever?"

Lancelot laughed. "My friend, I'm sure I wouldn't know. You'll just have to ask her." With that he walked away, still laughing.

18. Midsummer

Rebecca and Heather were in Rebeca's bedroom preparing for the party. They had each changed clothes several times. Finally, they looked each other up and down and smiled with satisfaction.

"You look great." Heather said.

"You too."

"You know Randy really likes you."

Rebecca could feel her cheeks burning. "Really?"

"Oh my God, you're blushing! You like him too!"

"I don't! Well, maybe a little. When I first met him, he seemed like an arrogant jerk. But he's changed . . . I think."

"Well, he's definitely changed. I might even start to like him."

Rebecca laughed. "I don't know what to think. I think it might be fun to have a boyfriend. But then there is this *queen* thing. I don't even know what that means. I mean Queen of England, that is *something*—she has England. She knows what to do. What do I have? What do I do?" She could feel tears coming and covered her face with her hands.

"You have us—all of us." She hugged Rebecca. "From what I've seen you already know what to do. Now stop that crying, you'll ruin your makeup." She pulled back to look. "Too late. Let's get you fixed up. You're going to knock Randy's eyes out. We've got a party to go to."

"Thanks, Heather. I don't know what came over me."

On the way out to the porch they ran into Pip. He ran over to them "Rebecca, I have something for you." He held up a tiara. It was beautiful.

It was gold, delicate as lace and had small jewels embedded throughout. "A queen needs a crown. The fairies made this for you. It's not a real crown, of course. It hasn't been consecrated. But it will do for now. Now bend down so I can put it on you."

She bent low so Pip could place the tiara. It was so light she could barely feel it there. She kissed Pip on the forehead and said, "Thank you—for everything."

"It was my pleasure, my queen. Now let's greet your subjects. Wait here so I can announce you."

He picked up a long brass horn from beside the door and went out onto the porch. Rebecca heard the horn blow and Pip shout, "Announcing . . . Queen … Rebecca!" She went out onto the porch. Heather stayed behind. Rebecca stood there a few minutes while the crowd applauded. Then Pip whispered, "Don't just stand there, silly, go greet your subjects." So that's what she did.

* * *

Jake finally found Celestine in the crowd. "Lancelot said you wanted to talk to me."

"I did. I think it is about time we took care of that goblin, don't you?"

"I don't know what you are talking about. But if you think so, I'm game."

"Excellent. I had the fairies mix up this potion." She said, handing him a small bottle. "You must drink it all."

Jake took the bottle, pulled the cork, and downed the contents in one gulp. It almost came back up. In his military career he had been forced to eat some disgusting things. This was by a wide margin the most awful thing he had ever choked down. "That was aw . . ." Coughing interrupted him. He coughed until he was bending over with his hands on his knees. Then something flew out of his mouth and hit the ground. It looked like a little man. Celestine stomped on it and a flash of light could be seen around her delicate heel. "What in the . . ." He started.

"A goblin. I told you. You probably picked him up somewhere in your military career. He has been whispering in your ear and giving you nightmares for years. You will undoubtedly sleep better now."

Jake could already feel something had changed inside him. He felt more comfortable in his own skin. "Well, I'll be . . . I feel . . . better."

"Of course."

"Thank you . . . Celestine. I heard there was going to be dancing. I was wondering . . . Well, you're about the most beautiful woman I have ever seen. Would you come with me?"

Celestine smiled. "How could I turn down such a gracious invitation?"

She took his arm and they set off toward the bonfire.

* * *

As promised, it was quite a party. There was a big bonfire. Gnomes provided music—even Amaryllis sang a few songs. There were fabulous displays of acrobatics and other things. Merlin juggled six gnomes high into the air without touching any of them—the gnomes giggling the whole time. Even the Fairies performed a marvelous aerial ballet. There were exotic foods and beverages. And there was dancing.

After some dancing, Rebecca was resting on a very nice chair provided by the gnomes, with Heather sitting beside her on a block of wood. Heather leaned towards her and pointed across the fire. "Now's your chance."

Rebecca saw Randy standing by himself with his hands in his pocket. She walked up to him and said, "Randy, you want to dance?"

Randy looked at his feet, his cheeks burning. "I don't know how."

Rebecca smiled to herself at this. He was kind of cute when he was humble. "Nobody cares, silly. Just come with me and do what I do." She grabbed his wrist, pulling his hand out of his pocket and led him into the dancing crowd.

Rebecca and Randy had just started dancing when someone bellowed "What in Heaven's name is going on here?" The music stopped and everyone looked in the direction of the bellow. There, standing with his hands on his hips and a stern look on his face was sheriff's deputy Andy Turnquist.

Naomi walked up to him and extended her hand. "Andy, to what do we owe the pleasure of your company?"

Andy took her hand but kept his eyes on the crowd. He looked at the gnomes. He looked at Lancelot's ears. He looked at the fairies, flying around the bonfire. "What . . . is . . . going . . . on . . . here?"

"We're having a party—obviously"

"There was a big explosion last night. You wouldn't know anything about that, would you?"

"Explosion? Why, no."

"I better call this in," he said, turning toward his car. There, standing with one of his front feet on the roof of the patrol car was Cedric. He could be surprisingly quiet for one so big.

"I'm afraid you won't be calling anyone, constable." Cedric said quietly.

Andy, shaking visibly, reached for his pistol. Lancelot grabbed his wrist and gently removed the pistol from his hand. "You won't be needing this."

* * *

Andy sat at Naomi's kitchen table sipping coffee. He was a bit calmer now that he was no longer staring at a real dragon. "Ok, so let me get this straight. Naomi, you are a hundred and fifty-seven years old. You were able to live that long because that dragon was trapped inside you. And you," he pointed at Lancelot, "are an elf. You actually knew King Arthur. Pip here is a gnome and Rebecca is a queen." He looked at her. She smiled and waved. "Last night you all fought a pitched battle with trolls who wanted to kill Rebecca because their boss, Pan, wants to kill her. Is that about right?"

"That covers the main points, constable." Lancelot said.

"This all sounds pretty dangerous to me. I'm supposed to protect the public. How can I *not* report this?" Andy was staring into his coffee cup.

"Who would believe you?" Naomi asked.

"Well, I suppose you have a point there. I'm not sure I believe it myself. So, what do I do now?"

Merlin spoke up. "My suggestion is this, we give you back your gun, you go back to your station, say you didn't find anything, and we go on about our business. Otherwise, I couldn't say what might happen."

"That sounded like a threat!" Andy bristled.

"Call it what you will, but I will protect my queen and my people. I am quite a powerful wizard, you know. I could send you and your car to Antarctica in a flash. They would find you in maybe . . . fifty years."

Rebecca stood up. "Enough! We're not threatening anybody and Andy, you're not telling anybody. *My* job is to unite the magicals and humans. I can't do it if you're going to fight. Right now, there are probably at least fifty humans out there and hundreds of magicals, all having a great time together." She pointed toward the party. "You can either join us or go home. I don't care. If there is a problem you need to know about, we will contact you and only you. Is that clear?"

There was a long pause while all around the table seemed stunned at Rebecca's outburst. Finally, Merlin bowed his head and said, "Yes, your highness."

All turned to look at Officer Turnquist. Finally, he too bowed his head and said, "Yes . . . Your Highness."

* * *

Merlin and Naomi stood on the porch watching Andy drive away. "Well, that was something." Merlin said.

"I just hope he keeps quiet."

"I'm sure he will, but I was talking about Rebecca. She instinctively knows the right thing to do. She reminds me of Arthur in that way. This thing that is happening here is a marvelous thing—everyone pulling together. Making new friends. Long overdue. Simply marvelous."

"Yes, but I worry about Cedric."

"Cedric! Why would you worry about him?"

"Because he is the last of his kind. Surely, he must get lonely."

"But he isn't. I know of at least one other—female, I think."

Naomi looked him in the eyes, a grin on her face. "We simply must introduce them."

19. The Day After The Day After

It was a brilliant late summer day. Rebecca stood before her castle gate in her new armor, the sword Excalibur in her hand. She could see Pan standing with his hands on his hips about fifty yards in front of her, the sun glinting off his horns.

"Such a brave little girl. I almost wish I didn't have to kill you." Pan's voice boomed across the yard. "Why don't you put down that sword and come to me that I may finish this."

"How about this?" she replied. "I'll come to you, but I think I'll keep Excalibur if you don't mind."

Pan laughed. "As you wish."

Rebecca advanced toward Pan cautiously, Excalibur held high over her right shoulder with both hands. Her pace quickened as she got closer and the last ten yards she was running. When she got close enough, she swung Excalibur as hard as she could. Much to her surprise the sword cut through his torso as if there was nothing there. She was shocked to see the wound close right behind the sword.

He reached for her. She cut right through his arm and again the wound healed as soon as it was made. Nearly blind with rage and fear, she attacked with the fury of a dragon. Each cut healed as soon as she made it. She stepped back, panting, frustrated.

Pan laughed. "You can't hurt me. I am a god. Surrender to me and I will make your death swift."

"Will you let the others go?"

"Only the magicals."

Rebecca thought of her magical friends, Lancelot, Pip and Cedric. Even a dragon like Cedric would not be able to defeat Pan. She also thought about Naomi, her grandmother and all her human friends—especially Heather and her brother, Randy. Especially Randy. But she could do nothing for them. If her willing death would save the magicals, then so be it.

"Alright, you win. I won't fight any more." She fell to her knees and hung her head.

Pan came toward her, drawing his sword. Then he swung.

"No!" Rebecca sprang up in bed. She was covered in sweat and panting like she had just run a hundred-yard dash. It took her a moment to get her bearings. She was in her own bed. It had all been a dream. Relief swept over her. It was still dark outside. She laid back down and tried to think of something else. She needed to put that dream out of her mind or she would never fall asleep. But blessed sleep came sooner than she thought.

* * *

"You're sure?" Pan says, hardly believing the good news.

"Gronk see girl dead. No human survive beating like that." Gronk, like all trolls, talks like he is staring in an old Tarzan movie. "You ask others. Girl dead. Gronk wish he could kill her again for all that die trying to get her. She die too quick."

Pan, clearly delighted with the news, sits on his throne with an evil grin—no longer listening to Gronk. He stands up and begins to pace. Gronk continues to prattle on, but Pan ignores him. "MARID!" He yells.

Marid, who has been eavesdropping in the form of a beetle behind a tree, returns to his true gremlin form, looking a bit like an angry teddy bear, and steps out. "Yes, Boss?"

"Did you hear that? This simpleton and his cronies have accomplished what you could not. The girl is dead. The great Rebecca will trouble us no more. I want you to gather my council to make a plan to rid the world of the human plague once and for all."

"Excellent!! And might I say it's about time! I will attend to it at once." Marid turns into a crow and flies away.

* * *

"Wakee, wakee." Pip said as he tickled Rebecca's cheek with a chicken feather he found in the yard. Rebecca brushed at it, still sleeping. "Wakee, wakee," he repeated. He kept stroking her face with the feather until she woke with a start, flailing at her face with her hands.

"Oh, my! What a dream! I dreamt that birds were flying at my face." She sat up and rubbed the sleep from her eyes.

Pip stood with the feather behind his back, barely containing his laughter. "That must have been awful." He could stifle his glee no longer and burst into laughter.

Rebecca started laughing too, though she didn't know at what—only that a gnome's laughter is contagious. "What are we laughing at?"

"I was tickling you with this." He held up the feather. "And you were dreaming about birds! That is hilarious!"

Even though she kept laughing, Rebecca couldn't see as much humor in it as Pip. But then, gnomes were like that—never miss a chance to play a joke and find humor in almost anything. As the laughter died down, Rebecca stretched and was instantly reminded by her stiff muscles of the battle two nights ago and the dancing last night at the Midsummer celebration.

"Well, good morning, Pip." She said with a yawn.

"Morning? It's two o'clock in the afternoon! Well, no matter. You needed the sleep. After all, in the last week you visited the Oracle, fought a battle, were dead for a couple of minutes and then brought back, only to find out you are our queen. What a week! Are you hungry?"

"Starving!"

"Well, why don't you get dressed and come down. We'll find you something to eat."

* * *

Naomi and Merlin sat on the front porch of the farmhouse sipping coffee and watching Cedric the dragon flying around over the woods. At length Naomi put her cup down and turned to Merlin. "So, Merlin, tell me about that second dragon."

"Certainly, but I'm sure you already know about it. Everyone has heard of the 'Loch Ness Monster'."

"What?. . . You're joking!"

"I assure you I am quite serious. You didn't think all those sightings were bogus, did you? I have to laugh when I hear some scientist banging on about how there couldn't possibly be a large carnivore living in that ecosystem or speculating about a population of dinosaurs surviving in the Loch. Such absurdity. She flies out in the dead of night and feeds at sea. That's the long and short of it, I guess." Merlin returned to sipping his coffee.

"What's the rest of her story? Why does she stay there?" Naomi was starting to get a bit frustrated with Merlin's tight-lipped communication style.

"You've heard of St. George?"

"Isn't he the patron saint of England, supposedly killed a dragon?"

"Yes, yes, quite. Well, the story is basically true. He did slay a dragon. It wasn't like in the story, however. The story would have you believe that the dragon was fond of eating young maidens. Nothing could be further from the truth. George was a young knight seeking make a name for himself. He heard there was a dragon living in a certain lake and sought him out to kill him for the glory. You see, by this time most people hated dragons—including kings. George went on to become a saint, so I guess he got what he was looking for."

He took another sip of coffee, then went on. "Anyway, he killed the dragon and the one currently living in Lock Ness was his mate. She probably believes, like Cedric does, that she is the last of her kind."

"That's awful. It must have been a terrible time for magicals back then."

"And for wizards, I'm afraid. There is a reason I was hiding out in Avalon, you know."

"Things seem to be changing for the better, if the Oracle's prophesy about Rebecca is true."

"I've never known her to be wrong. Reuniting the magical world and the human is a worthy goal. I wonder how it will be accomplished."

"As do I. . . Anyway, about this second dragon, do you suppose we could convince her to come here? It seems a shame if there are only two dragons in the world that they live on separate continents. They should be together."

"Are you trying to be a matchmaker? Remember, dragons are different than people. They may try to kill each other."

"Well, there's only one way to find out. I'll talk to Cedric."

"And so you should. Might be quite an adventure. In fact, I'll go with you."

They set their cups down and started out for the pasture. As she gazed across her yard at the sea of tents that housed the magical army, she couldn't help but wonder how it would all end. Rebecca had barely survived the attack of the troll army. True, they now had a large and growing army—both magical and human. And they would have time to prepare a better defense because Pan thought he had succeeded in his quest to kill Rebecca. Still, there was plenty to worry about. But, as Cedric would say, this present moment was pretty good—great even.

Cedric saw Naomi and Merlin approaching and gently touched down in the pasture. "Merlin old friend, it is so good to see you after all these years. I want to thank you for saving the two humans I love the most-and releasing me from my prison, pleasant though it may have been. Well done, old man, well done."

"You are most welcome. It is good to see you and good to be out in the world again, doing something useful. Anyway, now that the pleasantries are out of the way, we have something we wanted to talk to you about; some news."

"News you say? Do tell."

"Well, Naomi tells me that you have been under the impression that you are the only dragon left in the world."

"You say that as if I am not."

"That's because you aren't"

Cedric drew his head back and puffs of smoke came out of his nostrils. He clearly was surprised by the news and took a moment to gather his thoughts. "What do you mean, I'm not the only one?"

"I know of at least one more." Merlin folded his arms and looked up at Cedric, appearing quite satisfied with himself.

After a few moments Cedric spoke. "Merlin, really you are the most exasperating fellow. Why must one pry information from you that you came here to tell me?"

Naomi could remain silent no longer. "Isn't it wonderful, Cedric? She lives in Lock Ness, Scotland. I thought maybe we should go there and see if she would consider moving here."

Cedric started to chuckle. "Of course, the Loch Ness Monster. . . Naomi, I had almost forgotten how impetuous you can be. I look at you now and I still see that young girl I met so long ago." Cedric paused, clearly mulling things over. "You said 'she'. Does she have a name?"

"A name . . . a name . . . let's see. Granya, I think. Yes, Granya." In spite of his vast knowledge Merlin always seemed a bit confused when you asked him a simple question.

"Granya? . . . I was afraid of that." Cedric's eyes narrowed. "She will not help us."

"Why not!?" Naomi was shocked by his response.

"Her name means 'she who inspires terror'. She hates humans. When her mate was killed by that fool George, she went on a rampage. She laid waste to the Scottish countryside. That's when she got that name. Then she just disappeared. I had assumed her dead long ago. I guess she's been hiding in the lake, just as I hid until you found me. She would be more likely to help Pan."

"Perhaps." Merlin started to pace. "Perhaps we could convince her . . . if . . . if we could show her what's beginning here. Show her the folly of Pan's plan. The Creator put humans here for a purpose. It would be . . . wrong . . . to hunt us all down. Magicals need humans, just as humans need magicals. Surely, she wouldn't condemn an entire species for the foolishness of one individual."

"Well . . . "Naomi began. "There's only one way to find out."

"Indeed," Merlin agreed.

"Very well," Cedric said. "If nothing else it will be a fine adventure. We should discuss it with the others."

20. Councils of War

Pan sits on his throne, gazing at his war council. He looks around the circle at his war leaders. There is Marid, the gremlin, who commands the gremlins. Beside him sit the goblins and hob goblins. Only a few inches tall, their small size does not hint at the great power they can employ over the human mind. Then there are the furies, looking like ghosts but with the power to command a hurricane. Continuing around the circle, sits Gronk the troll, still proud of himself over the supposed death of Rebecca. Next sat Surtr, the fire demon with the power to command volcanos. Finally, Trezegruk the ogre—over twenty feet tall, with a taste for destruction and human flesh.

"Quite a crew indeed," Pan thought, then aloud: "The time has come to cleanse this world of the human plague that infests it. Marid, I want you and your kin to gum up the machines these humans depend on. If humans are killed, so much the better. Goblins, go forth and drive the humans mad, starting with those in authority. Create chaos wherever you can. Furies, I want two hurricanes—one in the Pacific and one in the Atlantic. In the Pacific, start in Indonesia, sweep north through China and Japan. In the Atlantic, hit the United States hard then cross to Europe. Move slowly and destroy as much as you can. Surtr, spew lava at will, wherever you want. Gronk and Trezegruk, follow the furies and mop up whatever humans remain."

"Master?" Marid says. "May I ask a question or two?"

"By all means," Pan replies. Not even Marid can spoil his mood today.

"All this sounds like a lot of fun, but you know this is going to take some time to organize. When do you expect this all to happen?"

"Start immediately, finish at your leisure. I have waited hundreds of years for this day and now that Rebecca is out of the way, nothing can stop us. Take your time, enjoy this. Savor it. When the wounds have healed and the world is once again a paradise, we will all feast and tell tales of how we took the world back."

"Thank you, master. We shall not disappoint you. May we get started?"

"By all means." As Pan watches his minions disperse, he feels a deep satisfaction. He is the starving man who knows a feast awaits.

* * *

Rebecca sat on the throne the gnomes had made and insisted she sit on. The meeting was held in the pasture so Cedric could attend. The others sat on the grass in a big circle—except Merlin, who stood facing the circle, Cedric towering above him.

"Thank you all for coming. I thought we should have a meeting. There are several things to discuss. Now that Pan thinks Rebecca is dead, at least for now, there are preparations we should make. First and foremost, we need better defenses—a wall around the farmyard at the very least. But I think a queen deserves a castle."

That last comment made Rebecca uneasy. So much had been given to her lately—so much that she didn't deserve. It was all a bit difficult to handle. "I don't know . . . "

"Of course you deserve a castle." Pip interrupted. "We, your subjects, expect a castle. In years to come dignitaries from around the world will visit, they will expect a castle. Besides, if you don't have a castle, where will I live?" Pip was grinning his widest.

Rebecca knew it was no use arguing with Pip—especially when he was grinning. No human could resist that grin. "OK, let's build a castle."

"Excellent!" Merlin replied. "I can get started right away. Although, I may be called away. I know of a great fellow. Lots of experience building things. History knows him as Imhotep, architect of the pharaohs."

Rebecca leaned forward in her chair. "Architect of the pharaohs? How old is he? . . . What is he?"

"He's a wizard like me, of course. His age? Only he can tell you. He's quite clever actually—invented the pyramid. How did you think all those huge blocks were moved to build the pyramids? Magic, that's how. Archeologists keep looking for his tomb, which doesn't exist because he isn't dead. . . Quite hilarious really. Shall I ask him to come?"

"How will you contact him?" Rebecca hated how new all this magic stuff was—so much she didn't know.

"We wizards have our way. Shall I call him?"

"Aah . . . Sure, go ahead." Rebecca, the new queen, would have to brush up on her decision-making skills. That last bit sounded a bit weak even to her.

"Excellent, leave all the details to me. Now on another matter, Cedric, Naomi, and I were just discussing earlier that Cedric is not the last dragon as they had previously thought." Merlin paused to let that truth sink in, then went on. "I—that is—we thought we might go and see if we could recruit her to our cause. Funny thing is M'lady, you probably have heard of her—the Loch Ness Monster."

Pip burst out laughing. "What shall we call her when we meet? 'Hello, Miss Monster'?" Pip continued laughing and slapping his knee. Rebecca was starting to chuckle too.

"Granya, I suppose, that is her name after all." Merlin replied calmly.

Pip stopped laughing. Apparently, he knew the story. "Oh . . . I don't like this idea. She's mean. She won't help anyway. She hates humans. Maybe she should stay hidden."

"I'm afraid I must agree with Pip on this, though it pains me to say it." Lancelot said. "However, . . . what if Pan recruits her? That would severely damage our cause. We want humans to think we magicals are their friends. Perhaps we need to recruit her first. . . Or kill her. . . Who would you see going on this expedition?"

"Well, there's me of course." Merlin answered. "And Cedric—and Rebecca."

Lancelot bristled. "I can't agree to that. It's too dangerous."

"But she must go." Merlin insisted. "Granya must meet the Queen. She must hear the Oracles words. How else can we convince her of the merit of our cause?"

There was a long pause while all eyes turned to Rebecca, who looked only to her grandmother, Naomi. At some length Naomi gave a subtle nod.

"I'm going." Rebecca declared.

"Not without me." Lancelot declared.

"Or me," Both Pip and Naomi chimed in.

"Then it's settled." Merlin said.

"Not by half." Finnian the fairy prince, who had been silent, flew into the center of the circle. "I must go. Things will go a lot smoother if you have someone to smooth the way with the Scottish fairies. They can be a bit suspicious of strangers. In fact, I will leave at once-if there are no objections."

No one said anything so he flew up out of sight. He was no sooner gone than he flew back. "I nearly forgot; we should arrange a meeting. Do you know Urquhart Castle?"

"Yes, the only castle on Loch Ness. It is in ruins, but I think it is a park now." Merlin replied.

"There is a small dock below the castle. I'll meet you there in a week's time."

"Very well," Merlin nodded in agreement. Finnian nodded in reply and was off again.

"What an odd little fellow," Merlin said as he watched Finnian fly away.

"Indeed," Lancelot agreed. "You know, it strikes me that our plan has a flaw. How are we going to get our large friend Cedric to Scotland? I mean to say, humans have this thing called radar. Flying around here is one thing. Flying across the continent is another. Jets will be scrambled. He will probably be shot at and have to defend himself. If we want to bring more humans into the fold, that simply won't do."

Merlin stroked his chin as he thought. "I see . . . I see. Tell me, did Cedric go with you to the Oracle? . . . Wait, of course he did. He was inside of Naomi. . . Why couldn't we just do that?"

"Would it be safe? Naomi almost died when I came out of her." Cedric said.

"So she did . . . so she did. Of course, you know a little magic goes a long way in these kinds of situations. I could arrange things so you could come and go at will."

"Really!?" Naomi was shocked but intrigued. While sometimes it had been a bit much having Cedric living in her heart all those years, she had to admit that in the days following his release she did occasionally miss the intimacy. "How would that work?"

"Simple, really. . . I mix up a simple potion, say a few special words and you drink it. Presto-changeo, you are permanently fortified for dragon residence."

"Excellent!" Lancelot finally seemed excited about the expedition. "I'll gather a few of the lads and we'll pop over to the Loch on the appointed day."

"I would like to stop by Avalon and pick up a few things. We left in such a hurry. Perhaps we could leave a couple of days early."

"By all means," Lancelot replied. "Everyone should visit Avalon at least once in their lifetime."

* * *

After the meeting Pip ran to the spring where he knew he would find the water nymph Amaryllis.

"I didn't want you to worry about me, so I thought I'd let you know I will be gone for a couple of days." Pip told Amaryllis, the love of his life—or so he said.

"Very considerate of you, but you needn't worry. I never worry about you. You're far too clever." Though this was not entirely true. She did worry a bit. Even though she was sure there could never really be anything between them. They were, after all, so different. "So where are you going?"

"It's kind of hush-hush, but I guess it would be alright to tell you. It seems that there is another dragon—Granya. She's been hiding in Loch Ness in Scotland since her rampage. Anyway, we're going to ask her to join our happy band."

"That won't be easy."

"Don't I know it. If we find her, she is as likely to try to roast us as talk to us."

"You know. . . I might be able to help. The Earth's waters are all connected. I'm sure I could find her. I may even be able to convince her to talk to you. She can't hurt me, you know. How can fire hurt a water nymph?"

"My girl, you never cease to amaze me. That would be excellent. When could you start?"

"Right away." Amaryllis bent down and kissed Pip on the forehead. "I'll meet you in a week in Loch Ness. Don't be late." With that she turned into crystal clear water and disappeared into the spring.

Pip watched her go, then jumped into the air and clicked the heels of his curly-toed shoes together. "He-he, she kissed me!" As he started to merrily prance back to the house, he began to sing a happy, wordless tune, punctuated every so often with a "She kissed me!"—a very happy gnome indeed.

21. Revelations

After the meeting Lancelot approached Rebecca. "May I accompany you back to the house?"

"Sure."

"I've been thinking, Rebecca. Now that you have Excalibur, we'll need to change your training. First, you will have to practice summoning and dismissing it. Can you summon it now?"

Rebecca held her right hand out from her side and instantly Excalibur appeared in it. Rebecca marveled at its beauty and lightness. "OK, now what?"

"Throw it away."

"Ok." She threw it and it stuck in the ground about thirty feet away. "Now what?"

"Dismiss it, then summon it again."

Rebecca did as she was told. The sword disappeared and reappeared in her hand.

"That could come in handy." Rebecca said.

"Indeed. I want you to practice that for the next hour. Tomorrow, I'll expect you at the barn at eight sharp. We have three days until we depart. We mustn't waste them."

Rebecca was not terribly pleased at this news, but she knew it was for the best. Pan was still out there, and he would learn soon enough she had not died—and he would be back.

When Rebecca got back to the house, she was surprised to see Merlin watching TV. He was watching a news channel. He looked up as she came in. "Hello, Rebecca. This is a very handy device—a good way to see what's happening in the world. There were two plane crashes this morning—and an earthquake in California. Vesuvius is starting to erupt. I am starting to wonder if Pan is up to something. Now that he thinks you are gone, he may be directing his attention to something else."

Rebecca was somewhat taken aback by that last bit. If Pan was up to no-good, was she supposed to do something? Is that what queens do? She would have to remember to talk to Naomi and Lancelot about it. For now, she had a few questions for Merlin.

"Merlin, can we talk a few minutes?"

"Certainly, you are the queen after all." He shut off the TV. "Please, sit." He gestured to the couch beside him.

"Well, I have been wondering, how does this magic stuff work?"

"That's a pretty broad question. Could you narrow it down a bit?"

"OK, how come sometimes I can see magicals and sometimes I can't?"

"Do you know how radio works?"

"A bit. There are waves of some kind."

"Quite so. Waves or vibrations. All matter has its own particular frequency. Some frequencies are visible to the human eye, and some are not. Magicals can change their frequency—to be visible or invisible."

"I think I get it. It's like tuning the radio to a certain station."

"Quite so. Only in this case it's more like the station changing frequency so you can receive it."

Rebecca was quiet for a moment while she thought about it. "How do they do that?"

"Now we come to the essence of magic. A while back, physicists were experimenting with sub-atomic particles. They made a most interesting discovery. The experimenter's expectations influenced the outcome of the experiment. Consciousness is a component of everything. It is the consciousness of the Creator that holds the universe together. Humans are special. We are made in the image of the Creator—with the same creative abilities. We can learn to manipulate matter and energy at will. In fact, as scientists recently learned, all matter is energy. I could have told them that fifteen hundred years ago. Anyway, magicals instinctively know certain things—have certain abilities."

"I see. . . What about potions and such?"

"Each species or substance has its own vibration and properties. A wizard can use these as tools to enhance the effect of his conscious manipulations."

"Can anyone learn to do magic?"

"Yes, of course. However, some people have more of a natural talent—just like some people have more musical talent. Even then it takes a lot of practice. I could teach you if you like. In fact, I should teach you a few things. Excalibur is more than a sword—much more."

"What does that mean?" There was so much Rebecca had to learn, but she was eager to get to it.

"There are a few things. Let's start with the basics. With Excalibur you can summon almost unlimited power and direct it to an enemy—like a lightning bolt. Would you like to try that?"

"Absolutely!" If her enemies were going to use magic against her, Rebecca darn sure wanted to be able to fight fire with fire. "Before we do, I have another question. When I . . . When I was . . . I mean . . . When I died, I saw my parents. They told me it wasn't my time—that I had to go back. What happens when we die?"

Merlin started to chuckle. “No simple questions for you I see. How much you remind me of Arthur. Anyway, death is merely a transition when we leave our physical bodies behind—our frequency changes. The human sprit never dies. Everyone comes into this earth to learn something or, in your case to do something special. When we have accomplished our life’s work we may go. There is more learning in the next world. Most people are reborn to learn new lessons. Most of the time they can see us, but we can’t see them. Your parents knew it wasn’t your time. They came to reassure you—to keep you from being frightened.”

“But what about you? You’re human, aren’t you?”

“As human as you.”

“How are you still alive?”

“A wizard learns how to keep the body and spirit together. I’m nearly two thousand years old—and yet, I don’t think I have fulfilled my purpose yet. . . And that’s all I’m prepared to say about it. How about we step out and you learn how to throw lightning bolts?”

“OK, and thanks. I didn’t mean to be nosey, but this is all so fascinating.”

“Indeed, quite fascinating.”

The pair walked out of the house, across the yard and past the barn until Merlin said. “This will do nicely. See that old stump?” He pointed to a stump about thirty yards away.

“Yes.”

“Now I want you to summon Excalibur and visualize a ball of energy forming around it. See the energy coming from the grass, the trees, the sky, the very Earth itself. The sword will help you.”

Rebeca did as she was told. It was if she could actually see the energy flowing into the sword. A bright blue glow formed around Excalibur.

"Excellent," Merlin said. "Now point the sword at the stump and command the energy to hit it."

Again, Rebecca did as directed and a bolt of lightning flashed from the tip of Excalibur and hit the stump, blowing it to pieces. There was a loud bang that startled her. Almost immediately Lancelot appeared beside her, followed very quickly by many other elves, swords and bows at the ready.

"What in the name of all that's holy was that?" Lancelot spat out.

Rebecca looked around, somewhat shocked by it all. "We were practicing."

"Practicing? What on earth?" Lancelot seemed a bit miffed about something.

Merlin stepped in. "Show him."

Rebecca did as instructed. Again, she pointed Excalibur at what was left of the stump and a bolt of lightning flew from the sword's tip and disintegrated it.

Lancelot sheathed his sword. "Teach her what you will, old man. But if you are going to blow something up, please, please let us know in advance. Everyone is a bit on edge here. Someone could get hurt."

Merlin seemed a bit rattled by being chewed out by Lancelot, but he couldn't fault his logic. "Sorry. . . I didn't think . . . You're right, of course. But, since the damage is done, do you have any objections if we continue?"

"By all means, continue. But I think I'll stick around if you don't mind."

"Of course . . . of course. Rebecca, do you see that dead branch on that big oak?"

"Yes"

"Cut it off, please."

Rebecca aimed and fired. The branch fell to the ground.

"Impressive." Lancelot was clearly impressed. "What about defense?"

"Good idea." Merlin responded. "Defense is just as easy. Rebecca, hold Excalibur in front of you. I'm going to throw something at you. You stop it with Excalibur."

Rebecca stood ready while Merlin backed up a bit and tossed a pebble at her. Excalibur seemed to move itself to block it. Rebecca and Excalibur were one. Merlin kept throwing pebbles, faster each time. Soon Rebecca was blocking one after another. Then Merlin substituted balls of light for pebbles. Faster and faster, they came. Rebecca blocked each one, though she was starting to sweat. Then Merlin switched to lightning bolts. Excalibur absorbed each one. Finally, he held the lightning instead of letting it go. An arc of electricity thirty feet long leaped from his fingers and was absorbed into Excalibur. It crackled and buzzed, and Rebecca could feel the heat on her face. Then it was gone.

"That was absolutely excellent!" Merlin gushed. "If ever there was any doubt that you are Arthur's true heir, that performance certainly banished it."

There was a loud cheer and applause, which surprised Rebecca. She looked around only to realize that everyone had been watching her. She saw Randy, a strange look on his face, clapping. Clearly, he was having some kind of mixed emotions about something. Even Cedric, Naomi on his back had settled to the ground to watch. "Bravo!" His voice boomed out over the crowd. "Such excellence deserves a reward. Would you like to ride a dragon?"

"Absolutely!" Rebecca dismissed Excalibur and ran to Cedric.

Naomi helped her up. "I'll hang onto his horns, and you hang onto me."

"Ok Grandma, let's go."

Soon they were sailing effortlessly over the forest. Rebecca held tight to Naomi's waist—tighter than she needed to—and leaned against her. Much to her surprise she felt tears rolling down her cheeks. She was afraid there would be sobs pretty soon so she tried to stifle. That only worked for about two seconds. 'Yup, here come the sobs.' She thought.

Naomi turned to look. "What's this?"

"I don't kno-o-ow." The sobs stretching out the last word. "It's just . . . so much!"

"Cedric, we need to land."

"Way ahead of you, my dear." Cedric said as he glided to a gentle landing on the beach of Naomi's Pond.

After they both slid to the ground, they hugged for a good two minutes—though it seemed longer. The sobs finally stopped, so Rebecca stepped back and wiped her eyes with her sleeve—which was quite a trick, considering she was wearing a tee shirt. Naomi handed her a Kleenex and she promptly blew her nose. How is it Naomi always seemed to have whatever Rebecca needed right at her fingertips?

"Thanks." She blew her nose again.

"No problem. I was worried about the back of my shirt on the trip home." Naomi chuckled and Rebecca smiled a bit.

"Now let's talk about this. What's it all about?"

"I'm not sure. I think . . . I think it's just . . . everything. My life has changed so much in the last few months. Aside from all the usual trials of growing up, I . . . I have to be the Queen—the last Pendragon." Rebecca started to pace and wave her arms about. Naomi sat at the picnic table and Cedric lay on the beach as if he were getting a tan.

"I was actually dead a couple of days ago! By the way, I met my parents when I was dead—did I forget to mention that? Then I've got this sword that shoots lightning. Which is handy because half of the magicals in the world want to kill me! "

Rebecca paced in silence for a moment, then continued her rant. "Two months ago, I just wanted a few friends. Now everybody wants to be my friend . . . except the one guy I really want for a friend. I'm just starting to like boys and now I scare them. You should have seen Randy's face back there."

"I actually did. It was pretty interesting. First, he was worried about you. Then, when he saw how well you were doing, he sort of wilted. I suspect it occurred to him that if you two became a couple he would not be the strong one. He'll either get over it or you'll find someone who will accept you for who you are." Naomi paused while she studied Rebecca's face. She seemed as though she might burst into tears again. "I'm sorry." She reached for Rebecca's hand. "I know it has been hard for you. I have been very proud of how you handled it all. I'm sure I would not have done nearly so well. Anyway, I do have a suggestion. Cedric is the wisest being I have ever met. If anyone can teach you how to deal with all this stress, it is him."

Rebecca turned to Cedric, who had been watching the scene with a sort of amused look on his face. He had seen young girls rant before. "My Queen, it would be my pleasure to help you. You already have a good start with your mindfulness practice and even your training with Lancelot. Why don't you find a comfortable place to sit, and we'll begin."

Rebecca decided to sit on the bench beside Naomi.

"Before we start, I want to tell you a few things. The first thing to always keep in mind is that events in and of themselves do not cause distress. It is your reaction to events that do that. The more you can free yourself from the habit of judgmental thinking, the less distress events will cause you. Remember that everything that happens is supposed to happen—it falls to us to accept it or not. It is also important to not judge yourself if you fall short of perfection. Just do your best and that will be good enough. The second thing is that most present moments are ok. The more you stay in the present, the less distress you will feel. Do you understand?"

"I think I do. You know, I've heard all this before. But, somehow, having lived through the last few days . . . It makes more sense now. Thanks for reminding me." Rebecca was starting to feel better already.

"It is my pleasure, my Queen. You will have to get used to being called that you know. Accept it."

"I know" Rebecca groaned.

"Now I want to show you something. I want you to start meditating. When you have achieved a deep relaxation, I will join you in your mind. It will be like when you talk to Wildfire."

When Rebecca felt deeply relaxed, she heard Cedric's voice. "Do you hear me?"

"Yes," she replied in her mind

"I want you to gently direct your awareness inward until you can see a small point of light . . . Can you see it?"

"Yes."

"I want you to move gently toward it. I will help you."

The small point of light grew larger as Rebecca moved toward it. Soon it was so big and bright it was like standing on the Sun—only not hot. In fact, there was a very pleasant sensation coming from the light. It was like when she was little, and her mom hugged her—only stronger. She could feel the love. She reached out and as soon as she touched the light she was pulled inside.

It was as if time stopped and all there was in the universe was overwhelming, all-encompassing love. She floated there, soaking it all in, for what seemed like an eternity. She felt at one with the light and with everything in the universe—from the smallest microbe to the largest whale, to the whole earth and beyond. In an instant she felt all the pain and pleasure in the universe and the love from the light made it all OK. She knew with absolute certainty that this light was the Creator, the Source of all—and that she was part of it. She knew that everyone everywhere could have this connection, if only they would seek it . . . And she knew, having experienced this, her life would never be the same—and she needed to get back to it.

No sooner had she thought that, and she was outside of the light, which was slowly receding. She began to notice her breathing again and took a few deliberate, slow breaths. Rebecca opened her eyes to see Naomi and Cedric smiling at her. She was somewhat surprised that the Sun was still up. "Wow! That was really . . . something. . . How long?"

Cedric chuckled. "About five minutes."

"Five minutes!! It felt like. . ."

"An eternity?" Naomi interrupted.

"Yeah. An eternity." Rebecca's eyes met Naomi's and they shared a silent recognition of each having had the experience.

Cedric interrupted the silence. "What about all those pressing issues?"

"What issues?" Rebecca said with a wink. "All I see is my Grandma and a dragon that promised me a ride . . . and thank you, Cedric."

Cedric chuckled warmly. "It was my pleasure. Now climb aboard and I'll show you why riding dragons is fun."

22. The Beginnings of Change

Sherriff's Deputy Andy Turnquist sat at his desk catching up on paperwork. While he generally did not care much for paperwork, on this particular evening he had volunteered to man the phones and do paperwork. He really felt as if he'd had enough adventure for a while after meeting that dragon and his friends the other night. He had thought about taking some vacation time but decided it wouldn't change anything. He would just do his job like always and hope he never heard from them again.

Andy was ready for a break. He leaned back in his chair and rubbed the back of his neck, which was getting a bit stiff from bending over his desk. It was always a bit spooky in the station at night, but on this night, he couldn't shake the feeling someone was watching him. Then he saw it—a red pointy hat above a pair of eyes just peering over the front of his desk. He would have thought someone was playing a trick on him by sneaking in a garden gnome—except this particular gnome was waving at him.

"Andy, it is Andy, right? Andy, I wanted to talk to you. Some of us will be going on a little trip. I was wondering if you could just drive by, maybe once or twice a day—starting, say in a couple of days—and we'll let you know when to stop. It's just for a couple of days, really."

Andy just stared at Pip, completely dumbstruck, for a few minutes. The pause gave Pip time to climb up on the desk and snap his fingers in front of Andy's face. "Hello, is anyone home?" He just kept snapping his fingers.

Finally, Andy held up a hand to block Pip's. "OK . . . What are you doing here?"

“I came to ask you to keep an eye on the place while we’re gone.” Pip started to grin. Andy found himself grinning too, though he didn’t know why.

“Why me?”

“You’re the only cop I know.”

“Why do you even need a cop? Seems to me you had plenty of help out there. They’re not all leaving, are they?” Andy really hoped they would

“Well, no. You caught me. We’re trying to suck you into our evil plan.”

“What evil plan?”

“We’re going to take over the world.”

“No . . . really?”

“I told them you wouldn’t believe me.”

“. . . OK, fine. Don’t tell me. I suppose I could swing by once in a while.”

“Great!”

“When are you leaving?”

“In three days.”

“Where are you going?”

“If I tell you, I’d have to kill you.”

“I didn’t really want to know anyway. When will you be back?”

“Can’t really tell you that either. We’ll let you know when to quit.”

“OK. One last question. How will I know if something is ‘out of the ordinary’? Everything about you guys is out of the ordinary.”

Pip laughed at that one. “Truer words were never spoken. I guess we’ll just have to trust your instincts.” Still laughing, he just faded from sight.

Andy just sat there staring at the spot formerly occupied by Pip. He wondered if he would ever get used to that. Thinking coffee might help, he got up to get some. Coffee helped everything.

* * *

The Lund family sat down to the first family dinner they’d had since before the battle. Since the immediate danger had passed, they had returned to their own home. It felt good to get things back to “normal”—or rather a new normal in a world with magical beings.

“Rebecca called.” Heather announced. “She said training is going to start again tomorrow morning at eight.”

“Just don’t forget you have chores here, too.” Christi, her mother, responded.

“I’ll help with the horses in the morning.” Randy offered, much to everyone’s surprise. Christi and Steve were pleased with the changes they had seen in their son these last weeks. He had become less the self-centered teen and more considerate of others.

“You know,” Steve said. “I just can’t stop thinking about that night.” Everyone knew he meant the night of the battle. “The healing that took place was nothing short of miraculous. I know they want to keep things hush-hush, but if those techniques could be brought into general use . . . The lives that could be saved . . . The suffering that could be eased. My head is just spinning with the possibilities.”

“This is all pretty exciting once you get used to the idea that magic exists.” Christi responded. “I, for one, am just fascinated with this whole goblin issue. When I think that so much of the mental illness I see as a social worker is caused by a parasite—one that can be treated so simply. Like you said, Steve, the possibilities . . . “

She was interrupted by a knock at the door. "I'll get it." Heather said as she bounced from her chair. She returned with the elf healer Celestine in tow.

"Hello." Celestine noticed she was interrupting the family's meal. "If this is an inconvenient time, I could come back."

"Nonsense," Steve replied. "We were just talking about you—sort of. Please, sit down. Are you hungry?"

"No, thank you." Celestine sat. "I suppose I should tell you why I came. I couldn't help but notice when we were working that, from our point of view, your medical knowledge has . . . some gaps. I mean no disrespect. I couldn't help but notice your intelligence and passion for healing. You just haven't been exposed to . . . the true nature of things. I am here to offer help."

Steve wasn't offended by her comments, he knew she was right. "What kind of help?"

"I was thinking . . . Maybe I could get involved somehow in your medical practice. If I cover my ears I could pass for human."

Steve thought for a moment before responding. "I would love to know what you know, to be able to treat like you do. I would like to figure out a way to bring this knowledge into the mainstream. But, and it's a big but, if I let you treat anyone I could lose my license . . . "

"Steve, stop thinking like a doctor." Christi Interrupted. "There are ways to get around that licensing issue. She could be an herbalist, or a holistic healer, or something like that. You could refer select people to her. With her success rate it wouldn't be long before she would have more business than she could handle."

"I think you may have something there. There are a couple of vacant shops in town where she could set up. We'd have to figure out something about money."

"Why don't you talk to Rebecca about it? I saw Merlin turn a fork into solid gold. He said money would never a problem." Heather piped up.

Both Steve and Christi turned to Heather. "Really?" Then they looked at each other and laughed.

"Perhaps this can be Rebecca's first royally sponsored service." Celestine offered.

"OK, let's do it." Steve declared.

Randy, who had left the room during the discussion to make a phone call, poked his head in from the living room. "Dad, can I use the car?"

"Where are you going?"

"Some of the guys are going to the lake. I thought I'd go with."

"OK, don't stay out too late."

"Thanks, Dad. I won't."

* * *

Randy and his friend Jeff were setting on the hood of Jeff's car, leaning back against the windshield. They each sipped on a beer. Relaxing with a beer had recently become part of the routine with Randy and his jock friends.

"So, tell me again where you have been for the last three weeks." Jeff said.

"For the tenth time, I got involved in a special training program." Randy felt he had to say something, and he thought a half-truth was better than an outright lie.

"What's this place called?"

"It's just one of our neighbors. He's . . . a retired military Special Forces guy. He offered to help me train."

"Well, aren't you the lucky one? . . . I'm empty." Jeff dumped the last few drops of beer on the ground. "You want one?"

"Sure."

"You know, dedication to the sport is one thing; but you need to get out more." He pulled two beers out of the cooler and handed one to Randy. "I think you need some female companionship. As it happens, I have a date Friday night and she has this friend—really cute." He took a long drink. "In fact, you'd be doing me a favor if you came along . . . If you know what I mean."

Randy took a swig of his beer. "I'll have to get back to you on that. I may be out of town on Friday."

"Taking a trip? Where to?"

Randy took another long drink—longer than he really wanted. He was scrambling inside trying to think how to cover that slip. He had hopes of going to Scotland with the others, though he hadn't been invited. But he really didn't want to try to explain all that to Jeff. "It's not definite yet. Like I said, I'll have to get back to you."

"OK . . . Mysterious. Let me know by tomorrow night, though. Ok?"

"Sure."

"So, tell me more about this training."

"Well, it starts with mindfulness . . ."

"Oh, sure—like martial arts."

"Yeah, like that. Then there's physical conditioning and hand to hand combat training—even swordsmanship and archery. We even practice on horseback." Randy carefully left out the part about the horses flying.

"You keep saying 'we'. Who else is there?"

"Just my sister and her friend Rebecca."

"Rebecca . . . You mean that new girl? Say . . . Now the pieces are starting to fall into place. Skipping wrestling camp to do this training? She's cute, but isn't she a bit young? What are you? Some kind of cradle-robber?"

"It's not like that. She's cute and all, but she's . . . different. Anyway, it's definitely not like that. It's really good training."

"Me thinketh the boy doth protesteth too mucheth." Jeff's butchery of Shakespeare may have been influenced by the several beers under his belt. His hearty laughter certainly was.

Randy could feel his ears burning, but he didn't want to talk about this anymore. So, he hoisted his beer and drained it. Actually, he was starting to feel something. She was pretty cute . . . And she was in great shape. Maybe too great. That show she put on with that old wizard this afternoon was both awesome and scary at the same time. Then there was that whole "queen" business. This wasn't like Homecoming Queen. Those magicals clearly saw her as a real queen. But he was worried for her and her upcoming trip to bring back the Loch Ness Monster. It made him queasy just to think about it. Maybe another beer would help.

* * *

When Randy woke up his head was pounding, his mouth was dry, and he really had to pee. This was made all the more unpleasant by the fact that his bed seemed to be rocking back and forth. In fact, it was. His sister Heather had her foot on the corner of his mattress, shaking it back and forth. This rocking was starting to get to his stomach.

"Ok, I'm up!" he groaned.

"What did you do last night? It smells like stale beer in here."

"Never mind. Get out of here so I can get dressed."

"Ok, but you should hit the shower too."

Randy did hit the shower, and took some aspirin, and found himself drinking from the shower like he had just crossed the Sahara.

He was feeling better—still not good—when he arrived at Naomi's barn for the day's training session. In addition to Heather and Rebecca, Jake Hanson—Naomi's creepy neighbor, and several others were present.

"Hi Randy." Rebecca said with a big smile. Then her smile turned into a concerned look. "Are you ok? You don't look so good."

"I'm fine." He lied, with a fake smile.

As usual, Lancelot popped in at eight sharp. He looked over the group. His gaze settled on Randy.

"Good morning. It is gratifying to see so many willing to stand in defense of our queen." As he spoke, he walked around and through the group. He stopped in front of Randy. "I think this morning we'll start with a nice run down to the pond and back. Randy, you lead."

Randy started off at a brisk pace, but soon fell into an easy jog. Lancelot moved in beside him. "I heard you gave a good account of yourself in the battle."

"Thanks." Randy really didn't feel like chatting.

"Let's pick up the pace a bit, shall we?"

Lancelot sped up a bit and Randy kept pace with him, though his head started to pound again.

"You know," Lancelot began. "There was a time when drinking to the detriment of one's duty would earn a good flogging."

"I just had a few beers. All the guys do it."

“And are all the guys members of the Queen’s elite guard?”

“Elite guard?”

“Yes. What did you think was happening here? We’re building something—something important and permanent. You are privileged to be a part of it.”

Randy was feeling truly guilty about his behavior at this point. “It won’t happen again.”

“See that it doesn’t.” Lancelot picked up the pace yet again. “We’ll talk more about this later.”

The training session went along as usual for the rest of the morning. Randy felt completely shot by the end of it. As they broke for lunch Heather caught up to him.

“So, what happened last night? It’s not like you to get drunk.” Heather seemed genuinely concerned.

Much to his surprise, Randy was grateful for the chance to talk. Even more remarkable was the fact that his little sister seemed like the perfect choice. “Well, last night Jeff had some beer.”

“Obviously.”

“Anyway, I thought one or two wouldn’t hurt. Jeff kept pestering me about what I’d been up to since school ended. What could I say? I told him I’d been involved in a special training program. Then it sort of came out that you and Rebecca were the only other trainees. Then he started teasing me about Rebecca—like there is something going on between us. The beer just seemed to . . . help.”

“So, is there something going on between you and Rebecca?”

“Not you too? Rebecca is awesome. And I like her. But she is young and then there is this whole “queen” business. How could I even take her on a date? She’s always surrounded by . . . someone. I never thought I'd say this about anyone, but she may be out of my league. I just wish people would leave me alone to figure it out on my own."

"Well . . . Ok." Heather was clearly surprised by her brother's hidden depths. "Why don't you do what I'm going to do? Tell your friends. At least then you won't have to worry about letting something slip."

"Is that a good idea?"

"Sure. Remember Rebecca's destiny—to bring the magical and human world together. What kid do you know that doesn't want magic to be real? Think about it. Everything is going to change."

Having said her piece, Heather ran off to catch up with Rebecca, leaving Randy with his own thoughts. It wasn't long before Lancelot fell in beside him. Randy braced for the chewing out he was sure was coming.

"I wanted you to know that I'm not being judgmental of you. In fact, this particular bit of foolishness I find quite amusing. But I also wanted to tell you that this is how it starts—problems with drink. You have some issues that bother you, then discover that alcohol makes you feel better temporarily. Then you do something while you are in your cups that you're embarrassed or guilty about and it becomes all too easy to ease those feelings with more drink. It's a slippery slope my friend. You are much too valuable as a fighter and a person to go that route. If something is bothering you, it's much better to talk it out. I swear, if I live to be ten thousand, I will never understand the human inclination to poison their brain and body with mood altering chemicals."

"When you put it that way I guess it doesn't make much sense." Randy replied.

They had stopped their progress toward the food tent and stood facing each other as Lancelot continued. "Also, I couldn't help but over-hear your conversation with Heather. I do have a piece of advice about Rebecca if you are interested."

"Sure." How could he refuse?

"You are both very young and a lot of things are up in the air right now. Your feelings are what they are, but perhaps you should wait and see how things play out. Take things slowly. She probably needs time to adjust to all the changes in her world too. That doesn't mean you should stay away from her or anything like that. She still needs her friends."

Randy thought a minute. "That's probably good advice. Thanks." He extended his hand and Lancelot shook it.

"One more thing, Randy. If you have no one else to talk to about these issues, you can talk to me."

"Ok . . . Thanks again." Randy was actually grateful to have someone outside his family and friends to talk to. He resumed his trek to the food tent, then turned back to Lancelot. "Can I go with to Loch Ness?"

"'Fraid not, old man. Don't worry, we'll take good care of her. Remember, they also serve who only stand and wait."

While Randy felt disappointment about not going to Scotland, he felt decidedly better about a couple of other things. Perhaps things would work themselves out—or not. However, things were ok for the present. Perhaps Heather was right. Maybe he should bring his friends into the secret.

* * *

"Imhotep, old man, I'm so glad you could come." Merlin shook his hand vigorously.

"I am glad to be here. To have this chance to build something colossal in the old way is truly a pleasure." Imhotep replied. He was shorter than Merlin. His shaven head was covered with a white Panama hat that with his white linen shirt contrasted his deeply tanned complection. Tan shorts and sandals completed his outfit. The only thing his appearance had in common with Merlin's aging-hippie look was the ubiquitous fanny pack.

"Come. You must meet the queen, Rebecca. She's young, but she seems to have a kind of inner wisdom. She's a natural leader . . . "Merlin continued to gush about Rebecca as they walked off to find her. They found her with her friend Heather getting ready to ride their winged horses. "Rebecca, I'm so glad I caught you before you left. I wanted to introduce you to Imhotep. He'll be working on your castle while we're away."

"Nice to meet you, Imhotep." Rebecca said, extending her hand. To her surprise, Imhotep did not shake her hand, but took it, doffed his hat, bowed at the waist, and kissed it.

"The pleasure is mine, Highness." Imhotep spoke with an accent that Rebecca couldn't quite place.

"Imhotep, I've been thinking. What kind of place is this going to be? I've seen pictures of castles that didn't look like a very good places to live. I mean, will it have electricity and modern plumbing? What about Grandma's house? She's lived there a long time. Maybe she won't want to leave it. Had anyone asked her?"

"Highness," Imhotep began. "Unlike my friend Merlin I have not been hiding on some island all these years. I have kept up with advances in technology. Your palace will be warm in the winter and cool in the summer. It will be both beautiful and safe. I will talk to your grandmother. She will be satisfied, I'm sure. Do you have any special requests?"

Heather leaned in and loudly whispered, "Tell him you want a big closet and a place for Wildfire to land by your bedroom."

"Yeah, can you do that?" Rebecca asked with a smile.

"Most assuredly, Highness. Anything else?" Imhotep returned her smile.

"What about a place to have fabulous parties?" Heather offered.

"What castle would be complete without a Great Hall? Or a throne room? Or gardens? I would show you a model, but I understand that time is of the essence. When you return from your trip the building should be well underway. If you find something not to your liking when you return, we can certainly change it."

"Well . . . that sounds good. Is there anything else?" Rebecca was looking forward to her ride.

"I can think of nothing, Highness."

"OK, well . . . thank you." With that, Rebecca and Heather mounted their pegasi and flew off.

As Merlin and Imhotep watched them fly away, Merlin said, "Well, what do you think?"

"Delightful, simply delightful. It has been a very long time since any person of royalty thanked me for anything."

23. Avalon

The next few days were busy and passed quickly. Soon it was time to leave for Avalon. Rebecca was amazed at how quickly the outer wall of the castle was taking shape. Also, it pleased her to think that Heather's dad and the elf healers were starting to work together. Her world was changing, and it was starting to please her. Maybe being The Queen wouldn't be so bad after all.

Rebecca and Heather were in Rebecca's room, packing for the trip.

"I wish I could go." Heather whined.

"I wish I didn't have to. I've about had my fill of excitement for a while." Rebecca held up two shirts, trying to decide which one to take—finally deciding on both.

"I guess it has been quite a summer so far. Gail called the other day—wondered where I've been. I wanted to tell her, but I didn't. I think we should tell the rest of our friends, though. I mean, who am I going to talk to when you're off doing queen stuff?"

"I really wish you would wait until we get back." Rebecca snapped. "There's no telling what will happen when they find out. It would be nice to have Grandma or Lancelot here at least, in case something weird happened."

"You don't have to get huffy about it. If you want me to wait, I'll wait. I'm just not looking forward to lying to my friends about what I've been doing the last month." Heather's voice had an edge that matched Rebecca's.

Rebecca folded a pair of jeans and set it neatly in her bag. "I know." Her voice softened a bit. She turned to Heather with a mischievous grin. "Why don't you hang out with that Jake Hanson while were gone?"

"Jake Hanson!? You have got to be kidding!" Heather suddenly realized that she was kidding. "He's got the body, but he's nuts! Also, he spends all his free time with that Celestine. I wonder what's really going on there. I mean, they're not the same species."

"I don't know. Have you seen how Pip fauns over Amaryllis?"

"I just thought that was Pip being Pip—you know, joking around."

"I don't know. It seems like something more to me." Rebecca shook her head. "Maybe not. Pip is quite the joker. Sometimes I think he's so cute I just want to pinch his little cheeks. Did he ever pull that 'tree hugger' joke on you?"

"Yes. He seemed to think that was really funny. Sometimes he is a bit much, but he's hard not to like. Do you really think Amaryllis and him have something going?"

"I don't know. It's just that when she's around he's less jokey and more flirty."

"Well, maybe you're right. All I know is if we're going inter-species, I still think Lancelot is hot."

They both laughed.

* * *

Rebecca and Heather came downstairs to find the group gathered in Naomi's living room. Cedric was safely nestled in Naomi's heart once again, as evidenced by Naomi's red glowing eyes.

"Now that Rebecca is here, that makes everyone." Cedric said. "Though I don't understand why Pip is going."

"I told you; I'm going to see after Amaryllis. After what she is trying to do, I thought it only fair. If she can find Granya and at least convince her to meet with us, think of the time we'll save. We could be back in no time at all."

Rebecca and Heather gave each other knowing looks.

The humans and Pip each took an elf's hand, picked up their bags and the group popped out. Heather still wished she had gone but decided to go see what her brother was up to.

* * *

Rebecca's first impression of the hidden island of Avalon was of trees—very large trees. Her mother had once taken her to see the California Redwoods. This was much the same—widely spaced trees hundreds of feet tall with a thick canopy of leaves. She found herself staring.

"Amazing, isn't it?" Lancelot said. "This grove has been here since before recorded history."

"It's awesome!" Rebecca walked up to a particularly large oak and reached out to touch the deeply furrowed bark. She detected a subtle vibration, and it startled her. She gasped and pulled back.

"Who dares trespass?" The tree's deep voice rumbled.

"No one trespasses." Merlin responded. "These are my guests. This is Rebecca, the last Pendragon, and our queen. This is Naomi, her grandmother and bearer of the dragon Cedric. Lancelot I'm sure you remember. These others are his crew."

"I'm no one's crew!" Pip objected. "I'm Pip."

"I stand corrected." Merlin bowed at Pip.

The tree began to speak again. "Cedric the dragon, you say. I would see him come forth."

Naomi gasped and clutched Merlin's shoulder for support as the ball of light that was Cedric burst from her chest. The ball flew up and grew until it seemed as if the Sun had come to Earth. Out of the light Cedric materialized and the trees began to sing. It was a haunting and beautiful song, with rich deep harmonies that built slowly to a climax then stopped.

Cedric bowed his head. "I am honored by your greeting."

The trees all answered in unison, though of different pitches. "It is we who are honored by the presence of Cedric, called The Ancient by us. Please share in our sacred island. You and your guests may stay as long as you wish."

"Thank you, Honored Grove. I believe our stay will be a short one this time."

"Yes . . . yes we have an appointment in three days' time," Merlin said. "If you will all follow me, I will show you where we will be staying."

The group walked single file through the giant trees and up a hill. When they crested the hill, a broad meadow spread before them. Where it had been dark in the forest the meadow was filled with brilliant sunshine. There were hundreds of fairies busily working among wildflowers of every color. The meadow went on for about a quarter mile and appeared to end in a cliff overlooking the sea. Perched on the edge of the cliff was what appeared to be the ruins of an ancient castle.

"That's our destination." Merlin pointed at the castle.

"Couldn't we have popped in a bit closer? I've got short legs you know." Pip whined.

"You're not going to grouse like that the whole time, are you? The walk will do you good." Lancelot had little patience for whining.

"Well . . . not the whole time."

Lancelot rolled his eyes and sighed. "I suppose I won't get a moment's peace unless I pop you over there."

"Goody!"

"I would be happy to fly Naomi and Rebecca over." Cedric offered.

"Thanks," both Rebecca and Naomi said at the same time. Then they laughed and climbed aboard Cedric.

They did not fly directly to the castle—they took the scenic route. Avalon was not large as islands go, only a few miles across. But it was beautiful. From the air they could see there was a spring that fed a stream along the edge of the meadow. It ran past the castle and fell over the cliff to the sea. Beyond the stream the woods began. Beyond the woods there were rocky hills covered in grass and wildflowers. There were Fairies everywhere. There was even a small village at the base of the hills where elves and gnomes could be seen going about their business.

"Cedric, it's beautiful," Naomi shouted into the wind.

In response Cedric roared and blew fire. "Such a relief to be in a safe place where we don't have to hide."

They circled the island once more and settled just outside the castle. There was no one to be seen. This clearly had been a small castle—just a tower with a wall around it. Parts of the wall had collapsed, but the tower was mostly intact.

As they surveyed the scene Pip's head poked out a window. "This place is great! I'll be right down to give you the tour." His head disappeared again.

"If you don't mind, I want to go back to the grove where we arrived. I need to catch up with some old friends." Cedric said.

"Sure," Naomi began. "I understand. What was that they called you—The Ancient? You can be sure I'll be asking about that later."

Cedric had no sooner taken flight than Pip appeared. "If you step this way, ladies, your tour will begin." He bowed at the waist and swept his arm toward the castle gate. “Apparently Merlin has been hanging his hat here since the fall of Camelot. I’m not sure how—or even if—he maintained his sanity living alone here all those years. He said he was studying.”

“But he wasn’t alone. There is a village of gnomes and elves on the other side of the forest.” Rebecca corrected him.

“That guy! He has the most annoying habit of leaving things out of the conversation. I like to make sure everyone is in possession of all the facts.”

“We know!” Rebecca began. She could see Pip was taking that as a criticism, so she added, “But that is just part of your charm.”

Pip’s grin returned and they continued into the tower. Rebecca’s first impression of the tower was one of darkness. They were in a dark hallway with a door at the end. But as the door swung open a spacious great hall came into view. It was illuminated with baseball-sized balls of light that appeared to be floating in space. There was a crackling fire in the fireplace at the far end. There were tables of various sizes throughout the room—most piled to overflowing with books, papers, and an assortment of devices of mysterious purpose. The finishing touch was a bookcase along one wall filled with ancient tomes, no doubt containing a wealth of magical knowledge.

“Welcome to my home, such as it is.” Merlin said. “Make yourself at home.” He removed an armload of scrolls from a chair and slid it over by the fire. “Here, Rebeca, sit by the fire. It gets kind of chilly in these old stone buildings.”

Rebecca sat while Naomi retrieved another chair. As they sat enjoying the fire, they heard rapid footsteps. Turning they saw Lancelot running down the stairs that wound up the curved wall.

“Merlin, there is a group of elves and gnomes approaching the castle. They seem friendly.”

"I'm sure they are. I'll see what they want." Merlin was quickly out the door, leaving it ajar. The rest of the group followed. They found not just a group of gnomes and elves, but numerous fairies waiting just outside the castle gate.

"Greetings, friends." Merlin extended his hand.

The elf in front shook it and smiled. "We heard you were back and have brought The Once and Future King."

"Sean, the trees have been tattling I see. One mistake though—not king but queen. Rebecca, come." Merlin beckoned with his hand. Rebecca stepped up beside him. Merlin leaned in and whispered, "Summon Excalibur."

Rebecca did as requested and stood holding Excalibur high for all to see. Instantly the magicals all kneeled and proclaimed, "Hail to the Queen."

While this did not surprise Rebecca, she couldn't help but be somewhat embarrassed by it. "Please stand." She walked through the crowd, shaking hands and asking for names.

When introductions were done Sean, the apparent leader, spoke up. "We saw the dragon. We would know more about him. Is he The Ancient, as the trees say?"

"He is," Merlin replied.

"What does that mean?" Rebecca enquired.

"Cedric comes from time before time. He knew the ancient groves when they were mere saplings. He protected them and taught men to revere them. Only he knows how old he is. He has fought for what is good and right for millennia. I met him when I was a Druid. He came to our sacred grove and took a special interest in me. I was never sure why. He is still revered because he uses his great power only when needed. He could have ruled the world but chose to teach compassion instead."

"That is . . . amazing," Naomi whispered. Then louder, "I wonder why he never chose to share any of this with me."

"In part humility and also, he probably never saw the need. He has been around so long if he were to tell everything it would take a very long time." Merlin explained. "Well, I see you have brought food. Please come in and we shall sup together."

* * *

After supper Rebecca climbed the stair to the top of the tower where Lancelot was standing watch.

"Correct me if I'm wrong, but it seems like you are growing a bit more comfortable with your new role." He said.

"I suppose I am." She responded, gazing out at the sea far below. "Cedric helped me. He showed me how we are all connected together—how we each have our part to play."

"And tomorrow you will make your first state visit—to the magical village of Avalon. How do you feel about that?"

"Pretty good, actually. I find myself looking forward to it."

"Good. You should enjoy it."

They were silent for a while as Rebecca continued to look out to sea. The Sun had long set, and the Moon was rising, making the sea sparkle as if it were full of diamonds. Occasionally a fish would jump. They appeared to be moving closer to shore and there seemed to be quite a few of them. As they drew closer, she could swear there were people among them. Finally, a head popped out of the water and an arm came up and waved to her.

Surprised, she waved back as more heads popped up. "Lancelot . . . Who or what are those?"

Lancelot chuckled. "Those are the mer-folk. I don't know why you are so surprised. If you've heard of it, it probably exists. I think they have come to meet the new queen. Would you like to meet them?"

"I would! Do you know where Pip went? I haven't seen him since supper."

"I don't. I would be happy to accompany you. I'll send one of the others to keep watch."

"How do we get down there?"

"Well, we could just pop down, or I believe Merlin mentioned there is a secret tunnel."

"If you don't mind, I'd like to see what the secret tunnel is like."

"As you wish, Highness"

* * *

Being unable to summon balls of light like Merlin, Lancelot retrieved a flashlight from his pack, and they were soon on their way down the dark stair to the sea. The stairs were steep, though every so often there was a landing with a door. Presumably, there were rooms of some kind behind them. Rebecca wondered what they might hold. The fourth landing they came to was illuminated by the door being open a crack. There were crashing and clanging sounds coming from behind the door. Lancelot pulled the door open with a loud creaking. Merlin, on his knees digging around under a table, looked up at them—clearly startled.

"What on earth are you doing, old man?" Lancelot asked.

Merlin stood up, dusting off his hands. "Just looking for a few things. It's amazing how much junk one can accumulate when you live in the same place for a few hundred years."

"Indeed." Lancelot looked around at the clutter. "There are some mer-folks below. I'm taking Rebecca down to meet them."

"Beware, the mer-folk have a strong independent streak." Merlin returned to his digging.

"Always, old man, always." Lancelot guided Rebecca out the door and they continued their descent.

"What did he mean, 'beware'?"

"I'm sure there's nothing to worry about."

They continued in silence until the tunnel opened to a small beach. There were a few mer-folk sitting on the beach and hundreds out in the water. They looked pretty much as she expected. They looked human from the waist up and instead of legs they looked like a fish, with scales that sparkled in the moonlight and a long, forked tail. Some of them carried three pronged spears.

"Greetings," matronly female said. "Are you she who would be queen?"

"I am"

"I am Alasandese, leader of this clan. Know that we mer-folk bow to no one who has not earned our allegiance."

Rebecca summoned Excalibur, thinking this would prove her claim.

"We care not for your trinkets. To earn our allegiance, you must prove your heart to us."

"How do I do that?"

"You must come with us."

"But . . . I can't breathe under water."

"We will see to that. But be warned, should your heart prove false, you may not survive."

Rebecca looked to Lancelot who said, "You need not do this. You can fulfill your destiny without them."

"Can I? Aren't they part of the magical world? How can I unite the magical world with the human world if I ignore a whole group? I think I need to go."

Lancelot sighed. "I suppose you are right, but I'm nervous about it because I can't go with you."

Rebecca pulled off her hiking boots and socks and walked into the surf. The mer-maid who had spoken swam up to her and took her hand.

"Whatever happens, do not let go of my hand. If you do, I cannot help you breathe. If your heart should prove false, we will desert you and you will be left on your own to return to land . . . or not."

"I understand."

They dove into the surf and followed the bottom out to sea. At first, she was afraid and it was weird not breathing. However, she looked within herself for the light that Cedric showed her. When she found it a sense connectedness and peace swept over her. She was no longer afraid.

A voice came into her head. "I will speak to you this way while we are under water. I sense your fear is gone. How did you accomplish this?"

"Cedric, the dragon taught me to find my center and draw strength from it."

"The Ancient? I had heard he has returned. He is a good teacher. It is good that you listen to him."

"Where are we going?"

"We go to our cave. It is our refuge. Save your questions until we get there."

They swam on into the murky depths of the sea. At length they swam into a cave and surfaced. In contrast to the darkness of the night sea, the cave was brightly lit by what appeared to some kind of moss growing on the walls. The only place where Rebecca could see dry land was a shelf of rock on the far end. This is where Alasandese took her.

Rebecca climbed up on the shelf and wiped the water from her eyes. It was chilly here. "So, what test would you have me do?"

"There is no test. You will wait here until we can get word to Pan and see what he wants us to do with you."

* * *

Pip walked along the stream that ran past the castle to the sea. While he was sure that Amaryllis could take care of herself, he still worried. He had the idea that perhaps the spirit of the spring that fed this stream may have some news of her. He hummed a little tune as he walked, thinking of the day Amaryllis kissed his forehead. What a day! He was quite surprised when a water nymph materialized from the stream.

"Are you one who travels with the Queen?" She asked.

"I am Pip, and yes, I travel with the Queen. And what is your name?"

"Verbena. Pip, there is no time to lose. The Mer-folk have taken the Queen and intend to turn her over to Pan."

Pip, for once in his life was speechless. He turned and ran as fast as his little legs could carry him—which was pretty fast, actually. All the while he shouted "LANCELOT!"

Lancelot appeared on the trail ahead of Pip. "What has gotten you so excited?"

"The mer-folk have taken Rebecca."

"Relax, old man. She went with them willingly. They want her to complete some kind of test before they pledge allegiance to her."

"It was a trick! They intend to give her to Pan."

"Oh dear!" Lancelot paused just a moment to think. "We need Merlin. Take my hand."

They re-appeared in the great hall, where Naomi and Merlin were chatting causally by the fireplace. The rest of Lancelot's lads were sharpening their swords and other weapons maintenance tasks.

"The mer-folk have taken Rebecca." Lancelot told Merlin. "We can rescue her, but we need to know where they have taken her."

"I see, I see. Most distressing."

"I agree. Can you tell me where they would have taken her?"

"Well . . . they have a cave—an underwater cave. That's probably where they are."

"That's just great. How can we find that? For us to pop in we have to have either been there before or have precise coordinates. But this . . ."

"I have an old map that may be helpful." Merlin rushed to a shelf full of scrolls and started digging through them. "Yes, here we are." He unrolled the map on a nearby table. "About twelve hundred years ago, give or take, there were some pirates who thought to use the cave to hide some of their ill-gotten treasure. Here," he pointed. "See where it shows the location and depth."

Lancelot frowned. "What language is that and can you read it?"

"Oh my yes, they're Nordic runes." Merlin scribbled something on a piece of paper and handed it to Lancelot. "Is that better?"

Lancelot studied the paper. "Perfect. Thanks." He handed the paper to one of his crew, who studied it briefly and passed it on the next. Lancelot stepped over to Naomi and Pip. "I think this is a job for elves alone. Do you agree?"

"Reluctantly," Naomi replied.

Pip chimed in, “Good luck, old man.”

“Luck has nothing to do with it,” Lancelot replied before he drew his sword, nodded to his men and popped away.

* * *

Rebecca stood and put her hands on her hips. “You might as well kill me now.” She summoned Excalibur. “But you should know it won’t be easy.”

There was an uneasy silence while the mer-folk glared back at Rebecca. Finally, the stand-off was broken by a three-pronged spear flying directly at her. She deflected it easily with Excalibur. It was soon replaced by another spear, and another, and another. She deflected every one. As she fought, Rebecca noticed muffled laughter coming from somewhere near her. As the spears came faster, the laughter got louder until someone was having a hearty belly-laugh at her expense. That made her mad. Bad enough they kidnaped her and are trying to kill her. But, laughing at her—that was the last straw. She started to move toward the laughter, deflecting more spears along the way. She may not leave this cave alive, but she was going to make that laughing stop. Someone shouted “Enough!” The spears stopped coming.

Alasandese, still chuckling, spoke. “You have passed your test, young one. We would not follow a queen that expected others to fight her battles. We mer-folk are warriors. We could only follow a warrior. You have shown us you have the heart of a warrior and the beginnings of wisdom as well. We will be proud to call you our queen.”

Shouts of “Hail Queen Rebecca!” echoed around the cave.

“Let us feast!” Alasandese declared. Soon music filled the cave and a large clam shell filled with all manner of raw seafood delicacies was placed in front of Rebecca. Though she had reservations she thought she should at least try some of them. Much to her surprise, they were delicious

* * *

Merlin's coordinates proved to be remarkably accurate, and the elves materialized right on the stone shelf. They were greeted with music and surprised looks from the mer-folk and Rebecca. It looked like they were interrupting a feast.

"Are you alright Highness?" Lancelot said.

"Yes, I'm fine. It was all a test, which I apparently passed."

"Indeed, you did." Alasandese added. "Is this the famous Lancelot of the Lake?"

"It is, m'lady."

"It is an honor to meet you. I am Alasandese, leader of this clan. Please join our feast."

"With pleasure, m'lady." He sheathed his sword and the other elves followed suit. "But first I must send word back to the castle. There are some very worried people back there."

Lancelot sent one of his lads to inform the others and sat beside Rebecca to partake in the feast. "You know, Alasandese, I'm not sure I approve of your methods. Rebecca could have been badly hurt, or even killed."

"I know our ways are harsh. However, a worthy queen would not have been in danger. As it turns out, Rebecca is a very worthy queen . . . what in the name of the sea is that?" She was looking right at Pip, who had returned with the messenger elf.

"Forgive me, Highness, I heard there was a party, and I couldn't resist." Pip announced. "Also, I have actually never seen a mer-maid and I just had to. I can see that reports I heard were not over-stated." That last bit he said while blatantly staring at a particularly stunning young mer-maid, whose charms were there for all to see.

Lancelot groaned. "Pip, old man, do grow up, will you?"

"Alasandese, meet Pip." Rebecca said. "He's harmless and he does grow on you."

"What a disturbing proposition." She replied.

* * *

Cedric was up most of the night talking and reminiscing with the sacred grove. It had been a very long time since he had visited a sacred grove. As he gradually came out of his slumber, he became aware of whispering. There appeared to be some kind of argument going on.

"I say we wake him."

"It would be disrespectful."

"We don't want to make him mad."

"Did he move? I think he moved."

Cedric opened his eyes a crack and saw a small delegation of elves and gnomes standing beside a large pile of various kinds of food. Upon seeing his eyes open one of the gnomes stepped forward.

"I am Nogotramard," He declared. "But you may call me Nog. We are from the village of Avalon. We have come here to pay homage to The Ancient. We have brought food, such as it is." He gestured to the pile of food.

"I am honored by your gift. Thank you."

"So, you are The Ancient, now known as Cedric?"

"I am."

"We need your advice. We have captured a human. He beached his boat, which is full of all manner of strange gadgets, by the way. He said he was looking for aliens, but he found us instead. He said we were 'the greatest find in this century', whatever that means. Anyway, what shall we do with him? Some of us thought you may want to eat him."

Cedric was somewhat taken aback by that last idea, though he didn't say so. "I think you should bring him to me . . . I want to talk to him."

"So, you're not going to eat him?" Nog seemed somewhat disappointed.

"Let's just start with a little conversation. Perhaps eating will come later." Cedric had no intention of eating anyone, but it amused him to humor this gnome.

"Very well, wait right here."

Two elves popped away and returned with a young man held between them. His hands were bound behind his back, and he had a cloth bag over his head.

"Unbind him," Cedric said.

The elves did as he bid. When the man's hands were free, he removed the bag from his head and beheld Cedric. He wet himself. Clearly, he had never seen a dragon before.

"Oh dear!" Cedric noticed the man's wet pants. "I will not hurt you. There is no need to fear me. Who are you and how did you find this island?"

"I'm George O'Reiley." George spoke with a thick Irish brogue. "I am a researcher. I have equipment in my boat to detect electro-magnetic anomalies. I thought I had found an alien base. My eyes told me there was nothing there. My instruments said there was. When I pierced the barrier I saw it plain as day—the island of Hy-Brasil . . . The island where aliens live." George pointed to the elves with their pointed ears and the diminutive gnomes. He managed to look pretty smug for a man who had just wet his pants.

"Oh dear, where to start." Cedric thought a bit before continuing. "The first thing you need to know is that there are no aliens on this island. These are elves and gnomes. I, as you might have guessed, am a dragon. My name is Cedric. Your presence here is a problem. That barrier you passed is there for a reason. We like our privacy. I'm not sure what we're going to do about that."

"What do you mean?" George looked a bit concerned for his safety, in spite of Cedric's assurances.

"This island's existence and location have been secret for hundreds of years. It must remain so. We will have to involve the queen."

"The queen? You mean Elizabeth? What kind of conspiracy is this?"

"Not quite. I refer to Rebecca—the last Pendragon. Which brings me to my second point. You have your stories mixed up. This island is not Hy-Brasil, it is Avalon."

"Avalon? You mean the Avalon from the Arthurian legend?"

"Is there another?" Now it was Cedric's turn to look smug. "Merlin put the barrier in place centuries ago. He has been here since."

"Merlin? The Merlin? You mean he still lives?"

"Of course."

"But . . . how?" George had long been intrigued with the unusual—hence his interest in the "Ancient Alien Theory". He was starting to realize that he had stumbled into something much more intriguing.

"You'll have to ask him. Why don't you go back to the village and get cleaned up? Remember you will be meeting the queen today. Dress appropriately."

With that, the two elves once again took his arms and popped away. The rest of the delegation thanked Cedric and returned to the village.

"Now we shall see how wise our young queen truly is." Cedric said to the trees.

"Indeed, we shall." The trees replied.

* * *

They arrived at the village right after lunch. The villagers had set up a throne in the village square and insisted she sit on it. She met the town council and discussed the Oracle's predictions and how they may come to pass. Rebecca was a bit bewildered by it all. The council asked questions she had no idea how to answer, but she gave it her best guess. They seemed to be pleased.

Toward the end of the meeting Cedric approached. "Your Highness, there is an urgent issue that requires your attention."

"What is it?"

"A man has crossed the barrier surrounding this island and learned our secret."

"Is that so bad? I mean, we are trying to unite the human and magical worlds."

"The problem is that we are not ready for everyone to know our secret yet."

"I see. I suppose you're right. So . . . where is he now?"

Cedric nodded to a couple of elves who stood guard outside a hut. They went inside and retrieved George, now dressed as if he was going to an opera circa 1910. The tails seemed a bit much in this rural village, but it was all the elves had resembling formal dress. The elves brought him before Rebecca and indicated he should kneel.

For his part, George looked at Rebecca with disbelief. He wasn't sure what he was expecting, but it certainly wasn't a teenage girl in jeans and a hoodie.

"My friend Cedric tells me you are a problem for us. Tell me what you are doing here." Rebecca tried to look stern.

George told her his whole story—how he had gone in search of the fabled island of Hy-Brasil and found Avalon instead, how he believed space-aliens had helped early mankind. Then he went on to say that what he found instead was the greatest discovery ever. How he was going to rock the scientific community by proving the existence of magicals. When he got to that part Rebecca gave Cedric a knowing look. Now she knew why he was a problem.

"Thank you, George. I think I've heard enough. Surely you realize we just can't let you go. I have been told that it is my destiny to unite the magical and human worlds. However, for now we need to remain secret, my life depends on it. So, what do we do about you? We could just kill you; I suppose. That would solve the problem." Rebecca studied George's face. He looked like he was going to cry. Then she heard Cedric's voice in her head.

"Stop playing with him. He'll wet his pants again."

"But we don't kill people unless we have to." She continued. "I think you have three choices. One, we could keep you here for the rest of your life or until you no longer represent a threat, whichever comes first. Or, two, we could let you go if you promise to keep our secret. But I'm not sure I trust you to do that. Or, choice number three, we could take you with us when we leave tomorrow."

The rest of Rebecca's entourage were quite shocked by this last suggestion. They each were formulating a response when George spoke.

"So . . . Your Highness, where might you be going tomorrow?"

"To find the Loch Ness Monster."

"Go on, pull the other one. Elves and pixies I can almost believe. The dragon without doubt is real. But I never bought into that Loch Ness malarkey. It's just stories to bring in the tourists." George scoffed.

"Actually, she is a dragon. We want to recruit her."

That seemed to silence him. He was clearly reviewing his options. Finally, he declared, “Ok, I’m in. What about my boat and equipment?”

“We’ll pull them up into the trees.” Lancelot said. “Take only what you can carry. I warn you, if you try to escape or get a message out it will not go well for you.” Lancelot gave him his most menacing look. Even Pip managed to look menacing.

The rest of the visit was uneventful. After the visit Merlin levitated George’s boat up into the woods by the shore. Pip decided it was his job to go invisible and follow George around, just in case. At one point he grabbed a notebook George was writing in and tossed it into the fireplace. George was quite shocked by this. When Pip materialized and waggled his finger at him, saying “No writing.” Lancelot actually laughed.

George spent the rest of the evening going from person to person, peppering them with questions. They were all getting a bit annoyed with him and turned in early to get away from him. All except for Pip, who kept his invisible vigil.

Cedric paid a final visit to the sacred grove. “What do you think of our young queen’s handling of our intruder?”

“We are pleased,” the trees sighed. “She turned a potential enemy into a potential friend. This bodes well for the future. You have taught her well.”

I feel I must tell you that this decision was all hers. Some things you cannot teach. True wisdom comes from the heart.”

“Even better.” The trees replied.

24. New Camelot

Jenny Miller was more than a reporter. She was also the editor, publisher and advertising salesperson for the Maple Ridge Chronicle—the local weekly newspaper. On this particular day, as she liked to do when she had the time, she was driving in the country looking for anything that might be newsworthy. For example, that's how she found the group of farmers that still harvested their small grain with an antique threshing-machine.

As she drove past Naomi's driveway, she thought she saw something. She had been down this road many times and there was definitely something new. Someone had built a huge wall. As she drew closer, she thought she saw crenellations on top of the wall, like a medieval castle. This was definitely worth investigating.

She slowly drove down the driveway until she got to a huge gate, closed by a huge iron portcullis. She wondered of this was some new theme park that had somehow avoided her notice until now. If so, this was big news. She simply had to get inside. She honked her horn and waited. There was no response, so she honked again. This time there was a metallic clanking sound as the portcullis slowly rose. The gate opened a crack and a man walked out.

She had to chuckle a bit when she saw him. He looked like Rambo, complete with compound bow and arrow quiver on his back. He was shirtless and clearly, he worked out frequently. As he approached her car she spoke first. "Hello. I'm Jenny Miller—reporter for the Maple Ridge Chronicle. I was driving by, and I couldn't help but see your new wall here. I'm sure my readers would be interested in what you are doing here."

The man squinted as he scrutinized her. He seemed to come to some kind of decision as his expression changed to a thin smile. “I’m sure they would. Would you like to come in?”

“That would be great.”

“I’ll open the gate and you can drive in.”

His muscles rippled as he pushed the heavy wooden doors open. She drove through and she heard the clanking sound again as the portcullis slid closed. She was kind of unnerved by this development, but Rambo seemed polite, and she was confident in her ability to take care of herself.

As she got out of the car Rambo extended his hand and said, “Jake Hanson. Pleased to meet you, Jenny.”

She shook his hand and smiled. “Pleased to meet you, Jake. What is this place?”

He frowned a bit as he thought about her question. She was starting to think that perhaps Jake was not the sharpest knife in the drawer. Finally, he spoke.

“Welcome to New Camelot. Feel free to look around, but I’m afraid you can’t leave.”

“WHAT?! What do you mean, I can’t leave?”

“Well . . . it’s pretty straightforward. Don’t you understand English? You—can’t—leave.”

Jenny looked at the shear fifty-foot walls and the heavy iron portcullis behind her car and the reality of her situation began to sink in. “Just who do you think you are? You can’t hold people against their will. That’s kidnapping. It’s against the law. You’re going to be in big trouble, Jake.”

“If you say so, Jenny.”

They stood scowling at each other for a few minutes when Jenny noticed another man standing beside Jake. She thought it odd that she didn't see him approach. "Another military type," she thought as she looked him up and down until her gaze came to rest on his ears. They were pointed.

"So, who are you supposed to be, Mr. Spock?"

"I am an elf, Ma'am. Is there a problem here?"

"I'll say! This jerk says I can't leave. . . Wait a minute. Did you say elf?"

"Yes, Ma'am. And I'm afraid that Jake is correct. You must remain here as our guest, for the time being. Perhaps it would be best, rather than debate it here, if we showed you around. Then I'm sure you will understand why your detention is necessary."

"Ok . . . let's go." Jenny was still determined to escape and maybe she would find a way if she looked around a bit. When she did get out, she would write the story of her life.

Several hours later, after meeting Imhotep, gnomes, elves, and fairies; and hearing the whole story, she was sitting on the porch steps resting her chin on her hands. She wasn't sure what to think. This whole situation challenged her whole concept of reality. She had always been a rational, logical person. Yet she could think of no rational explanation for the things she had seen. Apparently, magic was real. As she sat contemplating something above her caught her eye.

There were two winged horses with riders approaching. She thought "What next?" She was starting to expect the unexpected. The horses came to earth in front of her. The riders were a teenage boy and girl. She recognized the boy as Randy Lund, high school football star. The girl must be his sister. Perhaps she could convince them to help. The pair dismounted and walked up to her.

"Hello, Randy," she said, rising and extending her hand. "I'm Jenny Miller from the Chronicle. I interviewed you a few times."

"Yes, I remember." He shook her hand. "What are you doing here?"

"They won't let me leave."

Randy and his sister gave each other long knowing looks. This could end badly. Finally, Heather spoke up. "That's terrible."

"Yes, it is. Can you help me? They won't even let me make a call. They took my cell phone. We need to call the police." Jenny was starting to feel like she was getting somewhere.

"The police . . ."Again, the knowing looks before Heather continued. "I think I know just the guy. I'm Heather, by the way." She pulled her phone out of her pocket and dialed. "Andy Turnquist please. Hello? Officer Turnquist? This is Heather Lund. We met at Naomi's farm. Right. Well, we have kind of a situation here. Could you come out? That would be great, thanks." She put her phone back in her pocket. "He said he'll be right out."

"Oh, thank you so much. I don't know how to repay you." Jenny stepped forward and gave Heather a big hug.

They decided to wait for the police in the house. They made small talk until Andy walked in followed by Jake. Jenny stiffened when she saw him.

"That's him! That's the guy who tricked me in here then wouldn't let me out!" Jenny could hardly wait to see Jake get his comeuppance.

"I see," Andy responded. "Why don't we sit down, and you can tell me all about it?"

Jenny started at the beginning and left nothing out. She was about halfway through her story when she noticed Andy wasn't writing anything down. In fact, he didn't even have his notebook out. That struck her as very odd.

"Why aren't you writing anything down? What's going on here?" Jenny was starting to feel very paranoid. Were the police involved? If so, this was a much bigger story than she thought.

Andy rubbed the back of his neck as he thought about her question. Finally, he asked. "Did you see the dragon?"

"What? . . . The dragon?" Jenny was clearly shaken by this response to her question. "I . . . No, I didn't see the dragon."

"Too bad. When you see the dragon, that will make a believer out of you." Andy leaned back in his chair. "It made a believer out of me; I can tell you. As I see it, unfortunately, we have no choice but to hold you here until the queen gets back."

"Wait a minute. Queen? What queen are we talking about?"

Jake spoke up. "Rebecca, of course. She is out of town for a few days, so you'll just have to wait."

Jenny sagged. She had such high hopes of leaving with this police officer. Now, it appeared as though he was somehow part of this—whatever it is—conspiracy. Well . . . she might as well make the best of it.

"I have a paper to get out. If I am going to stay here, I'm going to need clothes and things. How long do you plan to hold me?"

Andy rubbed his neck again. This whole thing was giving him a headache. "I'm not sure how long . . ."

"Should only be a couple of days." Randy interjected.

"Ok, a couple of days." Andy was pleased to finally be in possession of that information. "When the queen gets back, we should be able to get this all sorted out. As far as the other. . . I could take you to your place to get some things. I don't know about your paper."

"Well, I suppose I could bring my laptop and work on it here if it's only a few days. I would need access to the internet. I suppose staying at New Camelot wouldn't be so bad." Jenny seemed to have resigned herself to the inevitable.

"New Camelot?" Both Heather and Randy blurted out, then, "Jinx!" then they laughed.

"Yeah," Jenny was somewhat surprised by their reaction. "That's what Jake called this place."

"I didn't know what else to call it."

"New Camelot." Heather said the words slowly to see how it sounded. "I like it."

25. Just Checking

Pan was very pleased with his minions' progress. Hurricanes were blowing. Volcanoes were erupting. Accidents were up across the globe. Goblins were driving more people crazy than ever. It was a good beginning. Only the ogres and trolls waited in reserve.

He sat upon his throne savoring the suffering he commanded when Marid flew in shaped as a raven. He landed at Pan's feet and returned to his normal angry teddy-bear form.

"Things continue to go well, Master. I just crashed another passenger plane. I haven't had this much fun in years." Marid clearly took pride in his work.

"You have done well, Marid. I have been thinking. I have a special task for you. I want you to go to that farm where the trolls killed the great Rebecca. I just want to make sure. Report back to me what you see."

"With pleasure, Master. At once, Master." Marid turned back into a raven and flew away.

* * *

As he glided over the trees approaching the farm Marid expected to see the same farm he had been so unceremoniously chased from. Instead, what he saw had him wondering if he was off course. He saw a castle. He flew higher to get a better view. He saw the barn where he had been interrogated by Cedric and his awful crew. He shuddered at the memory of it. He was clearly in the right place. When did this castle get here? This required closer investigation.

He glided down and landed behind the barn, changing into a mouse as he did so. As he scampered through the barn, he couldn't help the feeling that he was being watched. He scurried behind a post and peeked back behind him. Indeed, he was being watched—by a large tabby cat.

This just wouldn't do. Perhaps imitation was the best way to go. He turned into a cat. His pursuer arched her back, hissed and ran away. In her mind mice should not turn into cats. Marid chuckled. He'd have to remember that one. He continued on his way, the tip of his tail twisting back and forth as he walked.

He continued his trek toward the house. He saw the castle wall enclosing part of the pasture and the whole yard. There were quite a few tents with elves and gnomes busy at whatever elves and gnomes did. Behind the house a palace worthy of an emperor was taking shape.

He began to wonder if Rebecca was still alive. He almost wished she was. He would relish watching Pan punish those smug trolls for lying to him. This required a thorough investigation. He turned into a horse fly and took off to check things out.

He searched high and low. He searched in the giant kitchen and the great hall He looked in every bedroom and closet. He even searched every tunnel and sub-basement. He did not find Rebecca or her grandmother. All he found was a bald wizard, elves, and gnomes and one lonely human female. She was walking around taking pictures of everything. None of this made any sense. While it seemed as though Rebecca was gone, along with her grandmother and that meddling dragon, something was going on. He wondered what Pan would make of it.

* * *

"That is odd, I have to admit." Pan rubbed his furrowed brow. Things were going so well. "But if you are sure you didn't see any sign of Rebecca, I see no reason to change our plan. Perhaps I will drop by at some point to see what they are up to. Perhaps they plan to offer the palace to me as an act of contrition."

Marid hadn't thought of that, but then he lacked Pan's massive ego. He hoped it was so. "Yes Master . . . I'm sure that's it," he said. He was already thinking about what kind of mischief he could get into next.

26. Loch Ness

"Alright, let's review the plan." Lancelot began. "Cedric will return to Naomi's heart. We will pop over to Urquhart Castle, appearing under the old drawbridge to avoid being seen. We elves and Pip will remain invisible until dusk. Naomi, Merlin, and Rebecca will pretend to be tourists until dark. Then we will gather by the dock and hopefully meet Granya. Any questions?"

There were none, so they began. Cedric rose into the air and became a ball of light. He shrank until he was the size of a baseball. Lancelot steadied Naomi as Cedric flew smack into her chest.

"Are you alright, Grandma?" Rebecca held Naomi's hand.

Naomi took a deep breath and squeezed her hand. "I'm fine, dear. Let's get going."

The Humans and Pip each took an elf's hand and the group popped away. The next thing they knew they were standing under what used to be the drawbridge of Urquhart Castle. They looked around but couldn't see any people—though they could hear lots of them. They had made their entrance unobserved—so far, so good.

Lancelot turned to the humans. "Fortune is with us this day. Remember, even though you won't see us, we will be with you all day. You will see us after sunset."

With that the magicals faded from view. Rebecca, Naomi, Merlin, and George started exploring the ruins of the castle, looking to all the world like any other group of tourists. The castle was in fact crawling with tourists. The trio explored every inch of the castle ruins. Rebecca's favorite view was from the top of the keep. The lake was beautiful, with trees lining the surrounding hillsides.

"Imagine what it was like, Grandma, when this castle was whole. It must have been beautiful." Rebecca said while looking out over the ruins.

"Actually, it was rather ominous to behold. A great stone citadel perched on this hill." Merlin clearly had been here before. "This castle was attacked many times. Many men died here. Those were barbarous times. I'm glad I lived to see it, though. Even with all the things we have threatening the world now I'd much rather be alive now. Much safer . . . Yes, much safer indeed."

"Wow, I guess I never thought about it like that. I'm glad I live now too. I like running water and cell phones." Rebecca responded.

"Now, if it a beautiful castle you're after, just wait until you see your own. I'm not sure exactly what Imhotep has in mind, but I told him to make it beautiful. I'm sure the architect of the pharaohs will not disappoint." Merlin looked satisfied with himself.

"You know, when you first started talking about it, I wasn't excited about the idea. But now, standing here, I can see the appeal. I can't wait until I see it." The excitement of anticipation glowed in Rebecca's face.

Merlin chuckled. "I thought you'd come around. Now, these old bones could use a bench."

"Wait a minute," George said. "Imhotep? Architect of the pharaohs? You mean the pyramids weren't built by aliens?"

Merlin chuckled again. "My boy, how can a guy as seemingly smart as you be so ignorant of the facts? Of course, the pyramids were not built by aliens. Magic, old boy, magic."

"What about all the megalithic structures—like Stonehenge?"

"Magic. It's all magic. You have a lot to learn, but that must wait for another time. We're here to do a job."

George was clearly disappointed. “Alright, but rest assured we will be talking more about this later.”

They were heading toward a bench when a little boy’s voice came from behind them, “Look, Mommy, a garden gnome.”

When Rebecca turned, sure enough, there stood Pip still as a statue right beside the paved path. The boy, about Pip’s height, stood face to face with him. The boy’s mother, clearly unimpressed with garden gnomes, kept walking. She stopped about ten feet away to read a plaque. The three of them stood like that for a few minutes—the mother reading and Pip and the boy staring at each other. Then Pip winked.

“Mommy, he winked!” The boy shouted loud enough for everyone to hear. Most ignored it. “The gnome winked at me, Mommy.” He ran to her.

She bent down and grabbed the boy’s arm. “How many times have I told you to stop making things up?”

“But Mommy, look.” He pointed.

She looked, but Pip was gone. “No, you look. See there’s nothing there.”

“But Mommy I saw him.”

She took his hand and began pulling him toward the parking lot. “I think it’s time for us to go home now.”

“No, Mommy, I want to see the monster. Can’t we wait and see the monster?”

“I think it’s time for your nap, young man.”

As Rebecca watched the pair disappear down the path to the parking lot she felt an overwhelming urge to grin—an unmistakable clue that Pip was near. “Pip, you are a naughty, naughty boy.” She said under her breath.

"I know. I got bored." Though Pip could not be seen, he could be heard. "I haven't pulled that one in a long time. It's like finding money. I just couldn't resist. I promise I'll behave for the rest of the day."

The group continued on to a bench and sat down. Pip was true to his word and made no more trouble. The rest of the day passed uneventfully. Soon the tourists were thinning out. Merlin created a cloak of invisibility around them so no one would notice they were not leaving. In time the sun dropped below the western horizon, the elves and Pip reappeared, and they headed for the dock.

Before they made it to the dock, hundreds of fairies appeared blocking their path. One of them spoke. "Go no farther. I am Connor, leader of the Loch Ness fairies. We know what you're about and we'd like to keep our dragon, thank you very much."

Pip stepped forward. "Have you spoken to Finnian?"

"That we have." Connor waved his hand, and a bound and gagged Finnian was brought forth. They unbound him and he flew up and sat on Rebecca's shoulder.

"They were most discourteous, Your Majesty. I think you should punish them." Finnian was quite upset.

"Did they hurt you?" Rebecca asked.

"No, Highness. It takes more than these savages to harm me."

"I'm glad to hear it, Finnian. Let's hear what they have to say."

Pip spoke again. "Connor, you dishonor us and yourselves by treating an official emissary so. Why have you done such a thing?"

"As I said, we have no wish to lose our dragon. Also, it is by no means certain that you will triumph over Pan. What's in it for us if we help you?"

"What do you want?"

"If Pan is defeated, we would have the queen move her court here."

"Out of the question!" Merlin blurted out.

"Not so fast, Merlin." Lancelot counseled. "When the human world and the magical are once again united it will be a world-wide phenomenon. Perhaps some compromise can be reached."

"Or Rebecca could just overcome these sprites with Excalibur and be done with it." Merlin apparently had some anger issues.

"I will speak for myself!" Rebecca declared. "I am prepared to grant some concessions to these fairies provided they get out of our way and swear allegiance to me."

The rest of the group of travelers stared in open amazement at Rebecca. The maturity demonstrated by that statement surprised them all. Pip broke the silence. "What concessions would satisfy you, Connor?"

"We demand a gift. Something for the whole clan. And . . . We demand the queen spend at least part of the year here by the Loch."

There was a long silence while Rebecca considered her options. Remembered how the fairies she knew had a weakness for sweets. Then she remembered she had a bag of jellybeans in her backpack. She pulled it out and offered one to Connor.

He tasted it, held it over his head. "Delicious!" His band cheered. "Bring the gift!" he commanded. Two fairies flew forward, each holding the end of a string. A ring hung in between them. They placed it in Rebecca's hand. "We know you have Arthur's sword, Excalibur. We thought it only fair you had his ring as well. Put it on."

Rebecca hesitated, remembering the burning pain when Merlin placed Excalibur in her hand.

"Go ahead. It won't bite." Connor goaded.

Rebecca slowly slid the ring on, anticipating . . . something. To her surprise nothing happened. It was just a simple gold ring that was way too big for her. Where a stone might have been there was what looked like a tiny shield. As she looked at it, she could feel it starting to get warm. "Here we go," She thought, ready to pull it off. Then she noticed it was shrinking.

"Don't worry," Connor advised. "It won't squeeze your finger off."

The ring stopped shrinking when it was a perfect fit. Rebecca held it out, admiring it. "Thank you, Connor. This means a lot to me."

"Sentimental human," Connor chided. "Did you think Arthur's ring would not be magical? Hold your hand out and think 'shield'."

Rebecca did as instructed, and a shield appeared in her hand. It was light like Excalibur.

"Nothing can get through that shield, and it will never break. With Excalibur in your right hand and that shield in your left you will be virtually unbeatable. Now, what about the other thing?" Connor stood with his arms crossed, still looking defiant.

"I think we can figure something out. It would be my pleasure to visit my friends, the Scottish fairies, from time to time."

Connor stood with a victorious smirk on his face for a moment, then kneeled and proclaimed, "All hail Queen Rebecca." The rest of his band followed suit. Then he stood. "Finnian, no hard feelings, I hope. Just business, you understand. Come join us in our feast."

Finnian, never one to hold a grudge, flew down and grabbed a jellybean. "No hard feelings," he said to Connor, shaking his hand. The fairies all grabbed a jellybean and left, leaving the empty bag.

Pip spoke first. "Rebecca, you never cease to amaze."

Naomi gave her a hug. "I am so proud of you."

Lancelot added, "You become more a queen every day."

Merlin held her fingers, examining the ring. “I wondered what happened to this. I looked everywhere for it. I never thought about the fairies. Remarkable.”

Suddenly they all heard singing coming from the direction of the dock.

Pip took off running. “I’d recognize my beautiful Amaryllis’ singing anywhere.”

“I guess that’s our cue.” Lancelot steadied Naomi as Cedric burst forth from her chest. He flew off toward the lake and the rest followed on foot. When they got to the dock, they could see Pip sitting on the dock, his legs crossed, a look of rapt admiration on his face as he listened to Amaryllis sing.

Cedric circled around the lake and came to rest in the shallow water beside the dock. “What news of Granya? I thought perhaps I could spot her from the air, but I saw nothing.”

Amaryllis paused her singing to answer. “She has agreed to meet. She is far from convinced to join us. She asked me to sing to let her know when you get here.”

“Then by all means continue.”

Amaryllis continued to sing for nearly half an hour before Granya’s head broke the surface of the still water. She did not swim to shore, however. She scrutinized the group on the dock. “There are too many. I thought there would only be Cedric and the queen. Is this a trick of some kind?”

Rebecca stepped forward. “No trick. We need the elves to travel. This is my grandmother, Naomi. Pip, the gnome, is here because . . . Well, he’s no danger to you. And the other human, George . . . He’s sort of our prisoner. Please come closer so we can talk.”

Granya came right up to the dock. She wasn’t as big as Cedric, but she was still huge. She looked Cedric up and down for a time, then tipped her head back and roared. Cedric responded in kind. She blew fire and roared again, and again Cedric responded in kind.

Finally, she spoke again. "Cedric, glad I am to see that I am not the only one of our kind still on this earth. I thought you long dead."

"I am glad as well. Long I slumbered in the wilderness, hopeless and alone. Then I was given hope by this woman and this slip of a girl. This girl bears the sword Excalibur and according to the Oracle is destined to reunite the world of magic with the human world. Come join us in our glorious cause."

"Pretty words. I too have been without hope or purpose. And I admit that I have been terribly lonely. However, I hear that Pan has other plans. I hear he will kill this puny girl—queen or not. I hear he will wipe the abomination of humanity from the earth . . . And I just might help him. What do you think of that?"

"I think you forgot your training. Your mate, Quin, was my friend as well you know. I finished my grieving long ago—when it was appropriate. One human wronged you and you want to take it out on the whole race. You got your revenge long ago on innocent villagers. They named you Granya— 'she who inspires terror'. Isn't that enough retribution? Come, live in the present with me. Build a future with me."

"Oh, I see. You thought to come here and pull lonely old Granya out of her funk and whisk her away to a bright future—with you as my new mate? Think again! I'm nobody's pushover."

Cedric was clearly shocked by this development. He truly hadn't thought of that. "I assure you my lady, mating with you never entered my mind."

"Why not? Am I not pleasing to your eye?"

While Cedric was wise, he had very little experience dealing with this sort of thing. He was contemplating a response when Rebecca stepped forward.

"Granya, may I . . .

"Silence!" Granya cut her off. Then, to punctuate her remark she blew fire straight at Rebecca. Rebecca got her new shield up in time and Merlin shielded the rest with his magic. But when the fire died down Amaryllis was gone.

"No!" Pip cried out. He fell to his knees and whimpered, "Amaryllis, my beautiful Amaryllis." Then he stiffened and stood, pulling a dagger from inside his jacket. He started walking purposefully toward Granya. "You! You killed my beautiful Amaryllis!" His face was distorted into a look of pure hate.

Granya took to the air followed by Cedric. He bathed her in fire, and she roared in pain. The shocked group on the dock watched as the two dragons circled each other, blowing fire and attacking with fang and claw—a ballet of fire and pain. They watched in silence until the dragons were out of sight over the horizon.

Merlin broke the silence. "That went well."

Pip dropped his dagger and began to sob. Rebecca fell to her knees and held him while he cried.

"Why so sad, little man?" Amaryllis materialized behind him. "I told you that dragons couldn't hurt me."

Pip ran to her and hugged her legs. She picked him up and they just held each other.

"Don't ever do that to me again," Pip chided.

Amaryllis set him back on the dock. "I guess you do care about me."

"I keep telling you that."

"I promise to believe you from now on." She bent and kissed him on the forehead.

“I hate to interrupt you two.” Rebecca said. “But what do we do now? We came here to recruit a dragon, but we seem to have lost the one we had.”

There was a pause while everyone considered the question. Pip’s face brightened up and he held up a finger as if to say something. Then his brow wrinkled, and he dropped his hand.

Merlin cleared his throat. “It may not be as bad as all that. Cedric is strong and wise. I doubt she can hurt him much. My guess is at some point they will tire of fighting and go their separate ways. We could wait here for a while. If they aren’t back by dawn, we should probably go home.”

“I agree.” Lancelot said. “There is really nothing we can do for him at this point. He is the larger, stronger of the two. The odds are in his favor.”

Naomi continued to look concerned. “Cedric is my oldest and dearest friend. I won’t rest until I know he’s safe.”

Rebecca took Naomi’s hands and looked her in the eye. “I’m sure he’ll be ok Grandma.”

“Thanks, I’m just really worried about him.”

They waited in vain until the first light appeared on the eastern horizon and then went home.

* * *

Cedric and Granya battled across Scotland and out over the Atlantic. They were interrupted by a squadron of jets. They had been spotted on radar.

“Cedric, we need to get out of here!” Granya shouted.

“For once we are in agreement. Have any ideas?”

"Follow me." She folded her wings and dove through the clouds and into the sea far below.

The jets circled a couple of times and left. The pilots vowed to say they saw an unknown aircraft that flew away at high speed. No one would believe they saw dragons fighting.

The two dragons surfaced miles from where they splashed down. They swam in silence for a while.

Finally, Cedric spoke. "That was very clever. How did you know it would work?"

"Every couple of months or so I get a hankering for fish. Plus, I get bored. I like to mess with the pilots . . . Look, Cedric, I'm sorry . . . for everything."

"You spat fire at my queen."

"I know . . . I just . . . I was so worked up and she . . . surprised me. I just reacted—like a reflex. I'm so glad no one was hurt."

"As am I. Our queen is a very resilient. You were lucky."

"I know. And I am sorry. I if they . . . if you would have me, I would be glad to join your merry band."

"If you are sincere, I'm sure I could convince them. They trust me . . . You would have to apologize to the queen personally."

"Absolutely."

"Then I accept your apology. Welcome to our clan. Well . . . I suppose we should be on our way."

"On our way where?"

"I'll show you. Do what I do."

Cedric rose into the air and turned into a ball of light as he had to enter Naomi's heart. Granya did the same. They headed west—out of

British waters. They flew close to the water and very, very fast. When they got to the coast numerous calls went in to police stations across the country reporting UFO's. Those who saw them said they appeared to be playing tag, circling each other, and flying in a very erratic fashion. Reports differed, however, on one point. Some reported two lights, and some reported only one.

27. Back home

The group of travelers rematerialized in Naomi's living room. They were all weary, having been up all-night waiting for Cedric. Since they had traveled instantaneously from Scotland, even though it was dawn when they left, it was still night in Minnesota.

"I suggest we all get some rest," Lancelot said. "We can do little about finding Cedric now and things always look better in daylight. George, if you will come with me, I'll find you a place to sleep."

Lancelot, George, and the elves left. Pip climbed up in a chair by the fireplace and said, "Merlin, how about a fire?"

"A fire? What a good idea. That ought to cheer things up a bit." Merlin waved his hand in front of the fireplace and a roaring fire sprang to life.

Rebecca walked Naomi over to the fireplace and helped her into the wingback chair. She had never seen her look so old. "You look tired, Grandma."

"I am beat, but I don't know if I can sleep. I'm so worried about Cedric."

"You needn't be." Merlin took off his fanny pack and sat on the hearth. "Cedric is a master at combat. It was he who taught Arthur. Also, you never know about dragons. He may still be able to win her over. We'll just have to wait and see."

He reached in his fanny pack and pulled out a cloth bag that was much bigger than the pack. When he dropped it on the floor it rattled as if it was full of empty tin cans. The others looked on with fascination while he started pulling things out. "I brought a few things I thought we might need. Behold! Arthur's crown." He held it up for all to see before placing it on the hearth beside him. It was a marvelous thing—solid gold, encrusted with jewels and seven equally spaced points topped with diamonds as big as a thumb. "His scepter." It was an intricately carved silver rod with a fist sized ruby at one end and a slightly smaller emerald on the other. He placed it beside the crown. "The Holy Grail." A simple metal cup. "My scrying bowl." A simple copper bowl. "Let's see." He kept digging in the bag. "That's the main items of interest, I guess. These magical relics will help you in your quest to unite the two worlds. I'll teach you about them later . . . I wonder how Imhotep is coming with the castle. I think I'll go check before I sleep."

He picked up the items he had placed on the hearth and returned the bag to his pack. Then he left without another word.

The three that remained looked at each other in silence for a few minutes. A grin slowly started to form on Pip's face. The others followed suit. Finally, Rebecca said, "The Holy Grail?" and started to laugh. The others joined in.

"That old fossil," Pip began. "He never volunteers anything. I wonder what else he's got in that bag."

"The lost Ark?" Rebecca offered.

"The keys to El Dorado?" Pip countered.

"Montezuma's gold?"

"The crown jewels of Atlantis?"

"The Spear of Destiny?"

"Crystal skulls?"

"Bigfoot?"

Pip, who had been laughing and slapping his knee, suddenly looked serious. "Oh no, I assure you no Bigfoot would ever consent to be put in that bag."

"You mean Bigfoot is real?"

"Of course. How many times do we have to tell you? If you have heard of it, it probably exists."

Rebecca, still feeling playful, countered with, "What about . . . vampires?"

"Sure, though not very common or like you might think."

"Werewolves?"

"Of course."

"Space aliens?"

"Absolutely. You would be greatly surprised at how much life there is in this big universe. There are folks from several different planets living here, and on the Moon . . . and Mars. You know, I'd love to enlighten you on the topic, but I see Naomi has fallen asleep."

Rebecca looked and in fact Naomi had fallen asleep. Rebecca found a blanket and covered her. "I think I'll turn in too," she told Pip; and went upstairs to bed.

* * *

"Wake up! Wake up!" Pip shouted as he ran into Rebecca's room.

Rebecca sat up and rubbed her eyes. It was light out. She yawned and stretched. "I'm up, already. What's all the excitement about?"

"They're back! They're back! C'mon! Let's go see!"

Rebecca, too tired the night before to get undressed, was still wearing yesterday's clothes. She pulled on her shoes and hurried after Pip. When she got outside, she saw a crowd of magicals and humans alike gathered around not one, but two dragons. Naomi was already perched on Cedric's head. She waved to Rebecca. "Come talk to our newest recruit."

The crowd parted as Rebecca walked toward the dragons. Granya bowed her head. Rebecca spoke first. "You tried to roast me."

"Please forgive my foolishness. I have only known strife from humans. I reacted badly. If you will just give me the opportunity to prove my loyalty you will not be disappointed. I vow to protect you with my life." Granya appeared to be truly repentant.

Rebecca considered her response. "I forgive you. If Cedric trusts you, and he wouldn't have brought you here if he didn't, then so do I. However, you caused a very good friend of mine a great deal of pain. I would have you perform a service for Pip—whatever he chooses."

"With pleasure, my queen."

Pip pushed through the crowd. "Could you take me down to the lake? I want to see if Amaryllis is back."

"Easily." She lowered her head to the ground. "Climb on and we'll leave at once, with Queen Rebecca's permission, of course."

Rebecca was helping Pip climb up since in his struggle to climb he had used one of Granya's nostrils as a foot hold. "Sure, go ahead."

With Pip clinging tightly to one of her ears, Granya took to the air. Until that point Rebecca had been so focused on the dragons, she hadn't noticed the fifty foot wall out beyond the barn. It was shining white stone with crenellations along the top. Every hundred feet or so was a guard tower. The driveway ran through a huge gatehouse with an iron portcullis closing the opening. All she could think of to say was "Wow!"

"If you like the wall, you should see the castle." Lancelot said. "Turn around."

Her jaw literally dropped as she looked. Behind the house a huge castle of white polished stone rose to amazing height. There were turrets and towers and stained-glass windows. It was the most beautiful, magnificent thing she had ever seen.

Imhotep stepped forward through the crowd. "Highness, are you pleased with what you see so far?"

"Yes . . . it's . . . amazing!"

"I thought perhaps you might like to have breakfast in your new dining hall."

"I'm starving." She linked her arm with Imhotep's, and they walked arm in arm toward the castle. The crowd followed. The front door was a huge gothic arch, the thick double doors standing open. The reception hall was brightly lit by crystal chandeliers and huge windows, which surprised Rebecca. She had always thought of castles as being dark and gloomy. The hall was easily big enough to hold Naomi's entire house. Their footsteps echoed as they passed through the hall.

"I apologize that the walls are bare, Highness. We will finish the decorations soon. There will be tapestries on the wall and various pieces of statuary."

"It's beautiful, Imhotep. It amazes me how you could create something this huge in just a few days."

"Magic is a wonderful thing, Highness."

They approached a large ornately carved door and Imhotep pushed it open. "Behold your dining hall. We're actually finished in here."

The main feature of the dining hall was the table. It had to be fifty feet long. Each side was lined with ornately carved chairs, with the most ornate at the end. There were statues of every kind of magical creature imaginable and tapestries on the wall. Each tapestry depicted a scene from Rebecca's life since moving to Naomi's home—even Granya's attack at Loch Ness. Imhotep escorted her to the head of the table and pulled out her chair.

"If you will be seated, we can begin." Imhotep signaled to a gnome standing by a door behind Rebecca and a group of gnomes and elves began bringing in platters of food.

The group sat down and began to eat. Rebecca was hungry. She realized it had been nearly twenty-four hours since she had eaten. It felt good to be home surrounded by her friends and family. She looked around the table and her eyes came to rest on a blond woman she didn't recognize.

"Excuse me," she said. "Excuse me." The woman's gaze met hers. "I don't seem to know who you are."

"My name is Jenny Miller. I assume you are the famous Queen Rebecca."

"I am."

"Then I am your prisoner."

"My what?"

"Your prisoner."

Jake Hanson, who was sitting beside Jenny jumped into the conversation. "Maybe I can explain. She just showed up at the front gate a couple of days ago. I let her in and told her she couldn't leave. She runs the newspaper in town and wanted to publicize our new castle. I figured you could sort it out when you got back."

"I see . . . "Rebecca suddenly wasn't hungry as she thought about this new challenge.

George O'Reilly took advantage of the pause in the conversation to introduce himself. He stood and extended his hand across the table to Jenny. "George O'Reiley, fellow prisoner."

Jenny shook his hand. "Pleased to meet you."

"The pleasure is mine."

Lancelot joined in. "Perhaps introductions are in order all round. I am Lancelot of the Lake. Before you ask, yes, that Lancelot. I knew Arthur well. I am captain of Queen Rebecca's guard and her tutor."

The rest introduced themselves one by one. Then the group fell silent.

"Your Highness," Lancelot began. "It would seem we have an issue to discuss here. Now that the castle is built it will be impossible to keep this secret for long. Of course, that means that Pan will find out. We knew that would happen eventually, but if a story were to be published in a newspaper that would hasten the inevitable."

"I could cloak the castle with magic like I did with Avalon," Merlin offered.

At that point Pip walked in. "Why does everyone look so serious? We recruited our dragon without injury. We have a beautiful new home, and my beautiful Amaryllis has agreed to wed this happy gnome. We should be celebrating." He grinned his biggest grin and everyone followed suit.

Rebecca spoke first. "Congratulations, Pip." The others followed suit.

Pip climbed into an empty chair and began filling his plate. "So, what did I miss? You guys all look like this is a funeral."

Lancelot filled him in on the conversation so far. Pip looked thoughtful as he dug into his breakfast. He paused between bites. "You know, there is a good side in all of this. The integration of magicals and humans continues. I, for one, feel grateful for that. No one has been hurt—one more thing to be grateful for. Not only that we have gained two educated and talented people. What we need to do is find something for them to do.

George, you are a researcher. Do research. You must wait to publish, of course. But publish you will. Same goes for you, Jenny. You are a writer. Write. We'll let you know when you can go public."

"Pip old man, sometimes you amaze me. You are clearly smarter than you look." Lancelot said. "What say you, George and Jenny?"

George stood. "I have spent my career trying to solve many of history's riddles. I see this as the opportunity of a lifetime. I graciously accept this offer." He sat back down.

It was Jenny's turn to stand. "Since I got locked up here, I have seen things I thought existed only in fairy tales. I would love to write this story. It's the story of a lifetime. It will make my career . . . But I won't write a word unless I can come and go as I please."

"Would you agree to keep our secret until we say it's ok to go public? Our lives may depend on it." Rebecca asked.

Jenny looked into Rebecca's eyes. She saw innocence there, but wisdom as well. She also got a sense of integrity. "I agree."

"What about you, George?"

"I would like to be able to come and go as I please. An Irishman can keep a secret."

"Ok then, it's settled. Now let's finish breakfast. My pancakes are getting cold."

* * *

After breakfast the tour continued. There was the throne room, where Rebecca would receive visitors. Also, there was a library, game room, a gymnasium, an elevator, and many bedrooms. By far, Rebecca's favorite part of the tour was the Queens Chambers.

Imhotep told her they were going into the Queen's Chambers before he pushed open the double doors. What she saw was a big, beautiful room with a couch, chairs, and a fireplace, but no bed.

"Where's the bed?" she asked.

Imhotep chuckled. "This is but the antechamber. The bedroom lies beyond." He opened a door that sort of blended in with the other wall panels. Rebecca stepped in and looked around before flopping on her back on the king-sized canopied bed.

“This is awesome, Imhotep.” She said.

“Thank you, Highness. Through here is your bath, and here your closet and dressing room. And here,” He opened the double glass door. “Is the balcony you requested.”

Rebecca followed him out onto the balcony. Wildfire, her winged horse waited for her there. She greeted him by rubbing his velvet nose.

“Does this meet with your approval, Highness?”

“Yes, Imhotep. I don’t know what to say. I’m overwhelmed—and that takes a lot these days. Thank you.” Rebecca hugged him.

“It was my pleasure, Highness. It has been a long while since I had a free hand to build something of this scale. With your permission I will order your things moved in.”

“That would be great! Thanks.”

“One last thing, I should show you the secret escape passages. No castle is complete without them.”

“Cool! Then I’m going to try out that big tub. I reek.”

28. Meetings

"I think we should have a party to celebrate Pip and Amaryllis' engagement." Rebecca told her grandmother over lunch.

"That would be nice," Naomi replied. "We certainly have the space for it. We'll have to get together and plan something . . . You know Rebecca, I've been thinking. We should have regular meetings. There's a lot of stuff going on these days, and we need to stay on top of things or it's going to be pretty chaotic. Perhaps we could meet here in the dining hall—maybe over breakfast each day."

"That's a great idea, Grandma. I have been wondering about that. I feel like I'm just flailing around in the dark. At least this way I'll feel like, at least for that day, I know what's going on."

"Let's do it then. Who should we invite?"

"Well . . . you and me, Lancelot, and Pip . . . Finnian and both our wizards. I'd like Cedric here. He's so wise."

"Absolutely. Now that he can come and go as he pleases, he can attend with me. What about Celestine? I hear she's been working with Steve Lund to integrate elfin medical techniques into the mainstream. That could be an important part of bringing the two worlds together."

"I agree. But you know, if she comes, we'll probably get Jake Hanson too. I hear he follows her around like a puppy."

Naomi chuckled. "I've known Jake for a few years now and I've never seen him so calm. Who knew a goblin could cause such misery."

"I know. That one I had was awful. It seemed like the whole world crashed down on me. I'm so glad Pip was there." Rebecca was quiet for a moment, remembering that terrible time. She shook her head than smiled. I wonder what's really going on with those two."

Naomi smiled. "I'm sure I don't know . . . nor do I want to."

They both laughed.

After lunch Rebecca and Naomi spent the rest of the afternoon inviting people to the first breakfast council meeting. Naomi ran into Jenny, who was following Imhotep around. It occurred to her it would be nice if someone recorded their meetings, so she invited her. Rebecca found Randy working out in the gym.

"Rebecca, I'm so glad you're back!" He would have hugged her, but he was all sweaty.

Rebecca was thinking she wouldn't mind so much. "I'm glad I'm back too. Did you hear about Pip and Amaryllis?"

"Everybody's talking about it."

"Isn't it wonderful?"

"Yeah . . . I guess."

There was a long pause while they each struggled for something to say. Rebecca spoke first. "I was thinking of visiting Amaryllis. Do you want to walk with me?"

"I would, but I'm all sweaty. I should shower."

"I don't care about that. Wipe yourself off with a towel. I want to tell you about my trip."

She did just that as they walked out the front gate—the new wall blocking the old trail. When they were a hundred feet or so past the gate Rebecca turned back to view the castle. Her face went white.

"What's wrong?" Randy's hand went to his sword, which he was rarely without these days.

"It's the same as my dream. I had a dream where I was fighting Pan one on one in front of this castle. It didn't turn out well."

Randy took her right hand in his left and with his right turned her chin so he could look into her eyes. "It was just a dream. I'll tell you a secret. Freddy Kruger used to scare the crap out of me when I was a kid. But one day I realized it was just a movie. It's not scary anymore."

"But this is the exact castle from the dream."

"That still doesn't mean the dream will come true. I think we should ask Cedric or that Merlin guy. One of them should know what it means."

Rebecca thought a minute before replying. "I suppose you're right. At least I can't do anything about it in this moment Let's go talk to Amaryllis and then see if we can find someone who can explain my dream."

Which is exactly what they did.

* * *

Rebecca's first night in her new home passed without incident. Heather and Randy each had a guest room down the hall from the Queen's Chambers. In fact, most who had fought the trolls decided to move into the castle until Pan was no longer a threat. They had stayed up late watching movies on the theater-sized TV in the entertainment room. Rebecca had to admit it was pretty easy getting used to living in a castle.

All the invited guests were in attendance at breakfast, as well as Heather, Randy, and George O'Reiley. They decided to wait until after breakfast to start the meeting.

"I wanted to thank you all for coming." Rebecca began. "You have all been so much help to me so far and I couldn't think about being a queen without your help."

Merlin spoke next. "I think I can speak for everyone when I say it is an honor. I have taken the liberty of drawing up an agenda." He pulled a paper out of his shirt pocket, unfolded it, and handed it to Rebecca.

She looked it over and said, "This looks ok for a place to start. Thank you. Should I just go ahead?"

Merlin nodded.

"Ok, the first thing on the list is privacy."

Merlin picked it up from there. "I think it is clear to everyone that we need to hide this castle. I was able to hide Avalon from prying eyes for over fifteen hundred years by surrounding it with a magical shield. If you approve, I could start this morning."

Jake Hanson spoke up. "I think that's a great idea. It would cut down on uninvited guests." He was looking at Jenny while he spoke. She gave him the stink-eye in return.

"No offense, Jenny and George, but I agree." Rebecca responded. "If there are no objections I say we do it." No one objected, so she went on. "Code? What does that mean?"

"I was thinking we need a code of laws, a declaration of rights and so on. We are after all building a kingdom here. Which reminds me, what are we going to call our little kingdom?"

"I thought it was New Camelot." Jenny offered, looking at Jake. "I mean, it fits. You've got the last descendent of Arthur, Merlin, Lancelot and even a dragon."

"I like it." Rebecca declared. "If there are no objections . . ." She looked around the table. "Ok, New Camelot it is. Also, I think having a code of laws is a good idea. Maybe we could have a group, like a committee, working on it. What do you think?"

"I think a committee is a good idea." Naomi said. "Perhaps we could ask for volunteers."

"Volunteers is a good idea. Any objections?" Rebecca looked around the table. "Ok, let's do it . . . Let's see. What comes next? School. Merlin?"

"I am worried about school. I understand public school starts in a few weeks and Rebecca is still expected to attend?"

Naomi nodded.

"I think this is a very bad idea. The opportunities for disaster are incalculable."

"I agree," Lancelot spoke up. "Just showing up would eventually get back to Pan."

"We could do home-school." Naomi offered. "I would have to do some paperwork, but that's about it."

"Can I come too?" Heather asked.

"Could she, Grandma? That would so great!" Rebecca was clearly enthusiastic about the idea.

While Naomi considered this question Merlin spoke. "You know, we could get the finest teachers and provide the finest education available. Perhaps we could form another committee to put something together."

"Ok," Naomi began. "Let's put a committee together."

Everyone looked to Rebecca for approval. "Ok, I love this plan . . . That's everything on the list. I think we should plan a party to celebrate Pip's engagement."

"You know how I love a party." Pip said. "I would be happy to head up a committee for that."

"Objections?" There were none, so Rebecca said, "Ok, Pip, go ahead . . . What else do we need to talk about?"

"As long as you're forming committees, I think you need a committee to oversee bringing more humans in. My own experience wasn't pleasant." Jenny looked pointedly at Jake. "And I think you should involve that deputy—what was his name? Turnquist, Andy Turnquist."

The group was silent for a bit. Most thought the committee was a good idea but were not sure about Andy. At last Cedric spoke. "I think that is a good idea. We must think of the future."

"Here, here!" Merlin declared. "And in that vein, I feel I must bring something up. I watched the news yesterday and I think Pan is up to something. There have been plane crashes, erupting volcanoes, hurricanes, etc. The world seems to be going crazy. I'm not sure what, if anything, we can do; but I think, as a start, we should investigate."

"I could ask some of the lads to check things out." Lancelot offered.

Rebecca was saddened by this development. It really brought home the reality that being a real-life fairy princess had its downside. Clearly, there was an issue of responsibility here. At length she said, "Go ahead, Lancelot." She was just glad he wasn't going himself.

He nodded in response.

Merlin spoke again. "Now that that's settled, I have another matter." He reached in his ever-present fanny pack and pulled out the cloth bag of artifacts and set it on the table. "I thought we should go through these and talk about your coronation."

Rebecca was getting used to the idea of being a queen and was curious about the things she and Pip had seen the night they got back from Avalon. Her face lit up and she said, "Yeah, let's do that."

Merlin stood up and pulled out the crown. "The crown of Arthur. Here let me place it on your head." He walked to her and set it on her head. It slid down and sat on her ears. "I was afraid of that. Here let me fix that." He lifted the crown a bit with both hands and closed his eyes. The crown started to shrink until it was a perfect fit. "There, that's better. Now look at me."

As Rebecca did so, a wave of dizziness swept over her. There were gasps from some of the humans at the table. Though she couldn't see it, the gems on the points of the crown started to glow. Then beams of light connected the gems and a white glow appeared in the center, mere inches above her head.

"There is a reason men have long valued gold and jewels. Put together in the right configuration and worn, they can enhance human abilities. The crown of Arthur enhances your mental abilities. That's why you felt a bit dizzy when you put the crown on. How do you feel?"

"Well . . . I'm not dizzy any more. Everything does seem a bit brighter . . . and I can hear birds outside . . . and gnomes talking in the kitchen. Wow!"

Merlin removed the crown and set it on the table. He pulled out the scepter. "The Scepter of Arthur. No one can lie to you while you hold it and if you ask someone a question while pointing it at them, they must answer."

Rebecca took the scepter. She got a mischievous grin and pointed it at Heather. "What's the juiciest piece of gossip you know?"

"Becky Bjornson is pregnant." Heather blurted out before clamping both hands over her mouth.

"No way!" Rebecca gasped. She didn't know Becky well, only that she was older and the head cheerleader for the football team.

"It's true," Heather growled. "It has to be. You used that . . . thing on me. Which, by the way, don't ever do that to me again."

"I'm sorry. I won't. We'll have to talk more about that later."

Heather's smile returned. "You bet we will."

Merlin took the scepter and placed it on the table with the crown. "That's probably enough of that." He reached into the bag and pulled out the next object.

"The Grail," Lancelot whispered.

"My old friend is correct. The Grail is the most potent healing device known to man or magical. A drink from it can heal any wound, cure any illness. It can't raise the dead, but it can extend life."

"You old fox." Lancelot said. "You have been saving the crown jewels of Camelot all these years. I'll bet you've been drinking from the Grail too."

"From time to time, though it's been a while. I longed to see the day when Camelot rose again. I've had to wait a long time and I'm grateful to be here."

"As am I." Lancelot affirmed.

Pip was getting impatient. "We're all glad to be here and all; but what else is in that bag?"

Merlin scowled at Pip and resumed emptying his bag. He held up a copper bowl. "My scrying bowl. I had hoped to gain some insight into the Oracle's cryptic answer. 'There is nothing harder than stone and nothing softer than water. Yet water can prevail over stone' or something to that effect . . . Nothing so far."

Pip spoke up again. "I had an idea about that. I think the stone is Pan and the water is Rebecca."

"Thus proving that some things are obvious to even the simplest of minds," quipped Lancelot. "But what do you do with this knowledge? I had thought perhaps it was some martial arts reference, but frankly I'm at a loss."

Merlin continued looking in his bag, rummaging around with his hand. He finally decided to just empty the contents on the table. "The crown jewels of Camelot. Nice baubles, but not magical."

Rebecca pulled a necklace out of the pile. It was beautiful. It had diamonds, rubies and emeralds set in gold in a crescent pattern that, when she put it on, reached from the clasp in back and fell mid-way on her chest.

Heather stared at it, transfixed. "It's beautiful. It must be worth a fortune."

"Priceless, I suppose," Merlin replied. "It was part of Guinevere's dowry. She wore it at her wedding."

Rebecca held the necklace, scrutinizing it closely. She thought about her ancestor wearing this at her wedding—an arranged marriage, probably not much older than Rebecca is now. She suddenly felt a strong connection with this ancient woman. How hard it must have been for her—going into hiding with her infant daughter after Arthur's death. Stuck in a situation not of her making. Somehow that thought gave her strength.

"Thank you, Merlin, for saving all this for me." She stood up and kissed the old wizard on the cheek, his beard scratching her face. "I think maybe we could end the meeting for today; if that's ok."

The group got up to go on about their business for the day.

* * *

After the meeting Cedric went looking for Granya. He hadn't seen her at all this morning, and he was starting to worry. He flew up and over the woods and soon spotted her in a small valley in the far corner of Naomi's farm. She seemed to be feverishly digging. He circled around and landed beside her.

"Granya, what are you doing?"

"Digging." She didn't even look up.

"I can see that, but why?" He hated these kinds of games.

"I can't very well build a nest without digging a hole, now can I?"

Smoke puffed out of Cedric's nostrils. "A nest? You mean . . ."

"Yes, I'm going to lay eggs. If all these changes you talk about are coming, I wanted our children to be part of it. Also, I think we have a duty to bring our kind back from the brink of extinction."

“I am pleased, Granya.”

“Then perhaps instead of standing there crowing you could gather some cattails for bedding.”

“As you wish, Granya. As you wish.” Cedric took off in the direction of the swamp.

29. The Party

Rebecca was practicing archery behind the barn when she heard someone calling. She turned to look and saw Imhotep striding toward her followed closely by Pip.

"Highness," Imhotep began. "We need a decision. Pip here is insisting I put a fountain right in the middle of the reception hall. The hall is nearly complete. His fountain would disrupt the traffic flow. Impossible, simply impossible."

"What's the big deal?" Pip insisted. "All he needs to do is wave that staff of his. He can change things around however he wants. He's just angry because he wants to keep his elegant design."

Rebecca held up her hands in a "hush" gesture. She hated to contradict Imhotep. He had, after all, built her the most beautiful castle. However, Pip was her special friend. She couldn't make this decision lightly.

"I think we better go look," she said. They started off for the castle and soon stood in the grand reception hall. She turned to Pip. "So, what do you want?"

He strode to the middle of the huge black-and-white checkered floor. "The problem is that, as a water nymph, Amaryllis must remain near to her spring—or at least water that's connected to her spring. As things are now, she can't even attend her own engagement party. I want a spring right here—with a fountain and a sculpture of Amaryllis and me pouring water from a pot. It would be easy for him." He pointed at Imhotep. "But he won't do it."

"How hard would it be?" Rebecca asked Imhotep.

"Not difficult at all. He never told me why he wanted it." Imhotep explained. He held out his hand and an intricately carved wooden staff appeared in his hand. It was covered with some kind of writing and had a purple crystal as big as a fist fastened on top. The crystal started to glow.

He walked over to where Pip was standing and struck the floor hard with the bottom end of the staff. The floor cracked. There was a rumble from deep underground. Water started to flow from the crack. He then drew a circle about eight feet in diameter around the crack. The floor started to shimmer where he drew the circle. Then a circular wall started to rise from the floor. It rose to a height of about two feet, forming a basin that started to fill with water. He waved his hand and an intricate relief carving started to emerge from the stone wall. It was a forest motif.

Then he turned his attention to the center. He moved his hands as if sculpting. A pillar of stone rose from the center, water pouring from the top. Slowly it started to take shape. It formed into a life-size sculpture of Pip and Amaryllis holding a pot between them, water pouring from the spout. Pip stood on a stump.

"It's beautiful!" Rebecca exclaimed.

As she watched, a column of water rose from the fountain and Amaryllis took shape. She stepped out on the floor and hugged Pip, picking him up. "Thank you, Pip."

Imhotep turned to Rebecca and said. "Isn't that typical. I do all the work and he gets the credit."

Amaryllis put Pip down and kissed Imhotep on the cheek. "And thank you. I will not forget."

"It was my pleasure, my dear . . . Well, I have things to do." Imhotep walked away.

Amaryllis turned to Rebecca. "And thank you, Your Highness. You have a way of making your subjects feel important."

"You are important to me . . . and call me Rebecca."

* * *

The next morning at breakfast Rebecca brought up a kind of a touchy subject. She had argued with Heather about it the night before.

"I feel we need to discuss something. Apparently, Heather and Randy have told some of their friends our secret. I thought the rest of you should know."

Her announcement was met with silence. Randy nervously tapped his fork on his plate. Heather glared at Rebecca.

Finally, Naomi spoke. "Well, I think it's a good thing. Now Rebecca can invite some people nearer her age to the party. Eventually everyone is going to know anyway. We can't un-tell them. So, let's make the most of the situation."

Heather perked up at this, feeling somewhat vindicated.

"Do you really think that is a good idea?" Rebecca asked.

"I think it's a great idea."

Rebecca smiled at Heather. "Oh good. That sounds like fun.

* * *

By any measure the party was a huge success. There was a feast in the dining hall followed by dancing in the reception hall. A band of gnomes and elves played a waltz while Amaryllis and Pip danced the first dance. Amaryllis actually picked Pip up and held him like a child while she danced gracefully around the hall. It was comical and sweet to watch, and the crowd applauded when the song ended.

Then the band picked up the pace and nearly everyone joined in. There were chairs set up along the walls for people who weren't dancing. Naomi found one of these. Merlin soon joined her.

"Not dancing?" He asked.

"I think I'm starting to feel my age after all these years."

"Nonsense! Just look at Imhotep dancing with that stunning water nymph. He's older than me—by thousands of years. If I didn't know the story, I would suspect he installed that spring just so Amaryllis' fellow water nymphs could attend."

They both laughed before Merlin continued. "All joking aside, I know that having Cedric inside you all those years slowed your aging process, allowing you to live well beyond the usual human lifespan—but aging none-the-less. I wanted to tell you that we could reverse all that."

"I know you hinted at that before; but I don't know if I want to. I've had a pretty good life compared to most."

"But don't you want to live to see Rebecca mature into a woman in her own right, have children of her own? Don't you want to share her adventure?"

"You make a compelling point, Merlin. What would I have to do?"

Merlin reached into his fanny pack and pulled out the Grail. "Drink from the Grail. I do it about every sixty years or so. There are other ways, of course. But this is by far the best. In a few moments time it will heal all the damage we call aging."

Naomi considered his proposal. It would be nice to feel young again. The trouble with aging slowly is that you spend so many years feeling old. And it would be nice to see Rebecca grow and have a family—more than she had dared hoped for, actually.

"Alright, I'll do it."

They walked arm in arm through the dancers to the fountain. Merlin held the Grail in the stream and filled it. Then he drank it dry. He filled it again and offered it to Naomi.

She took it, said, "Here's mud in your eye." and drained it. She handed it back and Merlin replaced it in his pack. She could see Merlin had already started to change. His hair and beard were rapidly losing their grey and his skin looked smooth and supple. She looked at her own hands. They were the hands of a young woman—no age spots or wrinkles. She pulled a handful of her hair around where she could see it. She hadn't seen that rich brunette color in her hair in at least fifty years. And she felt great.

Merlin offered his hand and said, "Would the lady care to dance?"

She took his hand and replied, "I would love to."

They started to step out onto the dance floor, and he stopped—holding Naomi's hand at arm's length. He looked both of them up and down. "This will never do. Are you familiar with the tale of Cinderella?"

"Of course."

"Good. You're about to re-enact it." He waved his hand over his body and in a flash the jeans and flannel shirt he always wore were replaced with a rather elegant tuxedo, complete with black tie and cufflinks. He looked quite handsome.

Then he turned to Naomi. He waved his hand and instantly she was clad in a gown of deep blue, sleeveless and form-fitting on top with a loose long skirt for dancing. He drew a circle in the air with his finger and a pearl necklace appeared. Next he poked his finger as if dotting an invisible I. Matching earrings appeared.

Naomi regarded their new outfits appreciatively and said, "Merlin, you do know how to turn a girl's head."

"Now we're ready to dance." The current song was a waltz and they swirled onto the floor.

As they were dancing, Merlin said, "You know, I've been thinking about taking an apprentice. Are you interested?"

"Why . . . Merlin, if I didn't know better, I'd think you were looking for an excuse to spend more time with me."

Merlin laughed. "Am I that obvious? It's the Grail. Every time I get young, I get yearnings. Very distracting. But my offer still stands."

"You know, Merlin, I've always wanted to know more about magic."

Soon the other dancers moved back and gave the couple room. When the song was over the crowd applauded. Rebecca came out of the crowd.

"Grandma? Is that you?" Rebecca had never even seen pictures of Naomi when she was young.

"Yes, isn't it wonderful?" They held hands like excited schoolgirls. "I have Merlin to thank. Oh . . . and he's going to teach me magic." The music started again. "I'm going to dance again. I haven't danced in years. Go have fun, dear."

As Rebecca watched the couple dance away, she couldn't help but think, "This is going to take some getting used to." But then considering everything she had already gotten used to, this was a relatively minor—yet wonderful—thing. She was happy for Naomi.

Before she could move from the spot Brad, one of Randy's friends from the football team, asked her to dance. She accepted. In fact, as the night wore on, she probably danced with most of the football team. At one point she just had to rest. She sat along the edge of the dance floor sipping punch, watching the dancers. This was people watching at its finest.

Merlin and her grandmother seemed to be having a really good time. She was happy for them. Somehow, Heather had convinced Lancelot to dance with her. She didn't quite know how she felt about that, but decided it was kind of funny. Then she saw the healer elf Celestine and Jake Hanson across the dance floor, talking. He had been following her around like a puppy since the battle. Everyone was talking about it. She wondered what they were talking about. In fact, her imaginings were not far from the truth.

Celestine leaned back in her chair and regarded Jake with a lock of mild amusement. Jake was talking, something he did often.

"So, just think about it. Doesn't this engagement mean that people don't have to be the same to be together? I'm not saying we need to get married. At least not right away. But we could have dates. We could tell people we're dating. You'd be able to say, 'Jake is my boyfriend'. I would be proud—the proudest—to refer to you as my girlfriend. So, what do you think?"

Celestine was not surprised by his declaration of affection. That part she had known for weeks—everyone had known for weeks. She had been pursued before in her long life. She had even been married a couple of times. But this human—this Jake—was different than anyone she had ever met. There was something charming, yet . . . untamed about him.

"What do I think? I think a lot of things. I think you are a great warrior. I think you are very resourceful. And I think you are cute when you try to talk about your tender feelings. I would love to go on a date with you and see where this goes. In fact, let's call this a date. Come dance with me."

She rose and held out her hand. Jake took it and they danced. Rebecca smiled. She was sure there was something going on between them and this just proved it. She was glad, even if Jake was a little odd.

Rebecca was not particularly surprised when she noticed George O'Reiley and Jenny Miller dancing. They had been spending a lot of time together. It seemed like everyone was getting together. There must be something in the air tonight—magic. She chuckled at that. She had heard that phrase many times, but tonight it might actually be true.

Then she noticed Amaryllis walking her way. Soon she was sitting beside her.

“Rebecca, I wanted to thank you again for this wonderful party. I haven’t been to many parties. Alas, the life of a nymph can be a lonely one.”

“I was happy to do it. Pip is such a wonderful little guy.”

“He’s the most wonderful guy—of any size.”

“May I ask you something personal?”

“Of course.”

“I was wondering, what made you suddenly decide to marry Pip?”

Amaryllis laughed. “You know, he’s been after me for the longest time. But I’ve known many a nymph who ended up with a broken heart because of some guy with charm and a sense of humor. And Pip could—can—make me laugh like no other.”

“He can be pretty funny sometimes.”

“Yes, and I thought him just a funny little distraction; a friend filled with mischief and jokes. But when I saw how devastated he was when he thought I had been killed by Granya, I knew he really cared for me. And I realized I really cared for him.”

Just then Pip appeared out of the crowd. “Amaryllis, I think it’s time.” He started pulling a chair toward the band. “Rebecca, find Randy. Amaryllis is going to sing.”

She found Randy talking to some of his friends just as Pip, standing on a chair, started to speak.

“If I could have your attention for a minute. I wanted to thank you all for sharing this happy occasion with us. As much as I’m sure you all would love to listen to me blather on, Amaryllis has agreed to sing for you. So, grab someone you like and dance to the music of my lovely bride-to-be."

Rebecca saw Naomi leading Merlin to the dance floor. She turned to Randy to ask him to dance, but he beat her to it. Amaryllis began to sing a beautiful ballad, and everyone began to dance. It was a slow dance.

Randy, who had never heard Amaryllis sing before was quite mesmerized by it. Rebecca's voice brought him out of his reverie.

"Earth to Randy. . . Aren't you supposed to be paying attention to your partner when you dance?"

Randy smiled down at her. "I'm sorry. It's just I've never heard her sing before . . . She's really something."

"Yes, I know . . . Your dancing is improving."

"Thanks . . . I noticed you were dancing with a lot of guys tonight."

"Are you jealous?"

"No . . . Maybe. I don't know what to think. Everything has changed. When I first met you just a few weeks ago you were just the friend of my kid sister. Now, you're the Queen—complete with a castle and an army. I wonder if you might be out of my league . . . Plus, I know those guys. Some of them don't have much respect for women."

Rebecca laughed. "I don't know about being out of your league. I'm still just a girl. But you've changed too. When I first met you, you were a big arrogant jerk. You didn't have much respect for women either. You've changed into someone I actually like."

"Really?"

"Yes really. Why do you think I keep bugging you to dance with me at these things? Anyway, since we're talking about this, I don't know what is going to happen here. Pan may break in here and kill everyone tomorrow. Plus, I do have a lot of responsibilities. So, I don't think I'm ready for a steady boyfriend right now. But I would like a special friend, a male friend—not a boyfriend."

"I see," Randy said rather glumly.

"I don't think you do. You are currently my male companion of choice. I have feelings for you. I just don't want to rush into anything."

"That's better, I guess . . . But, Rebecca, I'm older . . . A guy has needs.

Rebecca laughed. "I think you are confusing your wants with your needs . . . Wow, just listen to me. I'm starting to sound like Lancelot. Anyway, I have wants too. One of them is to wait until I'm ready for certain things. Some of the others might surprise you. As far as the age thing goes, think of this. When I'm eighteen, you'll be twenty-one. That's an acceptable age difference in anyone's book."

Randy did think about it for a while. Finally, he said, "Ok, so is one of your wants to kiss me?"

"I thought you'd never figure it out."

They stepped behind a statue, and he held her in his arms and gently kissed her lips. It was her first real kiss from a boy. They just stood there holding each other for a few minutes, enjoying the goodness of the moment. They walked out hand in hand.

"See?" Rebecca started. "Sometimes we want the same things, so don't be shy about telling me what you want. Just do it with respect and the knowledge that I might not want the same thing and we'll be alright."

"How did you get so smart, anyway?"

"The best teachers in the world."

* * *

Everyone had a good time that night except Granya. She had begged off, telling Cedric that she wanted to attend to her nest. In fact, she was ready to lay her eggs and as soon as Cedric was gone, she did. As she carefully covered the dozen eggs with leaves and cattails a single tear rolled down her cheek.

She knew what she had to do, and she knew it would be dangerous. If things went badly, she knew her eggs would hatch without her. It was the dragon's way. Cedric would teach her children well.

She rose into the air and took a last look at the castle. Then she turned into a ball of light and sped away. She had a long way to travel and wanted to be back before Cedric returned.

She found Pan standing on a hill watching a river of red-hot lava destroying a village, a look of smug satisfaction on his face. She resumed her natural form and called to him.

"Great Pan, I have news of great import."

Pan looked up at her. "Approach, dragon, and share your news."

Granya landed on the hill beside Pan. "I am Granya."

"Ah, yes. Granya, the 'Loch Ness Monster.' I know of you. I always found your exploits amusing. What news do you bring?"

"If you know me, you know I have no love for mankind."

"I know this."

"What you don't know is that your nemesis Rebecca lives."

"What!?" His shout echoed across the valley. "I was assured she was dead. What evidence do you have?"

"I have seen her myself just yesterday. Her followers recruited me and brought me to their castle stronghold. Their numbers swell each day. They think I am with them, but I have eggs. I won't see my children grow up in the shadow of mankind."

Pan roared. He stomped his feet, and the earth shook. “I knew there was a castle, but I was assured she was gone. I can think of a gremlin and a troll who will answer for their incompetence. You will be rewarded for this if it proves true. If you will excuse me, I have some thinking to do.”

That was fine with Granya. She needed to get back as well.

30. The Battle

The morning after the party Rebecca slept in. She had been up until nearly dawn. It was quite a party. She lay in bed a while, thinking . . . of a kiss. She was happy for Pip and Amaryllis . . . and for herself. She sat up and stretched. Looking through the glass doors onto her balcony she could see it was a beautiful summer day. The late morning sun glistened off the polished railing on the balcony and there was . . . a crow preening himself there.

She opened the doors to the balcony and still the crow sat. He cawed. There was something strange about this crow. Suddenly she knew. In an instant she had Excalibur in hand and her shield up. "Marid!" She spat. In her next breath, "Guards!"

The crow jumped down to the floor and resumed his natural angry teddy bear shape. "At your service my queen." He kneeled before her.

Rebecca was unimpressed. "What do you want?" Two guards—a gnome and an elf—burst onto the balcony, swords raised.

"I bring a warning, my queen. Pan comes. He knows you are alive. I seek refuge. Pan will kill me if he finds me. I told him you were dead."

Fear swept over her. Then she stopped to consider his request. She turned to the guards. "Do we have somewhere we can lock him up?"

"Yes, Your Highness. There is a dungeon."

Dungeon? She could almost hear Imhotep say, "No castle is complete without a dungeon."

"Ok, lock him up and sound the alarm. We need to get ready for Pan."

* * *

Rebecca stood on the outer wall of her castle looking toward the woods. She was wearing her new armor—elfin armor. It looked just like regular clothes but would stop a bullet. Then a thought hit her like a hammer. "This is just like my dream."

Lancelot, standing beside her, noticed the color leave her face. He bent down to whisper. "Steady on, old girl. We have two wizards, two dragons and hundreds of the best fighters in the world. Nobody is going to hurt you today. Chin up, you don't want to invite a goblin in."

She smiled at him. "I know. Thanks . . . for everything."

Lancelot look at her quizzically. "That almost sounded like you were saying goodbye."

"Maybe I am . . . Lancelot, I had a dream. It was just like this. My armor was the same. The castle was the same. Only I had the dream before the castle was built . . . and I didn't win."

"I see . . . Well, I can see how that might be a little unsettling. Remember your mindfulness training. What should you do now?"

"Be in the present moment—without evaluating it."

"Very good. You are my best student—and I've had a few."

Rebecca hugged him. "Thanks, Dad."

Lancelot laughed.

As they looked out over the battlement Pan strode proudly out into the pasture. He stopped about a hundred yards away. "Rebecca, come out and face me." He called.

"I don't think so," She replied. "I heard you play rough. Can't we talk this out? I think we want many of the same things."

"We may indeed want many of the same things; but there is one thing I want that you don't—the end of humanity. There can be no peace while you and the other human vermin live."

The two dragons were standing with their hind feet on the ground and front feet on the wall, observing the whole scene. At this point in the conversation Granya took to the air. She flew directly to Pan and lit in front of him. He didn't react. It was clear they were not enemies.

Cedric gasped. "Granya . . . What have you done?"

The army watched nervously as Granya walked up to Pan. They could see them speaking but couldn't hear what was being said. Cedric hung his head in shame at what his new mate had done.

Suddenly, Granya blew fire directly into Pan's face. He flailed his arms wildly and finally connected to Granya's jaw and she tumbled through the air and landed—motionless.

But Pan was clearly blind—his eyes completely gone. The archers took that as their cue and hundreds of arrows flew at Pan. Most of them hit and Pan fell. A cheer went up from those manning the wall. These were the same arrows that only took one to kill a troll. They were sure he was dead even though he didn't "flash out" like the trolls. He just lay still.

"That seems too easy." Lancelot observed.

"I'm going to go make sure he's dead." Rebecca started for the stairs.

Lancelot ran after her. He grabbed her arm and turned her around. "It isn't safe. Let others do this."

There was fire in her eyes. "I am the queen. He was here to kill me. I'm doing this."

She ran down the stairs and out the gate. She soon stood next to Pan; Excalibur raised in both hands—ready to behead her mortal enemy. Quick as a wink Pan's hand lashed out and he had Rebecca by the ankle. He stood and started to grow. Soon he stood twenty feet tall, holding Rebecca upside down by the ankle. She bent at the waist and swung Excalibur at his arm. It sliced through like it was nothing and she fell, landing on her feet. She ran twenty feet or so and turned, sword high and shield up.

She gasped when she saw Pan. His arm was whole—just like her dream. Unlike her dream, Lancelot stood beside her, sword in hand. He was soon joined by hundreds of others. Cedric circled overhead.

She turned to Lancelot. “I’m sorry, you were right. What do we do now?”

“Get you back to the castle for a start.”

He had no sooner finished when Pan waved his hand. Lancelot and the soldiers behind him flew away like leaves in an autumn storm. He waved his other hand and the soldiers on the other side of Rebecca flew away. Cedric circled above—watching.

This was just like her dream, and she knew how it would end. She accepted it, but she refused to surrender. Her focus was as sharp as a dragon’s tooth. She looked up to Cedric’s eyes and saw the wisdom and love there. She thought of her grandmother and the day they rode Cedric together. Suddenly she knew what to do.

Her focus shifted inside, and time seemed to stop. She looked for the connection Cedric had shown her—and found it. She followed the connection to the Source. A wave of nearly overwhelming unconditional love swept over her, and she gasped. Instead of being pulled into the light like before, the light was filling her. She could feel it in every fiber of her being. She felt connected to everything.

She looked at Pan and saw him through new eyes. She could see hatred flowing from him in waves. Behind the hatred was fear. But deep inside there was a small flicker, a shadow of what he used to be and could be again. It was trapped by millennia of anger and poor decisions. She could literally feel his pain—the pain of being cut off from the Source for thousands of years; the pain of knowing it had all been by his own choice.

The Oracle's words suddenly made sense. Pan can't be killed, but he can be defeated. Nothing is harder than stone—Pan. Nothing is softer than water—Rebecca. They had figured out that much. They just couldn't figure out what to do with that knowledge. Now she knew—live in the present, and in that present moment she would make an ally of Pan or die trying. She could think of only one way to do that.

She spoke, though she was sure the voice wasn't her own and just a whisper. "I forgive you."

Pan grimaced as if in pain. "What did you say!?" He sounded shocked.

Louder this time. "I forgive you"

"HOW DARE YOU? I am the Great God Pan. It is mine to forgive or not."

She put away her sword and shield. This time she spoke so loudly the ground shook and the trees trembled—definitely not her own voice. "I forgive you. You killed my mother and I forgive you."

He grimaced again.

"You tried to kill me, not just once but four times and I forgive you." She could feel unconditional love flowing through her from the Source. It was like a shield, deflecting Pan's hatred. Pan fell to his knees and shrank back to the size of a man.

"You tried to wipe out humanity and I forgive you." She walked forward and placed her hand on his forehead. "You have murdered many and I forgive you."

Pan looked into her eyes, a plaintive look. "I'm begging you. Please stop."

"I forgive you," she responded.

Pan fell to the ground, balled up in pain.

Rebecca actually felt sorry to see him in that state. “I forgive you,” she repeated.

Pan started to glow, and Rebecca backed away, not knowing what to expect. Lancelot and Pip joined her. She saw Cedric land by Granya, who still lay motionless on the ground. Pan glowed brighter and brighter. Soon the onlookers had to shield their eyes and retreat farther. At length the glow stopped.

Rebecca opened her eyes and, in a year of astonishing surprises, could hardly believe her what she saw. There, standing in the sunlit bright green meadow, was a beautiful white unicorn. He seemed to glow in the sunlight. He shook his head and made that horse sound with his lips.

Then he spoke in a beautiful, melodious voice. “Thank you. Compassion is the strongest magic and your compassion redeemed me. So, I thought I would assume a pleasing shape.”

“Pan?” Rebecca inquired.

“None other, my queen.” He bowed. “If you will excuse me for a moment, there is someone who needs my immediate attention.”

He trotted over to Granya and lay his horn on her forehead. A soft glow came from it. At length she opened her eyes and stood up.

“Do not think ill of her. She knew I’d show up here eventually.” Pan explained. “She tricked me into thinking she was on my side and brought me here as soon as she thought you were ready. She was afraid if I came later her children would be in danger. Dragons are very good mothers.”

“Children?” Pip shouted. “Why Cedric, you old dog.”

The crowd cheered.

“You called me ‘my queen’. Does that mean you want to join our cause?” Rebecca inquired.

"If you will have me. I have many amends to make."

"I'd much rather have you as a friend than an enemy."

The crowd cheered again.

Rebecca turned and walked toward the castle, saying, "I have one last task to perform."

Soon she stood in the dungeon facing the gremlin, Marid. Unseen in the daylight, there was an unearthly glow around her face. It seemed to frighten Marid to no end.

He backed into a corner. "What are you going to do to me?" His voice shaking with fear.

"Something you won't expect. I'm going to forgive you."

When she was finished with him, much to everyone's surprise, he had transformed into a naked little gnome.

"Don't look so surprised. I was a gnome once . . . long ago." He pulled the blanket off his cot and wrapped it around himself. "I don't suppose I could borrow some clothes—unless you prefer me to run around naked."

"Believe me, no one wants to see that." Pip said. "I think I can find you something. Come with me."

As she watched the two gnomes walk away, she could feel the glow leaving her face. She knew it would be there again if she needed it.

31. Rebecca's Coronation.

Rebecca scrutinized herself in the full-length mirror. She was wearing a full-length white dress, covered with lace and tiny jewels. She wore Guinevere's dowry necklace and the most amazing diamond earrings. She looked closely for any flaws. After the coronation she was expected to make a speech and she was nervous.

"You look perfect." Heather, who had been helping her get ready for her coronation, opined. "Look, I know you are nervous. But just think about it. In the last few months, you have defeated an army of trolls, found the Loch Ness Monster, fought, and defeated a god, for crying out loud. This little ceremony is going to be a piece of cake."

"I think I'd rather fight another god than give this speech, but I suppose you are right . . . It's really something how Pan changed, isn't it. He wanted to kill us all and now he's the kindest . . . being I've ever met."

"The kindest god you've ever met . . . the only god you've ever met. I am curious about something" Heather chewed her lower lip as she formulated her question. "When you were fighting Pan, how did you know to forgive him. . . I mean, he was responsible for your mother's death. How could you forgive him?"

Now it was Rebecca's turn to think. "I'm not sure. When I knew I couldn't beat Pan in a fight, I contacted the Source like Cedric taught me. The Source kind of filled me up, and when that happened, I could see Pan as he really was—filed with hatred and evil, but there was also a kernel of goodness there. I also could sense he had cut himself off from the Source when he chose the path of hatred. I could feel the Source yearning to reconnect. I knew I couldn't beat him in a fight and even if I could it wouldn't bring my mom back. So. . . I decided the only way to not lose was to convert him to our side—to redeem him. I think by forgiving him I connected with and nurtured that kernel of goodness and that—his own goodness—defeated the evil in him and re-established his connection with the Source."

Heather looked at her wide eyed for a moment before responding. "Wow . . . and that's why you're the Queen."

"Really, it was the Source acting through me. I don't think I could have done it without the Source." She sat quietly for a moment before changing the subject. "You know, this has been the most amazing summer I think . . . anybody has ever had."

"I agree. That day I first talked to you in the lunchroom, never in my wildest dreams would I have thought any of this would happen . . . I've been wondering. That first day, Pip was there, wasn't he?"

"Yes. But I didn't know it until I got home."

"I thought so, you were just sitting there with the weirdest smile on your face . . . Well, I suppose we should get down there. People are waiting."

* * *

Rebecca sat on the throne, which was on the front steps of the castle so the dragons could attend. Also, there could be a bigger audience outside. A band was playing. There were at least two hundred chairs set up by the stairs. She could see all her friends and Naomi, her only family, sitting up front. She caught Randy's eye and smiled. He smiled back.

Beyond the chairs, fairies, gnomes, and elves sat on the ground almost all the way back to the wall. Behind the crowd stood Cedric and Granya, keeping a watchful eye on their newly hatched children. They were about the size a German Shepard and, though they could not yet fly or blow fire, had all the rambunctious inclination of a puppy. They wrestled and chased each other, their loud barks and growls drifted out over the crowd. Rebecca would have to talk loudly so those in the back by the dragons could hear.

At length the band stopped playing and Pan strode onto the dais. He looked more like the Pan Rebecca had first seen in the forest; except he was beautiful. His long black hair hung in curls down his back, held in place by a bright green ribbon. He wore short brown linen pants and a long green robe. His eyes, once so filled with hate, radiated pure unconditional love.

When he was filled with hatred he was locked into his former shape. Though he had changed into a unicorn—the rarest of all magicals—when Rebecca forgave him, apparently, he could appear as any shape he wanted to. When he turned into this shape, he explained to Rebecca that this was his natural form and "How else can I place the crown on your head?"

He stood before her now, Merlin holding the crown to her right and Imhotep the scepter to her left. She knelt and bowed her head.

Pan took the crown and began to speak. "Rebecca, do you swear to respect the rights of all, to rule with wisdom and compassion, to work with all your might to restore the unity of the magical and human domains?"

"I so swear."

Pan placed the crown of Arthur on her head and took the scepter. "Do you swear to seek the truth in others and in yourself?"

"I so swear."

He handed her the scepter. "Then I, the Great God Pan, declare you to be Rebecca Pendragon, Queen of the Realm of New Camelot, and Protector of the World. May your rule be long and prosperous. Rise and address your subjects."

She rose while Pan and the two wizards bowed and backed away.

"Citizens of New Camelot," she began. "Friends, first I want to express my gratitude to you all. You have been my protectors, my teachers, and my friends. Without you I would most likely be dead and humanity on its way to extinction. Thank you all.

Together we have won great victories and built this beautiful place. However, there is still much work to do. There are still gremlins, trolls, and ogres out there who refused Pan's call to stop their destruction. There are still humans that would destroy the nature that we all hold so dear. There are still humans that would prosper at the expense of others. And most humans do not believe the magical world exists.

With your help we will stop the predations of the destructive magicals. We will protect and heal this world we all hold so dear. We will return the world to the paradise it once was, the paradise the Source intended."

A cheer rose from the crowd. Then they began to chant. "Hail Rebecca, hail Rebecca . . .

Rebecca waved to the crowd. There was indeed much work to do. She felt confident that together they would get it done.

www.ingramcontent.com/pod-product-compliance
Ingram Content Group UK Ltd.
Pitfield, Milton Keynes, MK11 3LW, UK
UKHW041312190726
13845UKWH00025B/225

9 789395 131094